Teatimes

Teatimes
A World Tour

Helen Saberi

REAKTION BOOKS

This book is dedicated to my late mother,
Hilda Canning

Published by Reaktion Books Ltd
Unit 32, Waterside
44–48 Wharf Road
London N1 7UX, UK
www.reaktionbooks.co.uk

First published 2018
Copyright © Helen Saberi 2018

Printed and bound in China by 1010 Printing International Ltd

A catalogue record for this book is available
from the British Library

ISBN 978 1 78023 928 6

Contents

Introduction *7*

One Britain *11*

Two Europe *61*

Three United States of America *81*

Four Canada, Australia, New Zealand and South Africa *105*

Five India and the Subcontinent *143*

Six Tea Roads and Silk Roads *165*

Seven China, Japan, Korea and Taiwan *183*

Eight Other Teatimes from Around the World *205*

Recipes *211*

References *235*

Bibliography *241*

Acknowledgements *243*

Photo Acknowledgements *245*

Index *247*

Introduction

WRITING this book brought back many happy memories of teatimes. As a child growing up in Yorkshire in the 1950s and '60s I remember coming home from school, tired and hungry, and my mother would give me tea. In those days 'tea' was a meal in the late afternoon at about five or six o'clock. Our midday meal was called dinner. This custom prevailed in the north of England for a long time and some people still talk about dinner at lunchtime and tea at, well, teatime. My mother would give me a savoury dish to be eaten first. My favourite was smoked haddock poached in milk with bread and butter but I also liked cheese on toast, macaroni cheese, cauliflower cheese, egg and bacon pie and much more. In summer we often had salads such as corned beef salad (always with beetroot, lettuce, sliced boiled egg, tomato and salad cream) or Spam or ham. My mother loved baking so there was always something sweet for 'afters'. There were plenty of cakes and biscuits in her baking tins such as fairy cakes, raspberry buns, jam or lemon curd tarts and date and walnut cake. We drank tea – strong Indian black tea with milk and sugar. In winter we sometimes ate hot crumpets oozing with butter by the warm fireside. I also remember the afternoon teas on special occasions or for guests, when my mother would bring out her silver teapot, milk jug, sugar bowl, sugar tongs and best china. Tea would be served in the front room from a hostess trolley. Tea sandwiches were placed on the bottom shelf alongside scones (with jam and butter), and cakes such as butterfly cakes and perhaps slices of Madeira cake. Sometimes she baked a Victoria sponge cake filled with jam and buttercream, or a chocolate cake.

My later memories of special teatimes are from the time I lived in Afghanistan in the 1970s. Women of different nationalities who had married Afghans formed what we called the 'foreign wives tea circle'. Every first Thursday of the month we took turns hosting a tea party. It was an opportunity to get together and chat. We all tried to showcase our own country's traditions and specialities. The Germans, for example, would make wonderful cakes such as *Gugelhupf* and torte. The Scandinavians made open sandwiches and pastries. We British would make scones served with cream and jam, chocolate cake and tea sandwiches, while the Americans served angel food cake and strawberry shortcake. We often included Afghan teatime specialities such as *shami kebab* (a kind of rissole made with minced meat, mashed potatoes, split peas and onions formed into a sausage shape and fried), fried savoury stuffed pastries called *boulani*, pakoras (sliced vegetables such as potatoes or aubergines dipped in a spicy batter and fried) and sweet, crisp *gosh-e-feel* ('elephant ears') pastries sprinkled with ground pistachios. These teas were a wonderful opportunity for cultural mixing.

Common to all these meals is tea. The story of tea began long ago in China when it is said that some wild tea leaves accidentally fell into a pot of water. This infusion was sipped by the legendary Emperor Shennong, who declared that 'Tea gives vigour to the body, contentment to the mind and determination of purpose,' and recommended the infusion to his subjects. The leaves were from the plant *Camellia sinensis*. From these beginnings, and over successive dynasties in China, different styles of tea drinking evolved. By the eighth century AD tea began to spread east to Japan where the elaborate ritual of the tea ceremony was created. Tea also began to be transported along ancient caravan routes to Tibet, Burma, Central Asia and beyond. Tea reached Europe much later, in the seventeenth century, when Portuguese and Dutch traders brought it as a luxury alongside silk and spices. From Europe tea drinking spread to America, India and other places.

This book traces the history of tea drinking and teatimes and explores why and how tea has become the world's second most popular beverage after water. It also explores the social aspects of tea drinking and the different ways human beings across the planet drink their tea and what they eat with it.

Tea is not only drunk for enjoyment; it quenches thirst and brings feelings of well being, harmony, conviviality and hospitality. It is a versatile drink that is prepared in many different ways depending on the type of tea, the region and personal preferences. Tea has become very cosmopolitan. Nowadays people in London, Hamburg, Paris or New York can easily buy rare teas from Japan or Korea or expensive Pu-erh or first flush Darjeeling, not to mention the different styles of tea rooms or places to drink them: the *kissaten* of Japan; the *dim sum* restaurants of Hong Kong and China; the *chai khana* of Central Asia; the tea houses of the Far East; and the luxury hotels of North America and Europe.

Some kinds of tea, and the way they are drunk, are associated with men, others with women. For example working-class men in Britain tend to like their tea to be strong, with milk and lots of sugar and drunk from a sturdy mug, sometimes called 'builder's tea', while ladies in a sewing circle in Canada might prefer a lighter tea such as Darjeeling, served from dainty porcelain cups and saucers.

The word 'tea' (or teatime) can also mean a time in the day when people enjoy a refreshing drink of tea. This can be mid-morning or mid-afternoon, when tea might be served with a small snack, biscuit or piece of cake. Teatime can also mean 'afternoon tea' at 4 or 5 p.m. when dainty sandwiches and small cakes are served with tea. It can also indicate a more substantial meal in the early evening – often called 'high tea'

– which replaces dinner and consists of tea with hot dishes, meats, pies, cheese, large cakes and bread and butter.

Tea can also mean a social event. And, just as tea is drunk in many different ways, the rituals of teatime are also varied. Tea as a meal is usually associated with Britain, Ireland and some Commonwealth countries such as Canada, Australia and New Zealand, which pride themselves on their 'well filled tins' of home-baked cakes and biscuits. The focus of this book is mainly on the history of teatimes in these countries. Teatime traditions in the Netherlands, Germany, France and Ireland are also described. In the United States tearooms boasted homely food such as chicken pot pie and iced tea is the drink of choice. In India tea played an important social role during the Raj and continues to do so today, where teatime is often a fusion of East and West, with British-type cakes served alongside spicy Indian snacks.

Teatime traditions of other parts of the world are often different from those of the West, such as the butter tea of Tibet and the *lephet* (pickled tea) of Burma. How tea is made and how it is served is also described; in Russia and other countries along the Silk Road, for example, water for tea is often boiled in a samovar and the tea then served in ornate tea glasses.

China, Japan, Korea and Taiwan have their own distinct teatime traditions. China, where the story of tea began, has its own unique teatime called *yum cha* ('drink tea'), often taken late morning or midday, when small, delicious, bite-size snacks called *dim sum* are served. In Japan the meal served before the tea ceremony is called *cha-kaiseki*. Koreans have their own tea ceremony and enjoy a wide variety of herbal teas, while Taiwan has created a new trend of tea drinking in the form of bubble tea. The story of teatimes concludes with descriptions of other teatime traditions from around the world, including the mint teas of Morocco, the *onces* of Chile and the Welsh teas of Patagonia.

I hope that by reading this book you will enjoy your own memories of teatimes and take pleasure in reading about teatimes, past and present, from all over the world, in the comfort of your armchair while sipping a cup of your favourite tea.

Catherine of Braganza, wife of Charles II, giving a tea party at
Somerset House. Illustration by Kitty Shannon, 1926.

One

Britain

TEA ARRIVED on Britain's shores in the 1650s, brought over by Dutch trading companies, and quickly became fashionable among the rich upper classes. However, by the 1850s, when the cost of tea had become much lower and it had become more available, tea became the preferred beverage of everyone, rich and poor. It became part of the fabric of society and shaped the British way of life, appearing in almost every sphere of life from fashion to the decorative arts. Tea has become a defining symbol of Britishness.

Thomas De Quincey, an English essayist best known for writing *Confessions of an English Opium-eater* (1821), summed up the pleasures of taking tea in Britain:

> Surely everyone is aware of the divine pleasures which attend a wintry fireside: candles at four o'clock, warm hearth rugs, tea, a fair tea-maker, shutters closed, curtains flowering in ample draperies to the floor, whilst the wind and rain are raging audibly without.

The novelist A. P. Herbert wrote the following song in 1937. It became hugely popular, with music by Henry Sullivan, and sums up just how important a 'nice cup of tea' was for the British:

> I like a nice cup of tea in the morning
> For to start the day you see,
> And at half past eleven
> Well my idea of heaven
> Is a nice cup of tea.
> I like a nice cup of tea with my dinner,
> And a nice cup of tea with my tea,

And when it's time for bed
There's a lot to be said
For a nice cup of tea.

Tea drinking also led to the very British traditions of afternoon tea and high tea. Today, going out for afternoon tea at a hotel or tea room has become an essential stop for tourists who want to experience an important part of British culture.

Early days of tea drinking

THE FIRST newspaper advertisement for tea in Britain appeared in 1658: 'That excellent and by all physicians approved, China drink, called by the Chinese "Tcha" and by other nations "Tay", alias "Tee" is sold at the Sultaness Head Cophee [coffee] house in Sweetings Rents by the Royal Exchange, London.'

Although its acceptance as a drink was slow, it was to last. Of the three new exotic drinks in seventeenth-century Europe – cocoa, tea and coffee – the British at first preferred coffee and it was at the newly established coffee houses that tea was introduced to the public. Tea soon became the national drink, replacing ale. As Agnes Repplier says in her book *To Think of Tea!*:

Tea had come as a deliverer to a land that called for deliverance; a land of beef and ale, of heavy eating and abundant drunkenness; of grey skies and harsh winds; of strong nerved, stout-purposed, slow-thinking men and women. Above all, a land of sheltered homes and warm firesides – firesides that were waiting – waiting for the bubbling kettle and the fragrant breath of tea.

Samuel Pepys, the famous diarist, was an early devotee of tea drinking. In 1660 he wrote that he 'did send for a cup of tee, a China drink, of which I never had drunk before'. Seven years later on 28 June 1667 he recorded coming home to find his wife making tea, which 'Mr Pelling the potticary [an old word for a chemist via apothecary], tells her is good for her cold and defluxions.'

In 1662 Charles II married the Portuguese princess Catherine of Braganza. She was also a devotee of tea drinking and her dowry included a chest of China tea. It is said that the first thing she asked for when she landed on England's shores was a cup of tea.

Queen Catherine set the fashion for tea drinking. In 1663 the poet and politician Edmund Waller (1606–1687) celebrated her birthday with verses in praise of the Queen and 'the best of herbs':

Venus her Myrtle, Phoebus has his bays; Tea both excels, which she vouchsafes to praise. The best of Queens, the best of herbs, we owe To that bold nation which the way did show To the fair region where the sun doth rise, *Whose* rich productions we so justly prize. The Muse's friend, tea does our fancy aid, Regress those vapours which the head invade, And keep the palace of the soul serene, Fit on her birthday to salute the Queen.

The green tea from China was expensive and so remained, in those early days, a drink for the rich. Not everyone knew what to do with this new exotic ingredient. It is said that the widow of the Duke of Monmouth (who was executed in 1685) sent a pound of tea to one of her relatives in Scotland without indicating how it was to be prepared. The cook boiled the tea leaves, threw away the water and served the leaves as a vegetable, like spinach.

Tea was served in small handle-less bowls from small teapots made of stoneware or porcelain. The majority were fine glazed porcelain with blue and white designs and were often referred to as chinaware, reflecting their origins. When tea was shipped from China to Europe, alongside spices and other luxury goods, this chinaware was stowed in the bilges in specially constructed boxes which formed a floor for the tea above. Wooden ships always leaked, so while the teapots and tea bowls got wet but could withstand seawater without damage, the precious tea stayed protected and dry on top.[1]

Catherine of Braganza would have been served tea from a Chinese porcelain or stoneware teapot. Later she may have had a silver one. The earliest known silver teapot in England was made in 1670 and was presented to the Committee of the East India Company.

It wasn't until nearly a hundred years after the introduction of tea to Europe that the secret of porcelain manufacturing was discovered, by a German firm in Meissen. The first porcelain was produced there in 1710 and soon after exported to Britain. The secret spread beyond Germany in the mid-1700s. In 1745 the Chelsea Porcelain factory became the first British firm to produce porcelain, followed by Worcester, Minton Spode and Wedgwood, all producing exquisite tea services.

Tea continued to be popular with royalty in England and in Scotland. Mary of Modena, the beautiful second wife of the future James VII (James II of England), introduced tea drinking to Scotland in 1681 and it quickly became fashionable. James II's daughter Mary, from his first marriage to Anne Hyde, continued the custom of tea drinking in England, as did her sister Queen Anne who came to the throne in 1702. The custom of social tea drinking that developed in the

Silver teapot engraved with the words 'This silver tea-Pott was presented to ye Comtte of ye East India Company by ye Right Honul George Berkeley . . . of that Honourable and worthy Society, 1670.'

Queen Anne period produced a need for small movable chairs and tables, as well as for china cabinets in which to house the expensive tea service. The earliest tea service dates from her reign.

Queen Anne held court across her tea table, and, in imitation, fashionable women in England sipped Chinese tea from tiny porcelain bowls and ordered the new tea tables on which to serve it. Queen Anne was such an avid tea-drinker that she exchanged her tiny

Chinese teapots for a capacious bell-shaped silver one because it held more tea.

Tea equipage

IN THIS PAINTING from around 1727 attributed to Richard Collins, the artist portrays a fashionable family sitting around a tea table not only showing off their fine clothes but their expensive tea equipage, indicating their wealth and social status. The family is drinking from small Chinese porcelain tea bowls in a delicate manner. On the tea table is a typical silver tea service of the time: a sugar dish, sugar tongs, a hot water jug, a spoon boat with teaspoons, a slop bowl, a teapot with a lamp beneath it to keep the contents hot and a tea canister.

Because tea was so expensive and precious it was kept in the boudoir or drawing room in a Chinese jar or bottle called a canister or a catty (a word meaning a Malayan weight of approximately 21 oz., or 600 g).

Attrib. Richard Collins, *An English Family at Tea*, *c.* 1727, oil on canvas.

A beautiful and decorative tea chest of cedar and oak, veneered with maple, harewood, tulip wood, kingwood, satin wood, amaranth, holly and stained holly, with two caddies for green and black tea and a compartment in the middle probably for sugar or for mixing tea leaves, *c.* 1790.

These jars evolved into elegant boxes or caskets made of wood, tortoiseshell, papier maché or silver, with a lock and key and often containing two or more compartments for different types of tea, and some with a compartment in the middle for sugar. They became known as tea caddies.

A tea caddy spoon was used to measure out the tea leaves kept in the tea caddy before adding them to the teapot. When tea was first imported it came in tea chests and included was a scallop shell that was used to scoop the tea leaves. This is the first known form of a tea caddy spoon. Caddy spoons soon followed, which had a comparatively large bowl spoon with a disproportionately short handle. They are found in many different materials, including bone, pearl, tortoiseshell and silver. The shape and decorative style of the bowl varies from quite plain to imaginative designs such as a leaf, shell, shovel and jockey cap.

Mote spoons, also called mote skimmers, were considered an essential part of any upscale English tea service in those early days. (Mote is an old English word for a particle of dust or foreign matter, particularly in food and drink.) Mote spoons date from as early as 1697 and were made of silver, with small holes perforating the bowl or ladle and a long thin handle with a pointed end. Early shipments of Chinese teas arrived unsorted with a mixture of large and small tea leaves which would not only float in the tea poured out but also clog the spout. Society hostesses who served tea were aware that there might be a few motes floating on the surface of the tea and the mote spoon was an elegant accessory with which to remove them or any floating tea leaves. She would use the handle or shaft with the pointed end to unclog the spout of tea leaves. Teaspoons eventually replaced mote spoons when tea strainers came into use between 1790 and 1805 and

Modern silver-plated, shell design, tea caddy spoon.

teapots had integral straining holes set inside at the base of the spout.

Until the mid-eighteenth century tea was served in small handle-less bowls and people often talked about 'taking a dish of tea'. In about 1750 a man called Robert Adams incorporated a handle into the design of tea-cups. Although the cups were more costly to make than tea bowls and didn't pack tightly together for carriage to distant markets, this innovation was welcomed by English tea drinkers who found tea bowls difficult to use, and that they often burned their fingers. Adams designed teacups that were taller than their base and came with a saucer. Some tea drinkers liked to pour their hot tea into saucers, allowing the tea to cool before sipping. This habit also became known as taking 'a dish of tea'.

Tea kettles were used to refill the teapot while tea was being served. The lamp or burner was filled with camphorine, an odourless and inexpensive fuel that kept the water hot. For those who could afford it, a silver kettle would be preferred together with a silver teapot, milk jug and sugar bowl. The tea urn, heated by a charcoal burner, appeared in the 1760s and super-seded the kettle with a spirit burner. Sheffield plate tea urns did not appear until 1785.

When made, the tea would then be served from the tea table, which was first introduced in the late seventeenth century. Around 1700 over six thousand lacquered tea tables were imported to Britain. By the mid-eighteenth century London furniture makers were producing their own alternative form for the luxury market in mahogany embellished with brass inlay.

Some people had what is called a teapoy – a pedestal table with a top which lifts up revealing two lidded compartments for storing tea and two others containing cut-glass bowls for mixing the dried tea. It was a practical object but also a means for the hostess to display her modish taste in furniture as she presided over tea and gossip.[2]

Although servants would set everything up and aid the hostess, she was in charge of brewing the tea, which would then be served to guests. Both green and black tea were popular and sometimes sugar was added (although this, like tea, was a new import and expensive). In these early days it was still unusual for milk to be added to tea. So, while the men were drinking their tea in the noisy, smoky surroundings of the coffee shop and enjoying the gossip and politics of the day, the ladies were doing much the same thing but in more refined surroundings.

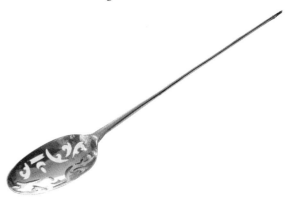

Silver mote spoon, 18th century.

Not everyone liked tea. In 1748 John Wesley, founder of the Methodist movement, argued for complete abstinence from tea on the grounds that it gave rise to 'numberless disorders, particularly those of a nervous kind'.

Tea was also denounced in Scotland by both medical men and the clergy. It was considered 'a highly improper article of diet, expensive, wasteful of time and likely to render the population weakly and effeminate'.[3] Some ministers of the Church of Scotland considered it a greater evil than whisky. A movement was even begun all over Scotland to stamp out the 'tea menace'. However, despite all the opposition, tea drinking became firmly established, especially with women, although gentlemen on the whole still preferred their alcohol.

Back in England Jonas Hanway, in his essay of 1757, branded tea 'as pernicious to health, obstructing industry and impoverishing the nation'. But Dr Johnson, who wrote the first *Dictionary of the English Language*, published in 1755, and who was perhaps the most celebrated of all tea drinkers, drinking, it is said, 25 cups of tea a day, came to tea's defence, calling himself 'A hardened and shameless tea-drinker who has for many years diluted his meals with only the infusion of this fascinating plant; whose kettle has scarcely time to cool; who with tea amuses the evening, with tea solaces the midnight – and with tea welcomes the morning.' Dr Johnson was known to frequent London's famed coffee houses. Gentlemen went there to discuss the politics and business of the day. They were smoky, noisy places. Women were not allowed and in any case no gentlewoman would have cared to set foot in one. Ladies took their tea at home. Some coffee houses sold tea in loose-leaf form so that it could be brewed at home. Thomas Twining, who opened Tom's Coffee House

Teapoy made with rosewood on a carved wooden pedestal with jelly mould feet, *c.* 1820s, at Felbrigg Hall, Norfolk.

on the Strand in 1706, was very well aware that lady customers would not venture inside a coffee house. In 1717 he renamed his establishment The Golden Lyon, a shop which specialized in selling a wide range of good quality teas and coffees.

This was London's first tea shop and ladies could enter without any impropriety. Jane Austen obtained her tea from Twining's shop. She wrote to her sister Cassandra in 1814 from London: 'I am sorry to hear that there has been a rise in tea. I do not mean to pay Twining till later in the day, when we may order a fresh supply.'[4] If Jane went in person to Twining's shop in the Strand she would have walked through a door which looks very much the same today.

Tea drinking remained largely a pastime for the wealthy until 1784 because it was heavily taxed. Smuggling was rife; so was adulteration.[5] The government came under pressure from legal tea merchants whose profits were being seriously undermined by all the smuggling so Prime Minister William Pitt the Younger drastically cut the tax on tea from 119 per cent to 12.5 per cent. Tea became affordable and the illegal smuggling trade was wiped out virtually overnight.

Tea gardens

TEA DRINKING now spread to the middle classes and replaced ale for breakfast and gin at other times of the day. Tea became Britain's most popular beverage and drinking coffee at coffee houses declined. Many coffee houses changed into men's clubs, some of which remain today in Pall Mall or the vicinity of St James's. Men joined the ladies and their families at one of the pleasure gardens, which were frequently referred to as 'tea gardens'. These large parks had shrubs, flowers, pools, fountains and statues. There were leafy arbours where people could sit, drink tea and eat bread and butter. As early as 1661 gardens were created at Vauxhall, on the south bank of the River Thames in London. In 1732 the gardens were developed further and they became the place to see and to be seen. The Prince Regent, later George IV, was a frequent visitor. Horace Walpole, Henry Fielding and Dr

Johnson also used to visit with their literary friends.[6] Later, other gardens were opened in London (such as Ranelagh, Marylebone, Cuper's and less famous ones such as St Helena Gardens in Rotherhithe and the Rosemary Branch in Islington) and in other major towns throughout the country.

Tea gardens provided outdoor entertainment for every class from April to September. The attractions included music, conjurors, acrobats, fireworks, riding and bowling, as well as tea and refreshments. Marylebone attracted famous people, including the composer Handel in the late 1750s. Leopold Mozart (father of Wolfgang, the child prodigy who came to London to amaze local music lovers) recorded visiting Ranelagh: 'On entering everyone pays 2*s*. 6*d*. For this he may have as much bread and butter as he can eat, and as much coffee and tea as he can drink.'[7]

Sadly, the rapid growth of London and of 'rowdyism' eventually led to the tea gardens being closed. Tea drinking became confined to the home.

Regency era

THE REGENCY era can refer to various stretches of time. The formal Regency (1811–20) was the period when King George III was deemed unfit to rule and his son ruled as Prince Regent. On the death of George III in 1820 the Prince Regent became George IV. However, the period 1795 to 1837 is often attributed as the Regency era, a time characterized by distinctive trends in British architecture, literature, fashions and so on. The era ended when Queen Victoria succeeded William IV.

During this period tea was taken at breakfast time and at the end of the day after dinner. Evening parties known as routs were much in vogue at the time. The name rout was also given to small biscuit-like cakes

George Morland, *The Tea Garden*, *c.* 1790. The scene depicts a middle-class family taking tea in Ranelagh Gardens.

which were often served with tea. Maria Rundell's recipe is from *A New System of Domestic Cookery* (1806):

> Mix two pounds of flour, one ditto butter, one ditto sugar, one ditto currants, clean and dry; then wet into a stiff paste, with 2 eggs, a large spoonful of orange-flower water, ditto rose-water, ditto sweet wine, ditto brandy drop on a tin-plate floured: a very short time bakes them.

Jane Austen liked drinking tea with her breakfast and in the evening after the late afternoon dinner, when the men joined them for tea, cakes, conversation, cards and music. The characters in her books also drink tea. For example, in *Mansfield Park* (1814) tea cannot come too soon for Fanny Price. Longing to escape Henry Crawford who has just proposed marriage, she wants to flee to her room to escape this unwelcome approach but etiquette forbids leaving until after tea:

She could have hardly kept her seat any longer had it not been for the sound of approaching relief, the very sound she had been waiting for, and long thinking it strangely delayed. The solemn procession . . . of the tea board, urn and cake bearers made its appearance and delivered her . . . Mr Crawford was forced to move away

Afternoon tea

There are few hours in life more agreeable
than the hour dedicated to the ceremony
known as afternoon tea.
Henry James, *The Portrait of a Lady*

ALTHOUGH THE tradition of afternoon tea is usually credited to Anna Maria, the seventh Duchess of Bedford, one of Queen Victoria's ladies-in-waiting, there is evidence suggesting that there was a custom of drinking tea accompanied by bread and cakes in the afternoon from the 1750s, with advertisements in the newspapers of main cities such as Oxford and Bath. This one is from the *Bath Chronicle and Weekly Gazette* (1766):

Spring Gardens are now open for the Summer season with Breakfasting and Afternoon Tea, as usual – Hot-Rolls, and Spring-Garden Cakes every Morning, from Half after Nine 'till Half after Ten, Sundays excepted.

However, afternoon tea taken at four or five o'clock does not seem to have been a regular institution until a quarter of a century after Jane Austen's death in 1817. Great social changes were taking place in Britain. The main meal of dinner had now shifted from the middle or late afternoon to much later in the evening, sometimes as late as eight or nine o'clock, and only a light lunch was taken at midday.

It is said the Duchess of Bedford complained of hunger or 'a sinking feeling' during the long gap between lunch and dinner and so she took all the necessary tea things and something to eat (probably some light cakes or bread and butter) to her private room. In a letter sent from Windsor Castle, she wrote to her brother-in-law in 1841: 'I forgot to name my old friend Prince Esterhazy who drank tea with me the other evening at 5 o'clock, or rather was my guest amongst eight ladies at the Castle.' The Duchess also took tea when staying at Belvoir Castle in Rutland and invited other ladies to take tea in her boudoir. The actress Fanny Kemble recollects in her autobiography, published in 1882, a visit to Belvoir Castle in March 1842:

My first introduction to 'afternoon tea' took place during this visit to Belvoir. When I received on several occasions private and rather mysterious invitations to the Duchess of Bedford's room, and found her with a 'small and select' circle of female guests of the castle, busily employed in brewing and drinking tea, with her grace's own private tea kettle. I do not believe that the now universally-honoured and observed institution of 'five o'clock tea' dates further back in the annals of English civilization than this very private and, I think, rather shamefaced practice of it.

It seems that tea drinking in the afternoon had long held a certain mystique, as seen in an article from eighty years earlier in *The Gentlemen's Magazine* for October 1758: 'Afternoon tea drinking is censured in

Thomas Rowlandson, *Ladies at Tea*, 1790–95, watercolour with pen and ink.
It is inscribed 'Would you please to have another Cup of Tea.'

the lower and middle classes as a waste of time and money, an occasion of gossiping, slander and sometime intrigue.' Gossip, slander and sometimes intrigue were not unknown at informal tea parties known as kettle-drums in the eighteenth and nineteenth centuries. Tea, drinking chocolate, cakes and sandwiches were served.

Scandal and gossip may have been entertaining but in the 1800s telling one's fortune by reading tea leaves was also fun.

By the mid-1850s afternoon tea had firmly estab-lished itself in British tradition. It was not long before other social hostesses picked up on the idea of after-noon tea and it became respectable enough for it to move into the drawing room. Georgiana Sitwell wrote that

It was not till about 1849 or 50 . . . that five o'clock tea in the drawing room was made an institution, and then only in a few fashionable houses where the dinner hour was as late as half past seven or eight o'clock. My mother was the first to intro-duce the custom to Scotland; and this was in consequence of Lord Alexander Russell, who was staying with us at Balmoral, telling her that his mother, the Duchess of Bedford, always had after-noon tea at Woburn [the Duchess's own home].[8]

Afternoon tea, an occasion for refined social con-tact, especially among women, became more elaborate. It was not long before all fashionable society was sip-ping tea with sandwiches and cakes. The portions were

'A Kettledrum in Knightsbridge', 1871. Ladies and gentlemen could mingle together and talk scandal at these parties.

Fortune teller reading the tea leaves, 1894.

usually small – just enough to stave off hunger pangs until dinnertime. Not everyone was so keen. Sir Henry Thompson in *Food and Feeding* (1901):

Here may be just named an invention of comparatively recent date, afternoon tea, which, however, cannot be reckoned as a meal. In reality, a pleasant excuse to mark the hour for friendly gossip

Reading the tea leaves

TEA-LEAF READING is also called tasseomancy, tasseography or teomancy. Tasseomancy comes from the Arabic word *tassa*, meaning cup, and the Greek word *mancy*, meaning divination. Like tea itself, tasseomancy originated in ancient China, but it became associated with gypsies who later started the spread of the practice throughout the world. Tea-leaf reading, or fortune-telling by tea leaves, first began to make its mark in England during the seventeenth century when tea was introduced into Europe from China. It began to grow in popularity during the 1800s as a means of telling one's future. Tea-leaf fortune-telling uses the symbols and the patterns formed by the way the tea leaves fall in a person's cup.

To read someone's tea leaves, you must first make a pot of tea, using loose leaves, and pour the tea without a strainer so that leaves pour into the cup. The inquirer is asked by the reader to sip the tea slowly and make a wish. The inquirer should drink from the cup until only a teaspoonful of tea remains. The dregs are swirled round the cup three times in an anti-clockwise direction with the left hand. The cup is turned over and placed on the saucer. The cup is then turned right side up. The handle of the cup should point to the inquirer. The reader takes the cup in both hands. The patterns of the leaves are examined and pictures and symbols formed by the leaves are looked for. This is where your imagination comes in or your intuition helps you decipher them. Leaves close to the brim relate to events soon to occur and those at the bottom of the cup

to bad tidings or the distant future. Those close to the handle concern matters at home.

Remember that a symbol or pattern may have its meaning altered by others nearby, so all symbols should be read in conjunction with each other. Good luck symbols include stars, triangles, trees, flowers, crowns and circles. Bad luck symbols include snakes, owls, crosses, cats, guns and cages.

Fortune-telling by tea leaves is still popular in Ireland, Scotland, Canada and the USA, as well as other places. Whether you believe it or not, reading the leaves can be an entertaining way of sharing tea with friends. I remember my mother, on dark, cold, winter teatimes, entertaining us by telling our fortunes. She was good at it and we all had a lot of fun.

There are many symbols and their meanings. Here are my favourites, chosen to foretell the future as I write this book:

Anchor – voyage or success
Book – revelations
Clouds – doubts or problems
Cross – suffering
Horse – ambition fulfilled
Ladder – advancement
Mountain – a strenuous climb ahead
Star – good luck
Palm tree – creativity
Wheel – a sign of progress
Windmill – success through hard work

with a hostess 'at home', it may be the occasion of undesirable habits, if enough solid food is eaten to impair digestion and 'spoil' the coming dinner. Nothing can be more undesirable at this hour than sweet and rich cake, hot buttered toast or muffins; nevertheless they are frequently offered. But a propos of tea, many of us might with advantage avoid the sugar and the cream, which at this hour interfere with the stomach far more than does the infusion itself, and add in their place a delicate slice of lemon no larger than a half-crown, the flavour of which – fragrant peel and a hint of acid – combines with the aroma of good tea, without in the least disguising or flattening it as the conventional additions do.

Nevertheless, in winter teas such as Assam with its rich pungent flavour, and warming foods such as cinnamon toast, hot buttered crumpets and rich fruitcakes, might be served round the fireside; in summer, delicate Earl Grey or the golden taste of Ceylon might accompany sandwiches, followed by a light Victoria sandwich cake, a light sponge with jam or buttercream filling named after Queen Victoria, who herself enjoyed tea and cakes. Her endorsement certainly helped establish the tradition of afternoon tea. Other cakes which might be served were small Balmorals (which were baked in moulds shaped like corrugated Nissen huts), Madeira cake or seed cake.

Muffins were also popular in Victorian times up to the First World War. The muffin man would walk through the streets at teatime ringing his bell, with his basket of muffins wrapped up well in flannel to keep them warm. The muffins, made from a soft yeast-leavened dough enriched with milk and butter to give them a light and spongy texture, were usually baked

A muffin man, with his basket of muffins on one arm, rings his hand bell to attract customers, 1841.

on a griddle, which made the top and bottom flat and golden brown, with a white band around the middle. For serving they were toasted, split in two and then spread with butter. The two halves were closed together again and kept warm.[9] The famous Victorian journalist Henry Mayhew quotes a muffin man in *London Labour and the London Poor* (1851) saying that the best sales for muffins were in the suburbs:

> it's best Hackney way, and Stoke Newington, and Dalston, and Balls Pond and Islington; where the gents that's in banks – the steady coves of them – goes home to their teas, and the missuses has muffins to welcome them . . .

The sandwich, which became an integral part of 'afternoon tea', had been named after John Montagu, the 4th Earl of Sandwich, who, it is said, one night before 1762 was too busy to stop for dinner and asked for some cold beef to be brought to him between two slices of bread. The common story is that at the time the earl was at a gaming table but an alternative explanation is that he, as First Lord of the Admiralty, was busily at work at his desk.[10] By the 1840s the sandwich had become commonplace. In early Victorian days sandwiches were usually made of ham, tongue or beef and not cucumber, which was thought to be poisonous. However, cucumber sandwiches did eventually become popular to the point that they were considered essential for a 'proper' afternoon tea.

Biscuits were also liked at teatime. Although many people in the early days of afternoon tea either made their own biscuits such as shortbreads, rout biscuits or Naples biscuits at home or bought them from confectioners, by the mid-nineteenth century biscuits were being produced in factories by companies such as Huntley & Palmer, who by the late 1830s were selling about twenty different kinds, from Abernethy and Oliver varieties to cracknels, macaroons, ratafias and sponge teacakes. Peek Freans, who started out as the Peek Brothers & Co. with a tea importation company, started producing the Garibaldi biscuit in 1861. Factory-made biscuits not only saved the housewife time, but cost less.

Both Indian and China teas would be served at afternoon tea. The first Indian tea arrived in 1839 and Ceylon teas soon after, in 1879. Milk or cream would be offered to add to the tea but had not been common additions before the 1720s. Milk may have been added to offset the bitterness of the Indian strong black tea. Sugar was also sometimes added for the same reason.

There has been much debate about whether milk should be added first to the cup or last. It has been suggested that milk was poured into the delicate porcelain cups first to prevent cracking. Victorian etiquette meant that tea was served ready-poured in cups and the milk or cream was added to the tea. George Orwell was definitely in the 'milk last' camp, writing in his essay 'A Nice Cup of Tea' for the *Evening Standard* in January 1946:

> one should pour tea into the cup first. This is one of the most controversial points of all; indeed in every family in Britain there are probably two schools of thought on the subject. The milk-first school can bring forward to fairly strong arguments, but I maintain that my own argument is unanswerable. This is that, by putting the tea in first and stirring as one pours, one can exactly regulate the amount of milk whereas one is liable to put in too much milk if one does it the other way round.

Opinions still vary all over Britain and no doubt the debate will continue.

Ornate Victorian serving tongs for sandwiches and cakes.

Italian 19th-century tea strainer.

Elegant teaware in silver or fine bone china, cake stands, sandwich trays, sugar tongs and tea strainers became the height of fashion. A tea trolley (sometimes called a tea cart or tea wagon) was often used to display the expensive teaware. Simply a serving cart on castors, usually with two shelves, the tea trolley not only displayed the teaware, but was used to serve the tea, cakes and sandwiches. The tea trolley remained popular through to the 1930s when formal teas were still part of daily life and entertainment.

Tables were laid with embroidered or lace cloths and serviettes. Afternoon tea became the focus for social visits and was treated as a special occasion. Mrs Beeton described the duties of the footman in her book *Beeton's Book of Household Management* in 1861:

As soon as the drawing-room bell rings for tea, the footman enters with the tray, which has been previously prepared; hands the tray round to the company, with cream and sugar, the tea and

Ornate Victorian silver sugar tongs.

coffee being generally poured out, while another attendant hands cakes, toast, or biscuits. If it is an ordinary family party, where this social meal is prepared by the mistress, he carries the urn or kettle, as the case may be; hands round the toast, or such other eatable as may be required, removing the whole in the same manner when tea is over.

Five o'clock teas, 'At Home' teas and tea receptions

FORMAL TEA parties became fashionable in Victorian times. Invitations to tea were issued verbally or by a small informal note or card. No answer was required. Guests just turned up if so disposed. Recommendations were given as to the correct time for afternoon tea. In 1884 Marie Bayard advised in *Hints on Etiquette* that 'the proper time is from four to seven'. Others thought a 'five o'clock' tea was best. Guests were not expected to stay for the whole time that tea was going on but to

come and go as they pleased during the allotted hours. Most guests stayed for about half an hour or so but it was expected that no one should stay later than seven o'clock.

The wealthy, possibly inspired by the habits of Queen Victoria, began to invite people to larger and more formal versions of afternoon teas, known as 'At Home' teas, and tea receptions. These sometimes catered for up to two hundred guests and usually took place between 4 and 7 p.m., during which time people could come and go. Ladies were escorted to the refreshments table by the gentlemen. A much more elaborate 'tea' would be provided, usually buffet style with small sandwiches such as foie gras, salmon or cucumber and cakes and biscuits of varying kinds such as Madeira cake, pound cake, small cakes, petit fours, macaroons and so on. Servants would serve ices and claret and champagne cups and, of course, tea. Guests or hosts might provide entertainment, but in more affluent households, professional musicians or singers might be employed.

Constance Spry, in her book *Come Into the Garden, Cook* (1942), gives an evocative account of her memories of 'At Homes' as a child growing up in a large household:

These were dressy affairs in more ways than one. Tatted doilies, ribbon-bound plate-handles, and tiered cakestands, impiously nicknamed curates, gave scope for competitive ingenuity and a source of revenue for bazaars. There was a complicated ritual about cards. White kid gloves were *de rigueur*. Woman's crowning glory was her hair, and she made the most of every bit of it. Glacé silk petticoats swished, veils twisted themselves into knots no sailor would care to name, and immense feather boas framed the face in a seductive and feminine manner.

The second Tuesday or fourth Thursday or whatever the hallowed day might be had a personality of its own; you could recognize it from the moment you came downstairs in the morning. The kitchen hummed with activity. The fire had to roar, the oven get hot, and there was to be no nonsense on the part of any one.

. . .

The kitchen heavyweights toiled up to their attics for a good wash. They polished their faces with yellow soap and water, dragged their hair back till the line of their eyebrows was lifted, buttoned up their black 'bodies', and showed discrimination in the matter of caps. The more important the occasion, the longer the streamer

. . .

The drawing-room contingent might take longer to dress, but never in our eyes achieved anything so smart as our Mary's best cap. Down the ladies came, curled and attired . . .

There was a Median law governing the time before which no well-mannered caller would arrive. From that mystic hour, however, answering the bell was a breathless affair. Hanging over the banisters we children might see the feathers and hear the frou-frou and get a nice sense of party goings-on.

. . . I have seen tightly gloved women balance a cup and saucer in the air, negotiate a knotted veil, and convey a tremulous cucumber sandwich from hand to mouth without a fault.

The delicate arrangement of the food, the fine quality of the teaware and the elegant setting made these

The Moustache Cup

DURING THIS period the British invented the moustache cup. Moustaches flourished throughout the Victorian era and often wax was applied to the moustache to keep it nice and stiff. This caused a problem when steaming cups of tea were drunk, for the steam melted the wax and sent it right into the cup. The moustache also often became stained. It is generally acknowledged that the moustache cup was invented by the innovative potter Harvey Adams in the 1860s. The cup had a semi-circular ledge inside, serving as a guard to support the moustache and keep it dry. The ledge has a half-moon-shaped opening to allow the passage of liquids. The invention spread all over Europe and many moustache cups were made by famous factories, such as Meissen, Limoges and others. The invention also spread to America.

Collection of moustache cups at the Tea Museum, Mariage Frères, Paris, France.

occasions a special affair. But so too, as implied by Constance Spry, was the way in which stylish ladies dressed for the occasion.

Tea gowns were introduced in the 1870s and, although the style changed somewhat, continued to be fashionable into the 1910s. Originally worn at home in the privacy of one's own boudoir, the tea gown was considered appropriate for receiving guests in the afternoon. In the magazine *Beauty and Fashion* (on 6 December 1890) this advice was given to hostesses:

> the first important item with a hostess in regard to afternoon tea is the selection of a becoming gown. The tea will taste sweeter and the cups will look prettier, if she is robed in some gauze like fabric of artistic make and a dainty tea-gown is of just as much consequence to her as the beverage itself and adds considerably to her good humour. If she knows that she is well clad, and that the pretty, flimsy lace and soft silk will bear the closest inspection of her particular friends, there is sure to be a charming air of satisfaction pervading her whole conversation and her manner will be more than usually affable and gracious.

One of the key points to note about the tea gown is that it could be worn without a corset, giving the wearer a little more comfort and ease than a dinner or day dress, with their constricting whalebones and laces. The tea gown was something between dress and undress, between a negligee and an evening dress, between a woman's private life and the public sphere of fashionable society. The gowns were often accessorized with chic gloves, parasols, fabulous hats and small handbags. It was not essential for ladies to wear gloves on these occasions but many did when there were large numbers

Tea and boudoir gowns being modelled by three ladies from the First World War period in an illustration for *The Queen* magazine.

of guests to receive; it was more pleasant for the hostess to do so, especially if she had warm hands. At afternoon dances ladies were required to retain their hats and bonnets.[11] In Edwardian times tea gowns were often referred to as 'teagies'. Many were made with pleated chiffon or silk muslin trimmed with lace or satin ribbons or fringed with crystals, jet or gold tassels. Loose fitting and feminine, they enabled ladies to move about gracefully and elegantly. They became essential female wear in the afternoons during country house weekends.

With the outbreak of the First World War in 1914, the Edwardian 'Golden Age' of elegance and indulgence came gradually to an end and lifestyles changed forever. Tea gowns slowly disappeared, merging with

Mrs Beeton's tea table, 1907.

the 'afternoon frock' or cocktail dress. A less grand 'At Home' was described in *Mrs Beeton's All-about Cookery* in the 1930s:

> tea is served upon small tables, the servant before bringing it in seeing that one is placed conveniently near her mistress, who generally dispenses the tea. No plates are given for a tea of this kind, then the servant or servants, after seeing that all is in readiness, leave the room, the gentlemen of the party doing all the waiting that is necessary.
>
> The tea equipage is usually placed upon a silver salver, the hot water is in a small silver or china kettle on a stand, and the cups are small. Thin bread and butter, sandwiches, cake, petit fours and sometimes fresh fruit are all the eatables given. These are daintily arranged on plates, spread with lace doilies.

High tea

IN CONTRAST to the elegant afternoon teas enjoyed by the upper classes, the tradition of high tea was finding a place in lower- and middle-class homes. High tea, like afternoon tea, came about because of social changes. During the seventeenth and eighteenth centuries most people worked in agriculture and tended to have their main meal of the day at midday with a light supper in the evening. After the Industrial Revolution it was not so convenient to have a hot midday meal and so when workers came home from their long, tiring shifts at the mine or factory, what they needed was a hearty meal which was supplemented by strong, sweet tea with milk. The Commutation Act of 1784 considerably reduced the tax on tea and it became affordable for everyone. And, by the mid-nineteenth century, cheaper Indian black tea was being imported into Britain. Working-class families were now able to afford to drink tea as their main beverage. This meal, usually served at about six o'clock, became known as 'high tea' or 'meat tea'. High tea was also often referred to as just 'tea', especially in the north where many of the mines and factories were.

Where did the term 'high tea' come from? Food historian Laura Mason suggests that the word 'high' carried a sense of richness during the seventeenth century and says that 'Possibly the expression high tea originally designated a more abundant meal than "tea" alone.'[12] Others suggest that 'high tea' meant sitting at a high table rather than the low one customary for afternoon tea.

Mrs Beeton's *The Book of Household Management* (1880 edn) goes someway to explain:

> There is Tea and Tea, the substantial family repast in the house of the early diner, and the afternoon cosy, chatty affairs that late diners have instituted . . . The family tea-meal is very like that of breakfast, only that more cakes and knicknackery in the way of sweet eatables are provided. A 'High Tea' is where meat takes a more prominent part and signifies really, what is a tea-dinner . . . The afternoon tea signifies little more than tea and bread and butter, and a few elegant trifles in the way of cake and fruit.

Typical dishes for high tea were cold meats such as ham (perhaps with fried eggs) and hot dishes such as sausages, macaroni cheese, Welsh rabbit, kippers and pies. Cheese, a cake or some biscuits were other items commonly served for high tea. For festive occasions, high days or holidays, other delicacies might feature such as roast pork, fish (usually in the form of salmon), a trifle and perhaps a jelly. Food served varied from home to home depending on the circumstances. Agricultural workers coming in from the fields would be treated to what is called a 'farmhouse tea'. These were hearty, family affairs with filling foods to satisfy big appetites. The smell of baking would pervade the air. Plenty of cakes, biscuits, scones and buns would be on the table as well as newly baked bread to be spread with butter or perhaps jam or preserves, home-made potted fish or meat pastes. Ham would probably be on the table too (high tea was also sometimes called 'ham tea').

There were also 'fish teas'. Margaret Drabble in *The Sea Lady* (2006) describes a typical 1950s seaside boarding house, whose tariff includes breakfast and a fish tea. What was meant by this was probably fish and chips or poached fish with mashed potatoes and parsley sauce.

'Shrimp teas' 'up north' were described by Dorothy Hartley in her book *Food in England* (1954):

> There was a little house that said 'Shrimp Teas'. We went through a little wicket gate down a flagged yard . . . There were three strong round wooden tables and against the three tables leant twelve strong square wooden chairs. On the tables were white cloths. You went to the door and told Betsy 'We've come'. Then you sat down and 'drew in'.

Betsy brought out a pot of tea, with a woollen tea-cosy on it, sugar and cream, a cup and saucer each, two big plates of thin bread and butter – brown and white – a big green plate of watercress, and a big pink plate of shrimps. And that was all, except an armoured salt cellar and a robin. Then you 'reached too'.

Presently Betsy Tattersall came out again, with a big white apron over her black gown, took the teapot in to replenish it, and see if you wanted any more bread and butter (you always did). And you ate, and talked, in desultory fashion (there is something very conversational about a shrimp tea), and the robin hopped about on the table.[13]

The Welsh have 'cockle teas'. Justina Evans shared her childhood memories of this teatime treat with food historian Alan Davidson:

Cockles, winkles and mussels were a teatime dish. Cockles we picked at the small seaside village of Ferryside, near Carmarthen. They were soaked overnight in a large enamel bowl of water, to which was added a lump of bar salt.

The following day the tap was left to run on them to remove any trace of sand. They were then boiled in a large iron saucepan on an open fire until the shells opened. They were dished up in the shells in one bowl with another bowl at the side for empty shells. The warm cockles were eaten with home-made bread and yellow, salted Welsh butter.

Cockles pickled with salt, pepper and vinegar were another teatime meal. They can also be sprinkled with oatmeal and fried with bacon.

The empty cockle shells were washed and dried and crushed, and used for grit for the chickens which most families kept in their back yards.[14]

Cockle pies and cockles and eggs were also popular.

Baked goods played an integral part at teatime when the baking skills of the housewife came to the fore. Food historian Laura Mason explains that many of the dishes served had their origins in much earlier times, such as raised pies, spiced and fruited breads, trifle, pound cake, seed cake and jam tarts:

The nineteenth century contributed to the repertoire yet more baked goods such as the Swiss tarts, walnut cake and chocolate roll. It was in the provision of the large range of home-baked goods – cakes, pastries and breads, so important to both afternoon and high tea – that the housewife really shone.

Mason goes on to explain that home baking was given a boost in the nineteenth century as refined flour and sugar, two important ingredients for baking, became cheaper and more readily available. Baking powder, which was easier and less time consuming to use than the traditional cake raising agents of yeast and beaten egg, also came into use in the middle of the century. Another boost was the cast-iron kitchen range with an integral oven, fired by coal. The range became commonplace, even in poorer households at this time, thus allowing more home baking. It was also at this time that canned foods became available. Salmon was first canned in California in 1864 and by the end of the nineteenth century tinned goods of all sorts were introduced into Britain. Canned salmon and canned peaches were considered a special treat for, say, birthdays or Sunday teas.[15]

In Scotland, in the words of F. Marian McNeill in *The Scots Kitchen* (1929), 'the Scottish tea-table reached as high a point of perfection as the breakfast table.' The Scottish housewife has always been celebrated for her baking skills in the form of bannocks, scones, drop scones, shortbreads, oatcakes, rich cakes such as Dundee, and tea breads. It was not just baked goods which excelled on the Scottish high-tea table. With a huge pot of tea, a variety of savoury dishes were served such as cold ham, pies, black and white puddings (with chips), bacon with eggs, eggs scrambled with cheese, tattie (potato) scones, herrings in oatmeal and squerr sausages (square sliced Lorne sausage) with fried potatoes. Standbys were tinned sardines or, for a special treat, tinned salmon. White bread with jam was a staple.[16]

The Welsh are also renowned for their baking skills, and baking lies at the heart of Welsh cooking. Many breads, scones and cakes were, and still are, cooked on a griddle or bakestone. On the tea table there might be the much-loved home-made breads such as bakestone bread (*bara planc*), fruited bread (*bara claddu*) or the traditional tea bread of Wales, *bara brith* (meaning speckled bread, the speckling meaning the fruit). Oatcakes, which have Celtic origins, are popular too. They are often eaten with butter and cheese. No Welsh teatime is complete without the traditional Welsh cakes (*pice ar y maen*), which are small, spicy flat cakes with currants and a dusting of sugar. These little cakes, which were made on a griddle or bakestone, were often served to travellers on their arrival at an inn. Also made on a bakestone are tinker's cakes (*teisennau tincar*). They date back to the time when tinkers travelled through Wales calling at farms and cottages to mend pots and pans. The cakes contain grated apple, giving them a soft and moist texture, and the cinnamon adds a bit of

spice. They were given to the tinkers when they called and were no doubt considered a tasty and welcome treat, offered with a cup of tea.

Various kinds of scones are made by the Welsh, with treacle, or Caerphilly cheese, or sometimes with currants. Lightcakes (*leicecs*) are similar to the Scottish drop scone but much lighter, made with the addition of buttermilk and bicarbonate of soda. The Welsh also love their pancakes and they are considered a birthday treat. There are many different kinds and they go under different names. Their popularity, apart from the taste of course, comes from the fact that they can be made at a moment's notice on the bakestone.

Cakes which come from the oven are, on the whole, a more recent tradition in Wales. Some cakes and buns were linked to the farming year, including sheep shearing time when whole communities worked together to shear some thousands of sheep. The task of catering for maybe a hundred hungry workers and guests over two whole days took days to prepare. Afternoon tea would be a plain meal of home-baked bread, butter, cheese and jam. Shearing cake (*Cacen gneifo*) flavoured with caraway, a rich yeasted fruitcake and gooseberry pie were considered shearing specialities in some regions. Similar fare would be served in the lowland areas for threshing parties, including a cake made with buttermilk and mixed fruit and harvest cake with a fruit (often apple) filling. A family's prestige was linked with the lavishness of a well-prepared feast.[17] Aberffraw cakes (*teisennau Aberffraw*), sometimes called James's cakes (*Cacennau Iago*), are small rich shortbread biscuits named after the small seaside village of Aberffraw on the south coast of Anglesey. Traditionally they are cut out in the shape of a scallop shell. The scallop shells which were, and still are, found on the wide beach near Aberffraw are not true scallops, but smaller 'queens'.

A porcelain 'Welsh tea party' fairing. In Victorian Britain china ornaments were given away as prizes at fairs and became known as fairings. They included the 'Welsh tea party', showing ladies in Welsh costumes sitting around the tea table. These figures first appeared in the mid-19th century and most were mass-produced in Germany by Conta & Boehme, as was the one pictured, specifically for the British market. They remained popular until the First World War.

The flat half of the shell is used to imprint the shortbread with its shell pattern.

Spices are added to other baked goods including caraway soda bread (*bara soda carawe*), caraway seed cake (*teisen carawe*) and cinnamon cake (*teisen sinamon*). Potato cakes (*teisennau tatws*) are spiced with

cinnamon or mixed spice and served hot, spread with butter. There are gingerbreads and ginger cakes too: honey and ginger cake, Fishguard gingerbread and oddly what is called Old Welsh gingerbread, which does not contain any ginger at all! By tradition this gingerbread sold at Welsh country fairs was always made in this way.

Not all teas in Britain were as sumptuous as those described above. Many working-class families had to make do with three basic ingredients, as Flora Thompson describes in her autobiographical account of her late nineteenth-century childhood in an Oxfordshire village, *Lark Rise to Candleford* (1945): 'Here then were the three chief ingredients of the one hot meal a day, bacon from the flitch [from the side of the pig], vegetables from the garden, and flour for a roly-poly.'

A popular teapot for many working-class families at this time was the Brown Betty, a round teapot made from a red clay which was discovered in the Stoke-on-Trent area in 1695 and with a distinctive brown glaze known as Rockingham glaze. No one knows how the teapot got its name. The teapot is brown, of course, but no one really knows where 'Betty' is from; perhaps, as some have speculated, Betty is the name of a girl or woman servant. What is known is that Brown Betty teapots made an excellent pot of tea. The round shape of the pot enabled the tea leaves to gently swirl around as the boiling water was poured into the pot, releasing more flavour with less bitterness, and the special clay seemed to retain heat better, keeping the tea warm.

Even with a Brown Betty the tea in the pot could become cold, especially in winter, so a tea cosy was often used, keeping the tea nice and hot. Tea cosies were made from wool, cloth and lace. It is thought that they first came into being in the 1860s, at the time

Mary Ellen Best, *Cottagers at Tea*, York or Yorkshire, 1830s. This is a prosperous cottage. The clock shows it is ten past five and the kettle is on the fire. The large bowl on the tea table is for slops: economical cottagers would make at least two brews from the same leaves.

when afternoon tea and high tea were becoming so popular, and that was when they were first mentioned. Gervas Huxley in *Talking of Tea* (1956) suggests that the idea may have come from large Chinese teapots brought to England in the nineteenth century, which sometimes arrived in a thickly padded cane basket with a small hole for the spout. Tea cosies were also a means for Victorian ladies to show off their needlework skills. Some were embroidered with glass beads or lined with silk. This sort of cosy would have been kept for special occasions and used with the 'best' silver or porcelain teapot when entertaining visitors. Every style of needlework was used – needlepoint, crewel, embroidery, ribbon work, and so on. Some tea cosies were crocheted or hand-knitted, resembling a woolly hat; some even featuring a bobble on top.

Nursery Teas

Afternoon tea – that pleasant hour
When children are from lessons free,
And gather round their social board
Brimful of mirth and childish glee.
J. C. Sowerby and H. H. Emmerson (1880)

CHILDREN HAD their own special nursery teatime in Victorian and Edwardian times, usually at four or five o'clock. Children led quite restricted lives and were only allowed out with their nanny, or occasionally their parents took them out. After lunch children rested before perhaps going for a walk. At teatime they were often spruced up and, on their best behaviour, were presented to any ladies taking afternoon tea with their mother in the drawing room. They did not stay long and at four or five o'clock would disappear upstairs for their own nursery or schoolroom tea, provided by the nanny in a more relaxed atmosphere. Sometimes the mother or 'mamma' would join the children in their nursery for tea. It was a precious time to spend with the children and give them her undivided attention. They might entertain her by playing their musical instruments or reciting some poetry. At holiday times the father might join them and play with them.

The fare provided at nursery teas was more substantial than the grown-up afternoon teas, more like a high tea as it was the last meal of the day for the children. Cook would produce all kinds of treats, especially for birthdays or if visitors were present. Bread and butter and jam or small finger sandwiches, small cakes, sponge cake filled with jam or butter icing, fancy biscuits, sometimes muffins or crumpets, were often on the tea table, perhaps served with cambric tea, often referred to as a 'nursery' or 'children's' tea. It was made primarily from hot water and heated milk or cream, sometimes sweetened and with perhaps a dash or two of strongly brewed tea.[18] Otherwise the children would drink milk, juice or perhaps cocoa. Dolls were sometimes treated to a tea party as well. They were served from miniature tea sets of china touted round by salesmen from the potteries.

In *The Nursery Cookery Book* written by Mrs K. Jameson in 1929, 'hoping that it may be of use to the mothers of little children', the teatime fare described for children was not so delicate. Instead of sandwiches with the crusts removed she suggested 'crusty bread and butter with honey or jelly – not thin bread and butter, but crusty corner pieces that take some chewing'. If possible the bread should be home-made of stone ground flour or fine ground wholemeal. 'Oat cakes with butter, or a Ryevita Crisp Bread, or Peek Frean's Vita-Wheat should be given occasionally, they give the jaws plenty of work to do.' Mrs Jameson suggested that 'sometimes

give for a change a little simple cake (home-made) or a sponge finger instead of honey and jam'. And 'Pure honey is the best natural sweet, and a great cleanser of the mouth of tongue, besides being most delicious and wholesome eaten on bread. If possible get it from a place where bees are kept, and then you will know it is pure.' No tea, not even cambric tea, but 'Plain milk warmed, or flavoured with Ovaltine or cocoa – one cupful.'

The writer Molly Keane in *Nursery Cooking* (1985) has mixed memories of her nursery teatimes, including one occasion when an enlightened hostess 'excited a solemn children's tea-party to ecstasy by the magical words, "Now! Let's start with the strawberries and

'Tea in the Nursery', *Punch* (1855). The head nurse tries to dissuade Miss Mary from stirring her tea with the candle-snuffers.

cream" rather than the usual way of starting with "bread and butter before cake". However, at another children's party she remembers that 'Nanny, stood behind her chair denying me all the pleasures of the table, and proclaiming to the hostess nanny, who was proffering sponge cake: "Thank-you, Nanny, no. We have our acid tum. We stick to bread and butter. Eat up dear."'

Happy memories of teatimes are described by Mrs McKee, cook to both Her Majesty the Queen and the late Queen Mother. A Swede by birth, she was working for the Queen and Prince Philip at Clarence House at the time of the accession. In her book *The Royal Cookery Book* (1964) she describes the carefree but numbered days when the Queen was Princess Elizabeth and how she would spend the afternoon playing on the lawn with Prince Charles and Princess Anne 'carefully folding up the rug and taking in the toys when it was time for tea'. Tea for Charles and Anne 'was always in the sun-filled nursery, informal and gay with Prince Charles chatting excitedly about the day's events'. According to McKee, Prince Charles liked rice croquettes with pineapple sauce when he was still in the nursery, but McKee, gives recipes for cakes too, such as ginger sponge cake, currant cake, Madeira cake, sponge sandwich cake, chocolate and coffee cake, pineapple cake and almond biscuits. For the Queen Mother and Princess Margaret, however, teatime was quite different; they took it at a small table laid with a white cloth in the drawing room. Another tablecloth was laid on the floor, on which the dogs were given their own 'tea'.

Mrs McKee tells us that for birthday teas there would always be a birthday cake such as meringue gateau. Sandwiches might include grated cheese and shredded lettuce, minced ham and mayonnaise with sliced tomato and watercress, and thinly sliced cucumber rolled up in brown bread and butter. Jam canapés

Sir James Gunn, *Conversation Piece at the Royal Lodge, Windsor*, 1950, oil on canvas. An intimate glimpse of King George VI and Queen Elizabeth (the late Queen Mother) in 1950 enjoying a simple and informal family tea at the Lodge at Windsor with Princess Elizabeth and Princess Margaret. The tea table is elegantly set and the simple food reflects the mood of the times with rationing and shortages.

made with puff pastry might feature alongside cream horns and sponge tea cakes.

Although nannies and nursery teas have become a thing of the past, in many homes giving children 'tea' when they come home from school, tired and hungry, still continues. Sandwiches or bread and butter (or jam) have now been replaced by such things as peanut or chocolate spread sandwiches, fish fingers or small pizzas, and, instead of fairy cakes, elaborately decorated cupcakes are the fashion.

Country teas

BY THE END OF the nineteenth century, afternoon tea had crossed all class barriers and had become popular in most British homes, including in the countryside.

In *Lark Rise to Candleford* Flora Thompson describes tea with Mrs Herring: 'the table was laid . . . there were the best tea things with a fat pink rose on the side of each cup; hearts of lettuce, thin bread and butter, and the crisp little cakes that had been baked in readiness that morning'. She also describes impromptu tea gatherings and how they were a regular event for the women of the village; how the 'younger set' would sometimes get together in one of their cottages and sip strong, sweet, milkless tea and chat and gossip: 'This tea drinking time was the woman's hour.'

In Wales, where tea drinking was slow to take on because it was expensive and scarce, village women formed Tea Clubs or Clwb Tê. As money was often short, the tea, food and equipment were pooled. As Marie Trevelyan explained in 1893, 'One woman would bring tea, one a cake, another a drop of gin or brandy to put in it. They visited the homes of the members in turn, and naturally gossiped about what interested women.' She also wrote: 'the hill women [of Wales] are fond of drinking tea in immoderate quantities . . . The teapot is always on the hob, there is no end to the potations. There is no limit to the sippings.'[19]

Florence White, in *Good Things in England* (1932), wrote of country and schoolroom teas:

These words conjure up pictures of the great halls of country houses with logs blazing and sizzling on the hearth; a table large enough to allow a man who hates afternoon tea to sit and spread scones with butter and home-made jam; a singing kettle; piping hot toast; and home-made cakes, dogs lying warming themselves in blissful happiness, never even troubling to stir as well-known footsteps are heard outside, and members of the houseparty and other friends come in, one after the other exhilarated but tired after a splendid run with some well-known pack, or a day with the guns.

Or in summer time long trestle tables literally weighed down with cups and saucers and good things for tea out of doors for the consolation or encouragement of rival cricket teams; or between sets of tennis.

Or in farmhouses where one knows a good tea will be spread if one calls in at the right time.

Or – perhaps best of all? – schoolrooms in town or country where the best toast is to be had, and a cut-and-come-again cake of which one never wearies.

White later quotes Lady Raglan from *Memories of Three Reigns*, who gives a vivid picture of country house teas in England in 1873:

That teatime! That was always a delightful hour in the country when we would gather beside a blazing log fire and retail to each other the news of the day. At one country house I remember that this meal was always served in the billiard room, because the men for what reason I could never imagine, liked to play billiards whilst we had tea.

A WELSH TEA PARTY.

Postcard from the 1920s or '30s depicting three Welsh women having tea and wearing national costume, including the tall, black hat.

Advertisement for Idolice Confectionery, 20th century, 'for tennis parties, picnics, at-homes etc'. A man is offering a plate containing chocolate Swiss roll to a woman in a deckchair, tennis racquet by her side.

Everything was home-made, the bread and the cakes and the scones. And there was a particular delicacy associated with this place which I particularly loved. It was ginger jumbles, which were served all hot and crisp and sticky like treacle.

Florence White not only mentions playing billiards while having tea, but explains that teas were often put on to add to the enjoyment of an afternoon of sport such as tennis, cricket or croquet, evoking the spirit of summer. The game of tennis as we know it today began to blossom in the 1860s and '70s and tennis parties were elegant affairs. Sandwiches, cakes and so on were served with iced tea, coffee and perhaps a 'tennis cup'. 'Cups' – cool and thirst-quenching drinks – often contained tea as one of the ingredients. Some 'cups' contained alcohol, which no doubt livened up many an occasion.

Ices were also popular. Mrs Marshall, in *Fancy Ices* (1894), gives a recipe for Canadian Tea Ice which she said could serve as a dessert ice, for tennis parties or a ball supper:

Canadian Tea Ice
Glace de Thé à la Canadienne

Take a quarter-pound of good tea; put it into a hot dry teapot and pour in one quart of perfectly boiling water; let it infuse for about five minutes, then strain off the liquid and set it aside till cold. Put in a basin six whole raw eggs that have been beaten with a whisk for about five minutes with a teaspoonful of Marshall's Vanilla Essence and six ounces of castor [caster] sugar; add the cold tea to it by degrees, whipping the mixture whilst doing so; then strain through a strainer and mix into it one pint of very thick whipped cream and put it into the charged freezer; freeze it well, put it into any little fancy ice moulds, place these in the charged ice-cave for about one and a half hours; when ready to use turn out the ices in the usual way on to a clean cloth, and arrange them in little fancy nougat or paper cases; place them on a dessert dish.

There was sometimes a tennis cake. This was a light fruitcake created to accompany the newly invented game of tennis. Over time the shape of tennis cakes changed from being round into an oblong shape which could be decorated depicting a miniature tennis court.

Mrs McKee in her *Royal Cookery Book* gives a tennis party menu: cucumber sandwiches (stressing that the bread and cucumber must be thinly sliced, with a sprinkling of salt and a drop of tarragon vinegar to each sandwich), biscuit crunchies with ice-cream, gooey chocolate cake, iced tea and iced coffee.

In the late 1860s and '70s the Spode company made some of the most exquisite chinaware known as tennis sets. These comprised of a teacup (or coffee cup) on an elongated 'saucer', which efficiently left room for a delicate cucumber sandwich, slice of cake or biscuit or two by the cup, thus saving having to juggle a teacup and saucer and a plate separately.

A cricket tea is quintessential to the whole ritual of cricket. Outdoors if possible, although sunshine, a gentle breeze, sitting in deck chairs listening to the 'thwack' of leather on willow, may be a slightly romantic view especially for those of us who have sat shivering and wrapped up in blankets or rugs watching the match on the village green or school playing field. The teas were, however, always a delight and definitely welcome, with lots of hot, comforting tea made in large teapots, the hot water bubbling in huge urns. If the weather was kind (or even unkind) there could be fruit squashes or even Pimms for 'grown-up' cricket matches. Usually prepared by the mothers, wives or girlfriends of the players, there was always a gentle competition for, say, the best coffee and walnut cake. Strawberries and cream also play an important part in the ritual of cricket teas and Eton Mess, the strawberry, meringue and cream dessert, became famous for being made for the long-standing annual Eton and Harrow cricket matches. In *Good Things in England* (1932), Florence White mentions cricket teas 'at Knightshayes, Tiverton, when Blundell's School played some other Eleven, and whether they won or lost Blundell's boys trickled golden syrup over substantial slices of bread and cream which they called "thunder and lightning".'

A summer's day picnic tea is one of the joys of English culture. There does not have to be any sport involved and it can be enjoyed out of doors when the weather is fine, either in the garden, in woods and orchards or on the beach at the seaside. The type of food made for picnics can vary considerably from some simple sandwiches eaten while sitting on a rug or blanket to much more elaborate affairs with savoury tarts or flans and salads followed by cakes and other sweet things. For the more adventurous, kebabs, sausages or steaks might be grilled over a transportable barbecue. Food might be served on a picnic table with people sitting around on picnic chairs. The tea itself might be served from a thermos in little cups or a primus stove might be used to boil water for a freshly brewed pot.

Claudia Roden, in *Picnic* (1982), remembers an illustration in a Cairo schoolbook of her childhood, showing a daintily set tea table on a well-mown lawn: tea caddy, silver teapot, cream and milk jugs, sugar bowl, slop basin with a silver strainer and fine bone china service laid out on a light Chantilly lace cloth. She said that they symbolized the mystique of Englishness.

Of course the English weather is not always reliable but, as Georgina Battiscombe says in *English Picnics* (1951), the English picnicker is a hardy species, above the vagaries of the weather. And for those of us who have weathered picnics on the beach, John Betjeman wrote nostalgically in 'Trebetherick':

Sand in the sandwiches, wasps in the tea,
Sun on our bathing dresses heavy with the wet,
Squelch of the bladder-rack waiting for the sea,
Fleas round the tamarisk, an early cigarette.

Happy days!

Perhaps the grandest 'picnic' of all, with lots of pomp and ceremony, is the grand tradition which began in the 1860s with Queen Victoria – the Buckingham Palace Garden Party. She began hosting 'breakfasts', despite the fact that they were held in the afternoon and tea was served. She invited diplomats, politicians and other professionals. They were such splendid and successful affairs that the tradition has been continued by Queen Elizabeth II who, every year, opens the private gardens at Buckingham Palace to host three afternoon tea parties, each attended by 8,000 guests. Invitations are sent to people from all walks of life. The dress code for gentlemen is morning dress, suit, uniform or national dress. Ladies wear afternoon dress, usually with hat and gloves, or national dress. Guests are invited for 3 p.m. so

Royal Albert Old Country Roses tennis tea set, *c.* 1962. Sometimes referred to as a hostess set.

Holyday, later also known as *The Picnic*, by French painter James Tissot, 1876. He had moved to England in 1871 and this painting portrays a picnic in the back garden of his London home in St John's Wood. The men are wearing the red, gold and black hats of the elite amateur I Zingari cricket club, so this might not have been an ordinary picnic but a cricket tea.

that they can enjoy walking in the Royal Gardens before tea. At 4 p.m. the Queen and the Duke of Edinburgh, accompanied by some members of the royal family, join the guests and the occasion is started by the rousing sound of the national anthem. Two military bands play alternately throughout the occasion. While high-ranking guests and dignitaries proceed to the royal tent for tea, the remaining guests are served afternoon tea from a long buffet table. The planning and organization of an afternoon tea on this scale is impressive. For the buffet there are 20,000 various tea sandwiches, 5,000 bridge rolls, 9,000 butter drop scones, 9,000 fruit tartlets, 3,000 butter cake fingers, 8,000 slices of chocolate or lemon cake, 4,500 slices of Dundee cake, 4,500 slices of Majorca cake and 3,500 slices of chocolate or jam Swiss roll. Twenty-seven thousand cups of tea are served as well as 10,000 glasses of iced coffee and 20,000 glasses of fruit squash. The tea served is a special blend called Maison Lyons, which is produced exclusively by

Twinings for Buckingham Palace Garden Parties. Apparently it is a blend of Darjeeling and Assam, perfect for a summer's day tea party.

Village fetes, school fetes and church and chapel teas

SUMMER IS ALSO the time for village and school fetes. They are a good opportunity for the community to get together. After growing up in a village in the 1950s, I have many happy memories of going to village and school fetes, enjoying competitions, sporting events, even maypole dancing. Teas were served in the village or church hall on long trestle tables or in a tea tent. The cakes, buns, sandwiches and other savouries such as sausage rolls were made by women, not without, I may say, some competitiveness. More recently at my own children's schools I remember making tea from the hissy tea urn in large heavy teapots and struggling to pour it out. Not much has really changed over the years except perhaps that the sandwiches might now be made with wholemeal bread with more sophisticated fillings, and quiches and other savouries, such as samosas and pakoras, reflecting our multi-cultural society. Some of the cakes have become more adventurous or healthier, such as carrot cake, but the Victoria sandwich cake remains as popular as ever, and, of course, scones with jam and cream or butter.

Churches and chapels also held teas (and still do) for their congregations and the local community, often to raise money for charity. There was a regular cycle of annual celebrations such as Whitsuntide, Sunday school outings in the summer, harvest festivals and grand Christmas bazaars. Extensive preparations were made, especially for the catering. Baking was home-made, ladies being asked to bring their specialities such as fairy cakes or chocolate cakes, and also to prepare a vast number of sandwiches, often made with potted meats and fish pastes. The ladies worked as a team, coping with hot and humid conditions, including the steam of boiling tea urns.[20]

A mention must be made of Christmas teas. Just as a child's birthday party must have jelly and blancmange, fairy cakes or butterfly buns and a birthday cake, the traditional fare for tea at Christmas includes mince pies, a trifle and, of course, a Christmas cake, usually iced and decorated with a Christmas theme.

Christmas afternoon tea out with turkey and cranberry sandwiches, crayfish cocktails, salmon blinis, mince pies, cupcakes and macarons, tea and a glass of bubbly.

A 'tea' seems to fit many occasions, including bridge parties. Elizabeth Craig, in *Enquire Within* (1952), suggests that they were the 'most delightful way of entertaining', whether it was bridge with refreshments only, tea for the afternoon and coffee and sandwiches for the evening. The usual afternoon time was from 3 to 6.30 p.m. For the tea, she suggests 'a variety of dainty cakes, éclairs and thinly buttered walnut and raisin bread and offer at the end tiny canapés of buttered toast spread with caviar, foie gras, and so on.' And, importantly, she advises: 'Remember to give guests tea serviettes before providing fare which will damage fingers for cards.' Tea à la Russe or à l'Americaine should be offered and so should both China and Ceylon or Indian infused, and cream for those who want it.

Funeral teas

THERE ARE ALSO sad occasions when tea is an important and indeed essential part of the ceremony. The funeral tea is one such occasion and it plays an important part in commemorating the end of life.

In the seventeenth and eighteenth centuries, before tea had become affordable for many people, beer or wine and cakes or biscuits were served to the mourners at funerals. Later, when tea had become the drink of the masses, tea was served as well but the custom of serving beer, wine or sherry also continued. Here is an account of the usual practice throughout the north of England:

> Before leaving the house for the grave-yard, the mourners have refreshment served to them – cheese, spice bread and beer for the men; biscuits and wine, both home-made for the women. On returning to the house, a funeral feast is prepared, the like of which is only seen at these

times . . . the expence [sic] was so great that families were impoverished for years.[21]

The biscuits served were sponge fingers, also called funeral biscuits. In *Food and England* Dorothy Hartley says that 'In some country districts they were nicknamed "funeral fingers", being laid out with the sherry to greet visiting mourners.' She also tells that her aunt told her 'that in Wales in the 'seventies [1870s] it was correct to give little faggots of these biscuits, neatly tied up with black tape and tissue paper, to children to eat on the long cold drive to the funeral.'

Food historian Peter Brears, in *A Taste of Leeds* (1998), records that everyone 'followed the cortege to the church, only a few "tea makers" remaining behind to prepare the refreshments for their return'. Brears goes on to say that funeral buns, along with ale, formed part of the funeral tea in the mid-nineteenth century and 'the remainder of the tea, which invariably included large quantities of boiled ham, was always of the very best which the family could afford, even if the expense might leave them with considerable debts.'

There is a rather awful but typical Yorkshire tale about ham and funerals. 'A terminally ill old man said of the ham cooking in the kitchen, "Ee luv, that smells good, can I 'ave some?" to which his old woman replied, "Th'as 'avin' non o' that theer. It's for t'buryin."'[22]

Ham also appears at many Welsh funeral teas. Traditionally, after the service only the men go to the graveside, while the women go home and prepare the tea. Minwel Tibbott, in her book *Domestic Life in Wales* (2002), describes the pattern which evolved in the second half of the nineteenth century: 'Funeral attenders returned from the burial to the house of the deceased for a meal of bread and butter, tea, home-boiled ham, pickled onions and fruitcake.' Even today

Cream Teas

A Devonshire cream tea – home-made scones
topped with cream and then jam.

THE WEST COUNTRY has been famous for its cream teas since the opening of the railways in the mid-nineteenth century and the resulting tourist boom. Hotels, tearooms, cafés and farmhouses specialized in cream teas. There are Cornish, Devonshire, Somerset and Dorset cream teas, with each county claiming the origin of the cream tea as their own. In 2004 the BBC reported that local historians in Tavistock, west Devon, had discovered evidence in ancient manuscripts to suggest that a tradition of eating bread with cream and jam existed in the eleventh century at Tavistock Abbey. (This is actually quite similar to a variation on the cream tea called 'thunder and lightning'.) The story goes that the Abbey had been plundered by the Vikings in 997 CE and the resident Benedictine monks had fed the local workers restoring the Abbey with bread, clotted cream and strawberry preserves.[23] While the manuscript may be one of the earliest written references to a dish of bread served with jam and cream, the Cornish claim that the way of making clotted cream was given to them by Phoenician traders (who were from modern day Lebanon and Syria) in search of Cornish tin around 500 BCE.

Originally the 'cream tea' was made with splits (Cornish or Devonshire, where they are sometimes called chudleighs). Splits are a type of slightly sweet bun made with yeast. The two counties are also divided over whether you spread cream or jam first. In Cornwall the split bun would first be spread with strawberry jam, topped with a spoonful (or two) of clotted cream. In Devon the cream is spread over the split bun first, then the jam added on top. Nowadays scones usually replace the split but the different ways of serving with the jam and cream still stand and traditionally the scones (or splits) should be warm (ideally, freshly baked). Whatever the origins or which way round you add cream or jam, what is certain is that the cream tea is one of the joys of afternoon tea both in the home and in many hotels and tea rooms all over Britain.

the funeral tea is prepared for family and friends, especially in rural areas. Sympathy towards a bereaved family would be expressed with gifts of food such as home-baked cakes. During the nineteenth century expensive items such as tea and sugar would be given by friends and neighbours. This would help the family and be a contribution towards the funeral tea. This custom still prevails in rural Wales today.

The baking of cakes, making of sandwiches and serving of lots of reviving cups of tea for mourners returning from the graveside were all part of the ritual. It was important to give the deceased a 'good send off' and provide a 'good spread'.

Out for tea

AT THE BEGINNING of the nineteenth century meals could be obtained at chophouses, coaching inns, hotels and coffee houses, yet these places were deemed unsuitable for respectable women. In the 1860s with the arrival of better railway hotels, and later on the appearance of restaurants such as the Holborn, the Criterion and the Gaiety, women were welcome. Tea and coffee shops, offering food and entertainment, also began to appear in London in the 1870s. They were run by temperance societies but because they were often mismanaged and of poor quality they were short lived.[24]

One venture which did turn out to be successful was when, in 1864, a resourceful manageress of the Aerated Bread Company (ABC) persuaded the firm's directors to open up a room at the back of the shop in the courtyard of Fenchurch Street railway station to provide tea and refreshments for customers. The venture proved popular, not just with ladies but with shop assistants, office workers and ordinary shoppers. The first tearoom was born and was a place where

women could take refreshments unaccompanied and meet their friends. Going out to tea became the new fashion. Tea shops and tearooms started to spring up all across Britain.

By the end of the century there were at least fifty ABC tearooms and when it reached its peak in the mid-1920s ABC were running over 150 branch shops and 250 tea shops. In 1955 the independent operation of ABC came to an end and nowadays the only traces to be found of ABC are faded signs above stores, such as at 232 The Strand, now a supermarket.

It was not long after the establishment of the ABC tearooms in London in 1864 that Glasgow was introduced to the delights of the tearoom. Stuart Cranston opened the first 'Cranston's Tearoom' in 1875 at 2 Queen Street on the corner of Argyll Street. Cranston was an enterprising tea merchant who owned a small retail tea business. An increased trade in tea and sugar imports was developing in Glasgow after the collapse of the tobacco trade. The consequences of poverty and urban deprivation had taken its toll in industrial cities like Glasgow, where alcoholism was a serious problem, so Cranston, who had strong family connections with the temperance movement, saw that working people needed somewhere to take refreshments during the day, and the idea that tea was 'the cups that cheer but not inebriate' certainly influenced him.[25] Developing the tearoom was to provide an alternative to the pub. He followed the custom of the day by allowing clients to taste a cup of tea before buying. He then decided to serve cups of tea with bread and butter and cakes. He also thought his customers, both men and women, might like to taste teas in comfort before buying so he provided tables for sixteen customers 'elbow to elbow'. He advertised a cup of China tea 'with sugar and cream, for 2d bread and cakes extra'.

Cranston's sister Kate also spotted the potential of tearooms and in 1878 she opened her own tearooms, Miss Cranston's Crown Tearooms, at 114 Argyle Street. They were on the ground floor of a temperance hotel, which was convenient for Glasgow's commercial workers. Stuart Cranston may have been the first to open a tearoom in Glasgow but it was Kate who became synonymous with the first Glasgow tearooms. With a distinctiveness described as 'Cranston from the chairs to the china', in 1886 she was ready to expand and took on new premises at 205 Ingram Street. Although we usually associate these early tearooms with ladies in hats, these tearooms developed in the first place to meet the needs of men.

In 1897 Kate commissioned the 28-year-old architect Charles Rennie Mackintosh to decorate the walls of her third tearoom in Buchanan Street with Art Nouveau murals. Her famous Willow Tearooms on the fashionable Sauchiehall Street in Glasgow, where the smartest new department stores were concentrated, opened in November 1903. They were the very epitome of chic and attracted customers who were predominantly female and fashion conscious.

During a twenty-year partnership Mackintosh created some of his most memorable interiors for Kate Cranston. Between 1887 and 1917 he designed or restyled, with amazing artistic flair, all four of her Glasgow tearooms. This included not only murals but structure, furniture, even the waitresses' stylish outfits, with chokers of pink beads. They created the 'new art' interior and what might be called 'designer' tearooms. It was this partnership which made Miss Cranston's tearooms legendary and internationally renowned.

By the turn of the century tearooms had caught on, particularly with more progressive women who needed a place to meet outside the home that was not a pub.

Illustration of the café of an Aerated Bread Shop, 1902.

Though many of the old male order found the idea of a tearoom extremely distasteful, there were others who felt differently. There was also the vast army of young city clerks, often with artistic temperaments, who felt at home in the Cranston atmosphere. Kate gave them tea and a place to smoke, talk, play cards or dominoes and, most importantly, she provided pretty waitresses with whom they could become friendly – even date.

A Cranston menu at the Scottish National Exhibition held in Glasgow in 1911 shows that the tearoom provided quite an extensive choice. Apart from tea (large or small, Russian or in a pot) and other beverages such as coffee, cocoa, chocolate and milk, bread, scones and pancakes were available, which could be supplemented by a pot of jam, jelly or marmalade. Sandwiches (varied), pies and snacks (such as sausage and chips) were also on the menu. People wanting lunches or high tea were well catered for with plenty of choice: soups, fish, egg, cheese dishes, hot meats, pies, savouries, cold viands and hot and cold sweets such as steamed fruit

Miss Cranston waitresses in the Room de Luxe of the Willow Tearooms wearing their uniforms and pink pearl choker necklaces, *c.* 1903.

of family bakeries also began to open tearooms. Craigs, Hubbards and Fullers were the leading bakers who brought to the tearoom an exceptionally high standard of baking. Fullers were known for their eclairs and marzipan and walnut cake with toffee topping. Hubbards made 'paving stones', square, chewy, crisp gingerbreads with a hard icing on top. Craigs, the most successful and popular of the bakery chains, were renowned for their chocolate liqueur cakes. They also brought in Continental bakers and the 'French cake' was introduced to the city.[27]

After the Second World War cheap female labour, on which the economic success of tearooms depended, became less available. Social habits also changed. The pre-war generation may have been happy with beautifully laundered tablecloths and good furniture, but young people in the post-war years wanted something more modern. Old bakery firms were taken over by conglomerates and only a few bakery tearooms have survived to the present day.[28] However, in December 1983 the Willow Tearooms were recreated and in 1997 Willow Tearooms opened in Buchanan Street, immediately next door to Miss Cranston's original Buchanan Tearooms. It contains recreations of the White Dining Room and Chinese Room from the Ingram Street site.

Back in London the most successful and well-known tearooms were those of the dynamic catering entrepreneur Joseph Lyons. He opened his first London tearoom in 1894 at 213 Piccadilly and by the end of 1895 had opened fourteen more. They were notable for their interior design and their art nouveau signs with gold lettering on white. They provided good cheap food with smartness and cleanliness. It cost 2*d* for a pot of tea (elsewhere it was 3*d* a cup), buns cost a penny and cream meringues 5*d*. The engaging waitresses, with their stylish but comfortable uniforms, were

pudding and custard sauce and charlotte russe. The menu also offered fixed price high teas and plain teas. For example, for high tea one could order a cup of tea with cold baked herring with sliced bread and butter, and a cake or scone 'from the stand' cost 9*d*. The plain tea for 6*d* consisted of just sliced buttered bread with a cake or for 1*s* you could have a pot of tea with sliced buttered bread, a buttered scone and two cakes, with a pot of jam![26]

In 1917, following the death of her husband, Kate Cranston sold her tearooms. Other Cranston-type women such as Miss Buick and Miss Rombach carried on with the same style of tearoom but a number

'Nippies' serving tea to some of the 1,000 disabled soldiers being entertained at Lyon's Coventry Street Corner House in London in 1926.

nicknamed 'nippies' because of their efficiency and speed in serving.

Tearooms and tea shops mushroomed in London, many of them owned and managed by women. In 1893 the Ladies' Own Tea Association opened in Bond Street. Others soon followed, including the Kettle-drum Tea Rooms. The decor in charming pink and primrose appealed to lady shoppers. Cakes and other delicacies were provided by Messrs Fuller, including their renowned iced walnut cake which became immortalized in both Nancy Mitford's *Love in a Cold Climate* (1949) and Evelyn Waugh's *Brideshead Revisited* (1945) when Charles tells the story of going up to Oxford and meeting his cousin Jasper, who stayed for tea and 'ate a very heavy meal of honey-buns, anchovy toast and Fuller's walnut cake'. Fullers' shop, which opened in Kensington High Street in 1892, although smaller than Lyons, appealed to many women because

of its cosy alcoves, palms and decor with small tables spread for tea with pastries and cakes, including the iced walnut cake.[29]

Other tearooms were opened, including in leading hotels and department stores. Liberty's in Regent Street, London, offered an exotic respite for shoppers in the form of its Eastern-themed tearoom. They could refresh themselves with tea and biscuits. For one person the cost was 6*d*, or for two 9*d*. They could choose which exotic blend of tea to drink: the Indian blend, the Lotus blend or the Yang Yin blend. Ladies coming here for tea were also offered the ultimate convenience of a ladies' cloakroom.

Some department stores such as Selfridges and Derry & Toms in Kensington enjoyed roof gardens. There were also tea gardens, such as Kensington Tea Gardens, Tewkesbury Abbey Garden or, further afield, Rushen Abbey on the Isle of Man, where tourists would

Postcard of Rushen Abbey tearoom on the Isle of Man, *c.* 1907. Originally a monastery,
gifted by King Olaf in 1134, Rushen Abbey has seen monks, raiders, demolition,
jam factories and strawberry tea dancing.

flock to dance on the large wooden dance floor situated in beautiful gardens or enjoy a strawberry cream tea while watching the dancing and listening to the orchestra.

Some theatres also opened up tearooms. The Coliseum boasted a tearoom on every tier: the Grand Tier Tearoom, the Balcony Tearoom and the Terrace Tearoom. Apart from enjoying 'dainty snacks at moderate charges' or a five o'clock tea served between 3 and 5 p.m., you could also purchase tickets for the next performance.

Tearooms sprang up all over the country. Yorkshire is famous for its Bettys. The first Bettys cafe opened in Harrogate on 17 July 1919. It was owned by another entrepreneur, originally from Switzerland, who, on becoming an English citizen, changed his name from Fritz Bützer to Frederick Belmont. Bettys café was exquisitely decorated and fitted out with showcases in precious wood and mirrors and glass on the walls. More Bettys followed in other towns of Yorkshire, including York and Ilkley. Bettys cafés today are still renowned for their combination of exquisite Swiss confectionery, cakes and patisserie with Yorkshire specialities such as Yorkshire curd tart, Yorkshire tea loaf and fat rascals.

Going out to tea played a key part in the independence and emancipation of women. Women now had a safe and respectable place for meeting their friends outside the home. The suffragettes often held their meetings over afternoon tea in tearooms or restaurants. The Criterion in Piccadilly was a favourite among members of the Women's Freedom League (WFL) and Emmeline Pankhurst mentioned it in her autobiography, *My Own Story* (1914), as a place that hosted many Women's Social and Political Union (WSPU) breakfasts and teas. The Gardenia was included in *The Vote Directory* – the WFL newspaper's list of recommended retailers – and was written up in the 6 May 1911 issue when, in the course of a suffragists' shopping day, the author has tea at the Gardenia: 'a fragrant cup of tea and some cress sandwiches made with Hovis bread'.[30]

Other tearooms frequented by the suffragettes included Lyons tearooms. But quite apart from the chains there was a proliferation of small tearooms particularly aimed at women and which were also likely to be run by women who may have had no training in anything other than running a home. These tearooms allowed women the possibility of running a business, while at the same time providing a place for women to meet and pause for refreshments. Alan's Tea Rooms was owned by Miss Marguerite Alan Liddle, sister of Helen Gordon Liddle, who was an active member of the WSPU, and it became particularly popular with

Detail from a 1920s Bettys café menu.

Postcard of one of the tea rooms at the London Coliseum, 1904.

suffragettes. It was situated upstairs at 263 Oxford Street and provided a discreet place for them to meet.

The Teacup Inn was another popular meeting place. It was opened in January 1910 in Portugal Street, just off Kingsway. In the WSPU's newspaper *Votes for Women* they advertised 'Dainty luncheons and afternoon teas at moderate charges. Home cookery. Vegetarian dishes and sandwiches. Entirely staffed and managed by women.'

Outside London the suffragettes frequented similar tearooms or cafés to hold their meetings and discuss politics. In Newcastle, Fenwick's café was the venue of choice. In Nottingham the WSPU held meetings at Morley's Café, a teetotal establishment, originally opened to provide an alternative to the pub. In Edinburgh the Café Vegetaria was particularly favoured by the local Women's Freedom League.

The tea dance (thé dansant)

IN CONTRAST TO the furtive meetings of the suffragettes, going out to tea, which reached its heyday in Edwardian times in England, on the Continent and in the USA, could also mean enjoying an afternoon out dancing. Afternoon teas were served in the lounges and palm courts of exclusive hotels to musical accompaniment. In about 1913 a new trend of 'tango teas' arrived in London. The tango was an exotic and risqué dance craze from Argentina and had already arrived on French dance floors around 1912 where 'tango teas' became the rage of high society. Some of London's grandest hotels held weekly tea dances or *thé dansants*, as they were fashionably called.

Gladys Crozier, a society hostess and leading authority on tea dancing, described the *thé dansant* scene in 1913:

Thé dansant menu at the Savoy, 1928.

THE DANSANT 5/-

Les Specialitées

Le THÉ RUSSE
Specially prepared by Russian Expert.

Les GAUFRES SAVOYARDES (chaudes)
(faites à la minute)

STRAWBERRY ICE CREAM.
SAVOY SUNDAE

Les Chocolats de Paris

AMERICAN COFFEE

Thé   Café   Chocolat
Buns   Buttered Toast   Gaufres

LES SANDWICHES de
Cresson   Tomate   Œuf   Concombre
Jambon   Langue   Saumon Fumé
(sur demande)

LA PÂTISSERIE FRANÇAISE.
Gâteau Mascotte   Choux à la Crème
Gâteau Monte Carlo   Mille Feuilles
        La Brioche Parisienne

La Salade de Fruits frais

LES GLACES À LA CRÈME.
Vanille   Fraise   Chocolat   Café

Savoy Fruit Cup
Orangeade   Citronnade   Café Viennois
        Thé Glacé

What could be pleasanter, for instance, on a dull wintry afternoon, at five o'clock or so, when calls or shopping are over, than to drop in to one of the cheery little 'Thé Dansant' clubs, which have sprung up all over the West End . . . to take one's place at a tiny table . . . to enjoy a most elaborate and delicious tea . . . whilst listening to an excellent string band (and) . . . joining in the dance . . .[31]

The Waldorf Hotel was one of the most popular venues, hosting tango teas in its stunning Palm Court where tables were placed around the dance floor and in a viewing gallery above, and guests could sit down and enjoy a refreshing cup of tea between dances. The Savoy was another popular venue. Susan Cohen describes these occasions in *Where to Take Tea* (2003): 'The tea-dance experience at the Savoy was the ultimate in good taste, style and sophistication. The tea-tables were beautifully set with the hotel's hallmark pink tablecloths, *le thé Russe* was prepared by a Russian expert and menus were presented in French to preserve the continental feel so loved by high society.' The 1928 menu reproduced here shows not only *Le Thé russe* but *Les Gaufres savoyardes*, Savoy sundae, *Les Sandwiches*, *La Pâtisserie française* and *Les Glaces à la crème*: lots of delicious food to sustain the dancers.

Scotland also had its own tea dances. Elizabeth Casciani describes how in Edinburgh in September 1926 the Plaza Salon de Danse and café opened its door for dancing and tea. Alcohol was not licensed for ballrooms but tea, coffee, Horlicks, cold milk, hot

A Parisian fashion come to London: the tango tea at Prince's restaurant, 1913.

milk or Bovril were all available. The food on offer was quite substantial, a high tea costing one and ninepence. Weddings cost more – four and sixpence per head – and the usual menu for these events was 'tea, coffee, various sandwiches, sandwich fingers, muffins, cakes, cut cake, shortbreads, assorted pastries, biscuits and chocolate biscuits, fruit and wine jellies and creams, trifle, fruit salad ices handed round later and "aerated waters" (lemonades).' For even grander affairs there was a five and sixpence menu consisting of soup or grapefruit, 'hot joints' or beefsteak pies served with vegetables and potatoes, cold meats and salad. There was a choice of two sweets plus the inevitable tea, coffee, biscuits and cheese, sandwiches and cakes, and biscuits followed by ices later.[32]

Tea gowns were already highly fashionable garments which were feminine but at the same time refined. Dressing for the *thé dansant*, however, called for garments that would allow even more freedom of movement. One of Mrs Crozier's favourite designers was Lady Duff Gordon – otherwise known by her professional name of Madame Lucile. Luxurious fabrics like chiffon, velvet, net and fur were combined with superb design and artistry to create beautiful frocks. By 1919 tango shoes were easy to identify by their cross-lacing ribbons and were seen worn with shorter dresses, often with a slit in the skirt to make dancing easier.

The craze for tango teas lasted into the early 1920s. Other dance crazes came and went on the tea dance floor: from the tango to the turkey trot; the shimmy to the shake; the bunny hug to the black bottom; the Castle walk to the Lindy hop (named after the American aviator Charles Lindbergh). In 1925 the first demonstration of the Charleston was given at a special *thé dansant* at the Carnival Club in London – to riotous results.[33] The Charleston became the next dance craze and, for the fashionable young set, cocktails instead of tea were the next trend. The Waldorf continued its tea dances until 1939 when a German bomb shattered the glass roof of the Palm Court and frivolities such as tea dances were cancelled.

Teatimes during the wars

TEA DANCES may have been cancelled but even two world wars could not stop British people from drinking tea and enjoying their teatimes, albeit in reduced circumstances. The British government was reluctant to ration tea when war broke out in 1914, realizing just how important it was to the British public. However, because of the difficulty of importing food from overseas during wartime, by the winter of 1917 Britain was running very short of basic foodstuffs. People, anxious about whether there was enough to go around, started to queue. The government introduced rationing of foodstuffs such as sugar, margarine and butter, but not tea.

Tea provided warmth and sustenance for soldiers fighting on the front in miserable conditions and despite the difficulties of brewing tea under the hardships of trench warfare, they drank a lot of it. Apart from regular packets of tea, they were provided with 'tea tabloids', small compressed tablets of tea which could be dissolved in boiling water.[34] Milk was also available in the form of tabloids or tinned, condensed or evaporated. Biscuits were available too. They were produced under government contract by Huntley & Palmers, which in 1914 was the world's largest biscuit manufacturer. They were made from salt, flour and water and the long suffering troops likened them to dog biscuits because they were notoriously hard and needed to be soaked in water or dunked in tea if cracked teeth were to be avoided.

On the home front, tea was also an essential. The YMCA performed a crucial role in supporting the troops. They set up recreation centres close to railways stations and other places where troops congregated, not only providing a place to rest, but serving tea, sandwiches or other refreshments. Women war workers who ran Red Cross canteens also brewed vast amounts of tea for tired soldiers on leave. A cup of tea and a snack were great morale boosters.

For families during and after the First World War it was often difficult to provide nourishing food for teatime. Dr Sprigg, in his wartime book *Food and How to Save It* (1918) issued by the Ministry of Food, gave ideas on the preparation of children's meals in the context of wartime food shortages and rationing. For tea he suggested bread, oatcake, margarine, dripping toast, currant bread, potato scones, barley scones, rice

The Soldiers and Sailors Buffet at Victoria Station, by Philip Dadd in *The Sphere*, 1915. An illustration of men either arriving on the leave train or departing for the Front. They are given free refreshments of tea or coffee, sandwiches and cake by volunteers, funded through charitable donations.

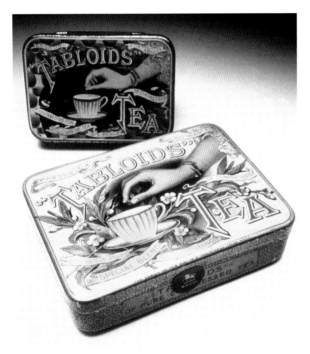

Two tabloid tea tins produced by Burroughs Wellcome and Co., *c.* 1900.

cakes, gingerbread made with oatmeal, syrup, jam, sandwiches of cress, tomato, lettuce and radish, green and fruit salads and stewed fruit.[35]

Just before the Second World War, when times were still hard, Elizabeth Craig's *1500 Everyday Menus* (*c.* 1940) gave ample scope and inspiration for the provision of appetizing but thrifty meals for high tea. She also advises on making the most of leftovers and gives daily menus using foods that are readily available and well within the reach of the modest purse. For example, for the Sunday in the first week of January she suggests sardines on toast, white bread, raisin bread, teacakes, Eccles cake, chocolate macaroons, gingerbread and green grapes. For Saturday in the second week of June she suggests Melton Mowbray pie, tomato and onion salad, brown bread, sultana scones, flapjacks, eclairs, devil's food cake, walnut wafers and compote of cherries.

During the Second World War, when times continued to be hard, tea played an important role in keeping up morale to the extent that it has been claimed that tea had a major impact on the outcome of the war. Winston Churchill claimed that tea was more important than ammunition. In 1942 historian A. A. Thompson wrote: 'They talk about Hitler's secret weapon, but what about England's secret weapon – tea. That's what keeps us going and that's what's going to carry us through – the army, the navy, the Women's Institute – what keeps 'em together is tea.'[36]

However, in July 1940 tea was rationed and the tight controls hit hard. The weekly allowance per person over the age of five was only 2 ounces (56 g). This was just enough for two or three cups of weak tea a day. There were extra allocations for people in vital jobs such as firefighters and steelworkers. Churchill, while he was First Lord of the Admiralty, also declared that tea was to be issued to sailors aboard naval vessels – as many cups of tea as they wanted. From 1944 onwards people over seventy were allowed 3 ounces. Tea rationing continued after the end of the war until 1952.

The Red Cross sent parcels to British prisoners of war abroad and by the end of the war twenty million or more were being sent. A quarter of a pound of tea (supplied by Twinings) was always included, along with cocoa powder, a bar of chocolate, processed cheese, condensed milk, dried eggs, a tin of sardines and a bar of soap.[37]

During the German bombing raids known as the Blitz, mobile canteens were set up on city streets by the Women's Voluntary Service. Volunteers would hand out cups of tea and coffee and snacks to rescue workers and the thousands of people affected by the bombing. Meanwhile Lyons tea shops took measures and arranged to get more out of their tea by making one hundred cups to the pound instead of the pre-war 85.

Food was rationed in Britain from 1940 until 1954. Allowances fluctuated, but at their lowest, one adult was allowed each week:

> 4 oz (113 g) bacon and ham
> 8 oz (226 g) sugar
> 2 oz (57 g) tea
> 1 shilling's worth of meat
> 1 oz (28 g) cheese
> 4 oz (113 g) butter

On top of this each person had an allowance of cooking fat and margarine and – once a month – some jam.

These meagre allowances proved quite a challenge for the British housewife to provide nourishing and tasty meals for the family, including for 'high tea'. The Ministry of Food published war cookery leaflets to help and give inspiration to people to make the most of their rations. In one of these leaflets, *No. 7: High Teas and Suppers*, there are many old teatime favourites, such as salmon croquettes served with a raw vegetable salad and bread, margarine and jam or macaroni cheese and tomatoes or watercress, followed by jam tart.

With rationing still in force in 1948 the Good Housekeeping Institute published a leaflet for *100 Ideas for Breakfast and High Tea*, hoping to inspire people to prepare nourishing and tasty meals. The recipes given are quite innovative, especially for 'substantial high teas', which include curried spaghetti and casseroled gnocchi with shredded cabbage. This followed their suggestions during the war years, when home-grown

Tea ladies and tea trolleys

TEA LADIES were used in an experiment to boost efficiency in workplaces for the war effort. They had such a hugely positive effect on morale that they became commonplace in all areas of work. By 1943 over ten thousand canteens were making sure that workers got some decent food and plenty of tea to keep them going through their long wartime shifts.

These were the first official tea breaks and a tea trolley was pushed along corridors and up and down office aisles by the 'tea lady' – something which was to become familiar in factories and offices in the 1950s and '60s. The tea trolley usually had everything needed for a tea break: an urn full of either hot water or already prepared tea and perhaps a selection of cakes, buns, cookies or other light treats.

With changing work patterns and the decline of the tradition of set tea breaks, along with the introduction of vending machines or cafeterias, the days of the office tea lady with her tea trolley gradually came to an end in the 1960s and '70s.

Tea trollies were also to be found at major railway stations such as York, Paddington and Euston from at least the beginning of the twentieth century.

Tea trolley providing tea and refreshments for passengers at Euston Station in 1908.

An army of tea ladies with their trolleys take tea to the workers at the Philips Lamps factory at Mitcham in Surrey in the 1940s.

vegetables were encouraged, that with vegetables from the garden attractive and nourishing dishes could be made for high tea, such as spinach and potato ring, cauliflower pie and colcannon. For meat dishes they admit that the meat ration 'does not usually stretch to provide many meat meals during the week, so for high teas the most welcome suggestions are probably those based on tinned "points" or unrationed meats, or using the odd quarter of a pound of minced meat or corned beef…to make the very meagre portion of such meats go as far as possible.' Recipes given include corned beef fritters and devilled sausages. Cheese dishes are said to be nourishing and quickly prepared, such as potato cheese toasts and savoury tartlets (using dried eggs). Salads too are encouraged as all-the-year-round favourites and made in a few minutes.

After the war there were many street tea parties, especially for children. Many remember putting on their best clothes. The sandwiches were often filled with Spam or meat or fish paste and jelly was topped with custard. Often there was a celebration cake with icing. Street tea parties have continued to be popular for big public occasions such as the Jubilee of 1977, the marriage of Prince Charles and Princess Diana in 1981, the Diamond Jubilee in 2012 and the Queen's ninetieth birthday in 2016.

During the war and into the 1950s going out to tea had declined. Legislation concerning wages and working conditions meant that running a tea shop became much more expensive. Self-service coffee bars became fashionable and popular. Afternoon tea in the grand hotels in large towns became dismal affairs and lost their appeal.

Tea, however, remained the favourite beverage in the home and gained ground in the 1950s with the arrival of the tea bag. Originally invented in the United States

Coronation street party, 1953. Villagers celebrating the Coronation of Elizabeth II with games, a brass band and, of course, a scrumptious tea party for the children.

by a New York City tea importer, Thomas Sullivan, in 1908, the tea bag was to revolutionize not only the tea industry but tea drinking as a whole. The centuries-old rituals of tea making had been turned into a quick and easy convenience. Today tea bags make up 96 per cent of the British tea market.

It was also at about this time that meal patterns changed again. Afternoon tea, except perhaps for a cup of tea and a biscuit or piece of cake mid-afternoon, more or less disappeared, and although many working-class people in parts of Britain, especially in the north, still had high tea at about five or six o'clock, working patterns for many people meant that this meal now moved to a later time and became dinner.

In the 1970s taking tea out started to become popular again when the National Trust began to offer visitors

Mad Hatter's tea party

John Tenniel's illustration of the Mad Hatter's Tea Party
from Lewis Carroll's *Alice's Adventures in Wonderland*.

THE THEME of the Mad Hatter's Tea Party has become very popular both in the home for parties and at tearooms and hotels. Created by Lewis Carroll in *Alice's Adventures in Wonderland* in 1865, it has become the most famous tea party in literature. It is full of riddles, nonsense and craziness. It is always teatime in the Mad Hatter's world because his watch is fixed at six o'clock.

'Take some more tea,' the March Hare said to Alice, very earnestly.

'I've had nothing yet,' Alice replied, in an offended tone, 'So I can't take more.' 'You mean you can't take less,' said the Hatter: 'It's very easy to take more than nothing.'

Alice gets no tea. There is only bread and butter on the table. For parties in the home mixed crockery may be used, odd cups and saucers, colourful tablecloths and napkins, unusual cakes and pastries such as marshmallow 'magic' mushrooms, rainbow sandwiches and Queen of Hearts jam tarts.

to their historic properties traditional afternoon tea. Today they have more than a hundred tearooms and cafés serving tea and home-made teatime treats across England, Wales and Northern Ireland.

When Jane Pettigrew opened her art deco tea shop in Clapham in 1983, the venture proved successful and popular and became part of this new trend. Today tearooms flourish all over Britain. One famous place to go for a special afternoon tea is the Pump Room in Bath, Somerset, which is adjacent to the historic Roman Baths. Regarded as the social heart of Bath for more than two centuries, the eighteenth-century Pump Room is an impressive neoclassical salon with tall windows, Corinthian columns, a glittering crystal chandelier and a fountain for drinking the hot spa water. There is plenty of choice for afternoon tea, including the traditional Bath bun of this region. For children, in the summer, there is a 'Little Mad Hatters Afternoon Tea' with a rabbit gingerbread biscuit, Queen of Hearts jam tart and 'Eat Me' cupcakes.

In London hotels such as the Ritz, the Savoy, the Waldorf, the Dorchester and the Lanesborough, to name just a few, provide elegant afternoon teas with a choice of speciality teas and, if desired, a glass of champagne. They are expensive and are enjoyed for special occasions or by tourists wanting to experience the very British tea tradition. Yet so intense is the competition that themed afternoon teas are becoming popular. You can enjoy an afternoon tea 'with a difference' at many of London's top venues, the difference being either a quirky theme (such as a Mad Hatter's tea), a unusual location (perhaps on a boat), or a global flavour, where in exchange for scones and sandwiches one can enjoy a Thai, sushi, *dim sum* or masala chai 'afternoon tea'. There is something to cater for all tastes, including the growing trend of gentlemen's teas, where there is not a

dainty sandwich or cake in sight. The menus created are more like high tea with substantial savoury dishes to cater for those who prefer savoury to sweet. The Athenaeum serves wild boar sausage rolls, mini steak and ale pies and cheddar and bacon scones and instead of champagne one can choose from the whisky menu. The customary tea can be sipped with sticky toffee pudding. Or treat yourself to a rabbit and pancetta pasty and poached oysters with Bloody Mary relish in between sips of Jack Daniel's 'Gentleman Jack' at the Sanctum Soho.

Two

Europe

M OST COUNTRIES IN EUROPE are better known for their coffee drinking. Tea was, however, first introduced to Europe by the Dutch in the early seventeenth century, and although the Portuguese were the first to sail round the Cape of Good Hope and enjoy a monopoly of Far Eastern trade in the sixteenth century, they did not pay much attention to trading in tea. It was their competitors, the Dutch, who brought the first shipment of green tea from Japan to Amsterdam in 1610. The Dutch marketed tea to other countries such as Germany, France and England (where it was to become the favoured beverage over coffee). Tea drinking traditions in Eastern Europe, including Poland, came via Russia in the seventeenth century.

The Netherlands

WHEN TEA FIRST ARRIVED it was an expensive, exotic novelty for the rich. It was also considered a medicinal beverage because of its bitter taste and purported health-giving properties. In 1657 Dr Brontekoë (nicknamed 'Mr Good Tea') publicly hailed the miraculous benefits of tea, prescribing forty to fifty cups of tea a day to reduce high fever.[1] From the outset, tea was not drunk at accepted mealtimes. Instead, a new meal was created. In the cities tea was accompanied by cakes, pastries and biscuits, whereas people living in the country might enjoy their tea with rusks or bread and cheese.[2]

Tea parties became a status symbol reflecting wealth and social standing. Dutch traders also brought with the tea exquisite and expensive Chinese porcelain tea sets, which were deemed necessary to serve the tea and accompanying delicacies. Potters began to imitate the Chinese porcelain teaware by making a tin-glazed earthenware known as faience. Dutch artists successfully captured the colour and charm

Jan Josef Horemans, *Tea Time*, 1750–1800.

of Chinese blue-and-white porcelain which, because it was made in and around Delft, became known as delftware. Japanese or Venetian dishes were also used, as well as golden spoons and forks.

Special rooms were set aside where the precious tea was prepared, served and drunk, usually sweetened with the equally precious sugar. 'The furniture consisted of tea-tables and chairs with cabinets for the cups and sugar boxes as well as for silver spoons and saffron pots . . . The tea and saffron were served together, the mixture being hot, sweetened and covered in a cup so as to preserve its aroma.'[3] The etiquette for drinking tea, especially for refined ladies, was to drink it from saucers. This is called *schotel drinken* in the Netherlands and the practice is still in use in some rural areas of the country.[4]

There was much competition between hostesses to provide the best delicacies to serve with the tea. 'Confituren were served in various forms: fruit might be candied, or pulp might be cooked with sugar and spread to dry in a thin sheet or the resulting jam-like

confection might be poured into teacups or special little moulds to set.'[5]

Today the Dutch import the majority of their tea from Indonesia (its former colony), with Sri Lanka a runner up. Although the Dutch tend to drink more coffee these days, tea is still popular for breakfast, at lunchtime and after dinner. Mid-morning usually means a coffee break in the Netherlands but mid-afternoon is reserved for *theetijd* – teatime – when sweet snacks such as biscuits (*koekjes*), pieces of chocolate (*chocolatjes*) and *muisjes* (sugar-coated aniseeds) are served with tea.[6] Tea is usually made on the weak side and no milk is added. Flavoured or fruit teas are also popular. Another teatime treat is a *stroopwafel* (a thin, crispy waffle 'sandwich' with a caramel-like syrup filling), which is originally from Gouda and said to have first been made in 1784 by a baker using leftovers from the bakery. The waffle is served on top of the teacup, the steam from the hot tea softens the syrup and at the same time a lovely aroma of cinnamon is released. For formal tea drinking the Dutch still like to use fine china teacups and saucers and many possess the iconic blue-and-white Dutch delftware.

There are plenty of places all over the Netherlands to take afternoon tea (usually referred to as 'high tea'),

Stroopwafel(s) with tea.

including The Royal Delft in Delft who serve their teas on delftware, and Gartine in Amsterdam, providing a variety of 'high teas' with soups, quiches, savoury choux pastries and various cakes.

Germany

THE FIRST TEA came to Germany via East Frisia close to the Dutch border around 1610, when East Frisian ships were contracted with the Dutch East India Company. Within a hundred years tea became the top beverage of East Frisia. (Tea was less expensive than domestically produced beer.) The Germans were also the first to discover the secrets of manufacturing china porcelain in Meissen in 1709. The designs of the tea services were based on Chinese models: the cups were tiny and without handles and saucers were deep, more like a shallow bowl. At this time the fashion for things Chinese gripped Europe. Many European princes and kings incorporated tea houses into their parks and gardens. One of the finest examples was the Chinese House built by Frederick II of Prussia in 1756 at Sanssouci chateau in Potsdam.

By the end of the eighteenth century tea drinking had become part of everyday life and replaced the customary morning bowl of soup. Tea drinking was popular in literary circles too. Goethe believed a tea party was the perfect way to receive friends. The poet Heinrich Heine wrote his famous poem on tea at the Stehelysh tea and pastry shop in Berlin where many painters, actors, writers and diplomats would meet and be stimulated by drinking tea:[7]

They sat round the tea-table drinking,
And speaking of love a great deal;
The men of aesthetics were thinking
The ladies more prone were to feel.[8]

The 'Chinese House' (tea house) is a charming and exotic garden pavilion in Sanssouci Park in Potsdam. It was commissioned by Frederick II of Prussia from 1754–64 to adorn his flower and vegetable garden. It was built in the then impressive and popular style of chinoiserie. Displayed around the pavilion's exterior are fairy-tale-like Chinese musicians and figures of tea-drinking men and women, which blend in with the columns shaped like gilded palms.

East Frisian *Tee mit Sahne* (tea with a cloud of cream) served in the famous 'Rood Dresmer' (red peony or rose pattern) teacup and saucer.

Although Germany today is usually associated with coffee drinking, tea drinking is taken very seriously. People in East Frisia still drink tea two to four times a day. In addition to breakfast and dinner there is morning teatime at around 11 a.m. and another at 3 p.m. The tea is usually a mix of Assam and Ceylon, which makes a strong, dark tea with a good aroma. East Frisians have their own special way of making tea, with rock sugar called *Kluntje* (also known as *Kandis*) and cream. First of all a lump of *Kluntje* is placed in a *Teeglas* (tea glass) or china cup. Strong, black tea is poured over the *Kluntje* (listen for the crack as the tea hits it), then, often with a special spoon called a *Rohmlepel* which has a round deep bowl, thick cream is poured carefully around the inside edge of the cup and rises like a cloud in the hot tea. The tea is not stirred, so the first thing the tea drinker tastes is the rich softness of the cream, then the bitterness of the hot tea and finally the sweetness of

the *Kluntje*. Traditionally three cups are drunk; in fact, as a guest, it is considered impolite to drink fewer than three cups. When you are finished the spoon is placed in the cup to signify you have had enough, otherwise your host will continue to refill.

East Frisians preferred drinking their tea from 'Dresmer Teegood' (Dresdner tea sets) from the Wallendorfer Porzellan manufacturing company, which has been in operation since 1764. Two patterns were popular: a blue one called 'Blau Dresmer' and the famous red peony (also called rose) pattern, the 'Rood Dresmer'. A set consisted of a cream canister, a teapot (*Treckpott*) and cups (*Koppen*, or *Kopkes*).

Tea is also popular in other parts of Germany, which is the largest consumer in the world of top-quality teas such as Darjeeling. Imports of tea rose to a record level in 2014. The port city of Hamburg acts as the centre for the wholesale tea trade in Europe and has a flourishing re-export trade, Canada being the major destination.[9] Bremen, with its seaport Bremerhaven, is also important for the tea trade and has a number of tearooms to cater for demand, including Teestübchen im Schnoor which is inside a medieval house. They serve eighty types of tea and a variety of home-made *Torten*. Teas are sold on the ground floor alongside handicrafts.

France

ALTHOUGH FRANCE is also better known for its coffee drinking, tea became a fashionable beverage for the rich when it arrived in the mid-seventeenth century. Later, afternoon tea became a social habit of the upper middle class, famously illustrated, for example, in Marcel Proust's novels. France today is still noted for its refined approach to tea and its drinking ritual, which has become known as 'French Tea', with scented

Jean-Étienne Liotard, *Still-life: Tea Set, c.* 1783, oil on canvas. This is one of five depictions of china tea sets
by Liotard. In this painting of teatime disarray, there is a tray set with six cups and saucers, a teapot, a sugar bowl,
a milk jug and a lidded jar probably containing tea leaves. The large bowl containing a teacup and saucer was
probably also used as a slop bowl and there is also a plate with some bread and butter.

tea blends, exquisite patisserie and a tea-based cuisine
including their famous tea-scented jellies.

The Dutch East India Company first shipped tea to
France in 1636. At first it was considered a medicine
or drug and was sold in pharmacies. The medical pro-
fession debated for quite some time the benefits of tea
drinking. Dr Gui Patin, a celebrated French physician
and writer, referred to tea as 'the impertinent novelty
of the century',[10] while Father Alexander Rhodes wrote
that 'People must regard it as a precious medicament;
it not only does positively cure nervous headache, but
it is a sovereign remedy for gravel and gout.'[11] Cardinal

Mazarin, chief minister to young Louis XIV (r. 1643–
1715), it is said, introduced tea drinking to the French
court, and drank it regularly to alleviate his symptoms
of gout. Later Louis was also to drink tea to alleviate
his own gout.

Madame de Sévigné, the famous letter writer,
recorded in one of her letters in 1684 that 'The Princess
of Tarente took twelve cups of tea daily, and Monsieur
le Landgrave forty. He was dying and this resuscitated
him visibly.'[12] Earlier, in a letter written in 1680 to a
friend who was in poor health, she advised her to drink
milk and recommended that to avoid the cold milk

clashing with the heat of the blood she should add it to hot tea. She went on to say that Madam de la Sablière recently took 'tea with her milk' because she liked it.

Many intellectuals, as well as the leaders of society, became enthusiastic tea drinkers, including the dramatists Paul Scarron and Jean Racine, but tea only really became more accessible and fashionable for the French when the *Amphitrite*, the first French ship to return from China, arrived with a rich cargo of tea and other exotic items of silk, lacquer and porcelain in 1700.

By the end of Louis XIV's reign tea had become fashionable in high society and was by now considered a pleasant and convivial beverage, even for the healthy. It remained, however, more expensive than coffee for a long time. There was also the expense of costly porcelain and silver teaware needed, unlike coffee which was being offered in the new, popular cafés.

The French started their own manufacture of soft paste porcelain in 1745 at the Chateau de Vincennes. In 1756 the factory moved to Sèvres and in 1772, after the discovery of kaolin at Limoges, Sèvres began

producing fine hard paste porcelain famous for its high quality. Exquisite tableware was designed. Tea sets were painted in dark blue, turquoise, yellow, apple-green and rose pink – called rose Pompadour, after Madame de Pompadour, who was Sèvres' most important patron.[13]

The famous French writer Honoré de Balzac (1799–1850) was a devotee of tea and associated tea drinking with elegant living. He possessed a small cache of extremely expensive tea, which he served only on rare occasions, and then only to his special friends.[14] He introduced tea into the social life of his characters in his *Illusions perdues* (Lost Illusions, 1843) and *La Cousine Bette* (Cousin Bette, 1846). In *Illusions perdues* the tea-loving Balzac tells of a woman from Angoulême who 'loudly informed the entire province of an evening party of ice cream, cake and tea, a great innovation in a city where tea was still sold at apothecaries as a remedy for indigestion.'[15]

The artist Claude Monet also liked tea. When he moved to his famous house at Giverny in 1883, he liked to serve afternoon tea in the garden whenever the weather permitted. Although Monet's daily routine revolved totally around his painting and he was a reserved and private person, he loved comfort and good food and enjoyed entertaining his friends. Many were leading figures of the time, such as the statesman Clemenceau, as well as his fellow Impressionists – in particular Renoir, Pissarro, Sisley, Degas and Cézanne. Other regular guests included Rodin, Whistler, Maupassant and Valéry. Tea would be served under the lime trees, on the balcony or near the pond. He liked strong tea, which came from the Kardomah shop. Scones, chestnut biscuits or cinnamon toast might be served. His other teatime favourites included Genoa cake, rich fruitcake, orange cake, madeleines and *pain perdu*. After tea his guests might climb up the stairs

Travelling tea service for the Duc d'Angoulême by Dihl et Guerhard, Paris, *c.* 1788.

Claude Monet, *The Tea Set*, 1872, oil on canvas.
The dramatic red lacquerware tray and the blue-and-white porcelain
illustrate Monet's fascination with Asian art and objects.

to look at Monet's private collection of paintings by Cézanne, Renoir, Pissarro, Degas and so on. No one was invited for dinner because Monet went to bed very early in order to rise at dawn.[16]

Tea drinking only really became popular at the end of the nineteenth century with the new bourgeoisie and the birth of the *salon de thé* (tea salon or tearoom), when it became known as 'le five o'clock'. The first tearoom in Paris opened in the 1880s when two English brothers with the surname Neal started serving tea and biscuits at their stationery and bookstore,

the Papeterie de la Concorde on the rue de Rivoli. At first the tea and biscuits were served at two tables, but eventually they set up a proper tearoom upstairs. The store was later to become W. H. Smith & Sons, a fine British bookshop famous for its tea rooms. In 1898 Auguste Fauchon opened a tearoom, the Grand Salon de Thé, on the place de la Madeleine. He hired and worked with the best chefs and pastry chefs in Paris for this venture.

Once launched in Paris the *salon de thé* thrived. Ladies who were not admitted to cafés, which were

Polite salon society taking 'five o'clock tea' in Paris in the Belle Epoque.

the exclusive domain of men, could meet their friends, perhaps after shopping, and enjoy refreshments and patisserie.

Ladurée was another early tea salon in Paris. It began in 1862 when Louis Ernest Ladurée created a bakery at 16 rue Royale in the heart of Paris. After a fire in 1871 the premises were reconstructed into a pastry shop and, with his wife Jeanne Souchard, he succeeded in combining the style of Parisian cafés with the delicacies of French patisserie, creating what would later be called a tearoom. Jules Chéret was entrusted with the interior decoration. The chubby cherubs dressed as pastry cooks painted by him on the ceiling form

the company's emblem. The walls lined with mirrors gave customers the opportunity to preen and be seen. Ladurée's rise to fame came in 1930 when his grandson, Pierre Desfontaines, had the idea of sandwiching two *macaron* shells together with a creamy ganache. Ladurée are now renowned for their delectable, dainty *macarons*, all in a rainbow of colours and flavours. At the same time Desfontaines also opened a tearoom at the pastry shop. It was a big success with ladies, who enjoyed meeting their friends in a tearoom rather than at home.

In 1903 the Austrian confectioner Antoine Rumpelmayer, who had made his name in the south of France for his delicious cakes and pastries, opened his *salon de thé* in Paris at 226 rue de Rivoli. Originally the salon was named 'Rumpelmayer' but later he renamed it in honour of his daughter-in-law, Angelina. The decor of Angelina was designed by the French architect Édouard-Jean Niermans and combined elegance, charm and refinement. Angelina quickly attracted fashionable Paris society including Marcel Proust, who famously and eloquently reminisced about tea and madeleines in *À La Recherche du temps perdu* (In Search of Lost Time, translated as *Remembrance of Things Past*), published in seven parts. In *Swann's Way* (1913) he captures the stylishness of the *salon de thé*:

> her [Odette's] expression grew serious, worried, petulant because she was afraid of missing the flower show, or merely of not being in time for tea, with muffins and toast, at the Rue Royale tearooms, where she believed that regular attendance was indispensable in order to set the seal upon a woman's certificate of elegance . . .

And as for madeleines, Proust's narrator, on recalling an episode from his childhood after tasting a madeleine dipped in tea, wrote,

> She sent out for one of those short, plump little cakes called 'petites madeleines,' which look as though they had been moulded in the fluted valve of a scallop shell. And soon, mechanically, dispirited after a dreary day with the prospect of a depressing morrow, I raised to my lips a spoonful of the tea in which I had soaked a morsel of the cake. No sooner had the warm liquid, and the crumbs with it, touched my palate, a shudder ran through me, and I stopped, intent upon the extraordinary thing that was happening to me. An exquisite pleasure had invaded my senses . . . And suddenly the memory revealed itself. The taste was that of the little piece of madeleine which on Sunday mornings at Combray (because on those mornings I did not go out before mass), when I went to say good morning

The Angelina tearoom in Paris, *c.* 1903.

Edmund Blampied, 'Le Five O'Clock' at Deauville, 1926. An impression of the polo ground at Deauville during the tea hour. Taking afternoon tea had become the fashion with *l'haut monde* on the Continent after the First World War.

to her in her bedroom, my aunt Léonie used to give me, dipping it first in her own cup of tea or tisane. The sight of the little madeleine had recalled nothing to my mind before I tasted it . . .[17]

Coco Chanel, so famous for her elegance, was regularly seated at table number ten at Angelina. It is said she was a daily customer just for the hot chocolate. The table is next to one of the mirrors and her biographers have written that she loved mirrors and used them to coyly observe the world around her.

Tea dances (*thé dansants*) were also held in Paris. On 20 March 1913 the *Chicago Daily Tribune* reported the following about 'Paris Tea Dances Popular with Society People':

Rumplemeyer's the famous tea place of the Rue de Rivoli, which is known to every Chicagoan who puts his foot in Paris, has started a new fashion in afternoon affairs, which they have christened the 'thé dansant,' and which has achieved an instant and immense success.

In the largest building they install a splendid orchestra and from 3 until 7 o'clock this plays strictly American tunes, rag time, all the waltzes, gallops, two-steps, and marches that come across the Atlantic. In the wide gallery which surrounds the huge hall tea is served, with all the wonderful accessories in the way of tarts and cakes, for which Rumplemeyer is noted. The entrance fee is 5 francs and this entitles one to as much of tea and all the accompanying dainties as can be managed, and to as many times they care to avail themselves of perfect music and a perfect floor for dancing.

The fashionable institution of the *salon de thé* spread to grand hotels such as the Ritz in Paris, although not to everyone's delight, with Escoffier declaring: 'How can one eat jam, cakes and pastries, and enjoy a dinner – the king of meals an hour or two later? How can one appreciate the food, the cooking or the wines?'[18] At grand hotels in seaside resorts, such as the Hôtel du Palais in Biarritz and the Grand Hôtel in Cabourg, afternoon tea could be taken on sunny verandas or in rooms with sea views. The decor of *salons de thé* was luxurious and sophisticated, with ornate mirrors, crystal chandeliers and marbled tables. *Thé dansant* were also held.

In France, *salons de thé*, as distinct from cafés, which were smoky places and the domain of men, were for a long time the only public place that women could frequent without endangering their reputations. Also, whereas French cafés were often noisy, convivial and open to the street, a typical *salon de thé* would be located on the second floor, away from the gazes of people passing by, enabling connoisseurs to savour fine teas in peace and intimacy. However, just how much tea Parisian ladies consumed is debatable. Many were more likely to prefer coffee or hot chocolate. In fact, as culinary historian Michael Krondl suggests in his book *Sweet Invention* (2011), neither the beverage nor the patisserie which accompanied it were really the point

for the French ladies of leisure. As novelist Jeanne Philomène Laperche (writing under the pseudonym Pierre de Coulevain) noted in 1903,

During the last five years, [tea rooms] have sprung up like mushrooms. They are to be found everywhere now, in the Rue Cambon, Rue de Rivoli, Rue St-Honoré, on the road to the Louvre and to the Bon Marche. Paris has gone beyond London in this respect. Does that mean that the Frenchwoman has become a tea drinker? Not at all, and what is more, she never will be. She neither knows how to drink it, how to prepare it, nor how to serve it. She swallows it in an absent-minded way, like any kind of infusion. It excites her nerves without making her gay. She is too fond of talking, and of showing off to advantage, to give the necessary attention to the teapot, samovar or kettle. She is incapable of repeating several times the prescribed questions: 'Strong or weak? How many pieces of sugar? Cream or lemon?' And when she does ask the questions she never listens to the answers. The tea-room, where, if she is not afraid of appearing too bourgeois, she takes her chocolate, makes a pleasant halting-place between her shopping and her trying-on [of clothes]. It answers two purposes – her wish to be sociable and at the same time exclusive.[19]

What makes French tea so unique is not only the refined approach to tea drinking and the exotic blends of tea drunk but its accompanying patisserie. This French art form, which was well established by the end of the seventeenth century, reached extravagant heights in the days of Marie-Antoine Carême (1783–1833), a

Patisserie counter at Angelina, Paris.

patissier who became the most celebrated chef in France in the nineteenth century. Since then other French pastry chefs have continued to create exquisite patisseries, such as millefeuille, tarte Tatin and gateaux such as Saint-Honoré and opéra. Also served at teatime are the not so sweet and rich: madeleines, financiers, croissants, brioche, *pains au chocolat* or 'le muffin' and 'le toast' accompanied by fruit conserves.

Angelina is still famous for its *chocolat l'africain* (African hot chocolate) and for its patisserie, including the Mont Blanc. Sweet favourites at Ladurée are caramelized pear tart, opéra gateau and brightly coloured *macarons*.

Since the 1970s more and more tearooms have opened. In 1985 the long-established Mariage Frères

company opened their first tea emporium and tea salon on rue Bourg-Tibourg in Paris. The Mariage family have been in the tea trade since the mid-seventeenth century and in 1854 Henri and Edouard Mariage founded the present-day Mariage Frères tea company. They opened their first wholesale shop in Paris and became renowned as suppliers of the world's most exclusive teas. Over a hundred years later, in 1983, the company transformed itself from selling wholesale into a retail company. Two 'outsiders', Kitti Cha Sangmanee from Thailand and Richard Bueno from Holland, breathed new life into the company and started opening tea houses within central Paris.

The two men were joined in 1987 by another great tea lover, Franck Desains. The three men developed what has become known as 'French Tea', a gourmet approach to the tea drinking ritual which includes new blends of smoked and perfumed teas. They also invented a tea-based cuisine, including their famous tea-scented jellies. Mariage Frères now has four tea salons where tea-loving customers can enjoy an exquisite afternoon tea in exotic and elegant surroundings with a choice of teas, an assortment of tea-flavoured mini-viennoiseries, sandwiches, patisserie or madeleines, financiers, scones or muffins. Sixty-five per cent of French people add sugar to their tea; some add milk (usually hot) but the majority flavour it with lemon or nothing at all.

Some people have argued that *salons de thé* have for long become a bit faded or old-fashioned, as places for ladies of a certain age to meet, or just catering for tourists. However, this image is swiftly changing today. *Salons de thé* are thriving, especially in Paris; they have evolved from strictly tea salons to more casual places where light meals and traditional teas are served, and they are attracting an increasingly younger clientele.

Meanwhile the trend which Mariage Frères set in the 1980s continues to expand. The French are further developing their refined approach to tea drinking by developing more fine blends of teas, often flavoured with flowers, fruits and spices. Many have exotic and evocative names such as Pondicherry, Roi de Siam, Grande Caravane, Casablanca and Marco Polo. Other tea shops such as those of the chain Le Palais du Thé and tea companies such as Dammann Frères are expanding too. Some have called it a silent tea revolution in France, and France is one of the few countries in which tea consumption continues to grow.

Tea at home

THE FRENCH (and Belgians and Swiss) have a tradition of an afternoon snack called *le goûter*, sometimes called 'le quatre heures' (four o'clock), served at home. It is mainly for children who, coming home from school, have a little snack to keep them going until dinnertime. The snack is usually a baguette or roll with butter and jam or perhaps chocolate spread or maybe a *pain au chocolat*. Tea (and coffee) are not, however, served, as they are considered 'too exciting' at the end of the day. Instead children are given hot chocolate or orange juice. *Thé*, on the other hand, is 'le five o'clock', usually taken between 5 and 7 p.m. It is sometimes a formal occasion for guests. As with taking tea at elegant *salons de thé*, the French sense of style on these occasions in the home is very important. The tea served is carefully chosen, as are the exquisite cakes, tarts and tartlets, colourful *macarons*, biscuits and patisserie, and the hostess's best silver, porcelain or pottery is set out on the table. In the past it was mainly taken by women and was often organized around a game such as bridge or canasta. Gisèle d'Assailly described in *La Cuisine sonsidérée comme un des beaux-arts* (1951) how tea should be served, no matter how unsophisticated it is:

We arrive at teatime: tea-and-a-chat, tea-and-bridge, tea-and-canasta . . . In private, the said tea makes its entrance on a trolley with its accompanying sandwiches and cakes. Sometimes it is laid out in the dining room and the teapot is the absolutely last thing to arrive, flanked by its jug of hot water. In any event, the silverware or pewter must be absolutely gleaming, while the serviettes or tablecloth must be embroidered or trimmed with lace.[20]

Ireland

One of the nicest times of day
I'm sure you will agree,
Is when you put the kettle on
At four o'clock for tea.

The little tray's arranged with care,
Especially for two,
With dainty, tasty sandwiches
And biscuits, just a few.

The bright, round teapot's waiting for
The kettle's cheerful tune,
And a friend has come to share with you
A happy afternoon.[22]

Ireland is the one of the largest tea consumers per capita of any country in the world.[23] It is claimed by Barry's Tea, founded in 1901 and one of Ireland's most famous brands of tea, that on average the Irish consume up to six cups of tea a day. And they like it strong with a generous amount of rich milk (milk in the cup first) and usually with sugar. There is a common saying in Ireland that a proper cup of tea should be 'strong enough for a mouse to trot on'. The tea they drink is usually a blend of full bodied Assam with Ceylon or African tea varieties. Tea is drunk at breakfast, 'elevenses' (at around 11 a.m.), mid-afternoon at about 4 p.m. and with high tea (the evening meal) at about 6 p.m.

Tea was not imported in volume to Ireland until the 1800s. Up until then tea had been imported into Ireland from England under the monopoly of the East India Company and was very expensive. It was a beverage for the wealthy. In 1833 the monopoly was broken; merchants could make their own arrangements and in

Silver tea service, Mappin & Webb postcard, Paris, 1920s.

Early in her career Coco Chanel liked to host stylish teas in her chic apartment above her shop at 31 rue Cambon. She used to invite an interesting mix of friends, journalists and associates and would serve Ceylon tea (which she liked served with lemon) from her vermeil teapot. Accompanying the tea were *macarons*, toast, jam, honey and crème fraîche ordered from the Ritz.[21]

1835 Charles Bewley, the enterprising son of Samuel Bewley, a successful Quaker businessman whose family were originally from France, imported an unprecedented cargo of 2,099 chests of tea on the *Hellas*. It was said to be the first ship ever freighted directly from Canton to Dublin. A few months later the *Mandarin* loaded a further 8,623 chests. This probably accounted for 40 per cent of the annual Irish consumption of tea at that time. Tea began to be imported directly into Dublin, Belfast and Cork. Tea was to remain a key product for the Bewley family's business for years.[24]

Between 1840 and 1890 the Irish diet changed dramatically and tea consumption also began to rise markedly. The Irish diet had been based on milk, bread, potatoes, eggs, butter and bacon. All this was to change after the failure of the potato crops during the Great Famine. New dietary habits were introduced, including the much-disliked maize, which was eaten as a form of porridge. Tea drinking, combined with a taste for sugar and white bread, spread rapidly through the country after the famine. Many people no doubt picked up the taste for tea while working as servants in the houses of the gentry. Elizabeth Smith of County Wicklow, who was having some trouble with a newly recruited servant, recorded in her diary 'the wish to have tea for her breakfast like the other maids! She, who has often and often had but one meal a day and that dry potatoes.'[25] One contributory cause to the spread of tea was the temperance movement. By 1890 people were drinking three to four cups of tea a day and doctors began to suggest that the habit of drinking such large quantities of long stewed tea, combined with a poor diet, contributed to rates of mental illness. 'Tea drinking is becoming a curse,' wrote Dr Moore of Letterkenny; 'the people are developing a craving for tea just as great as that which a drunkard has for alcohol.'[26]

The Bewley family expanded into the coffee trade and in 1894 opened Bewley's first oriental café in George's Street, Dublin. To stimulate the market for the relatively unknown coffee, Ernest Bewley gave demonstrations on coffee making at the back of the shop while his wife made scones and buns to go with it. This venture proved extremely popular, and so was started a unique mix of shops and cafés that Bewley's have run ever since. Two years later in 1896 another café was opened on Westmoreland Street. The café provided a meeting place and a refreshment stop for business people and shoppers. On the menu was tea, coffee, various rolls, rich and often elaborate cakes in the continental style, sticky buns and eggs (boiled, poached or scrambled).[27] More cafés were to follow in Fleet Street and in Grafton Street in 1927. The cafés were renowned for the quality of the ingredients, including pure sugar and butter, used for baking cakes (such as cherry logs, madeiras, raspberry creams, Dutch tarts and lady cakes), breads such as barm brack and confectionery.

The café in Grafton Street became legendary, and a hub of the literary, cultural, artistic, architectural and social life of Dublin. It was frequented by famous Irish literary and artistic figures including James Joyce, Patrick Kavanagh, Samuel Beckett and Sean O'Casey. One of its most famous assets is a set of six stained-glass windows by the Irish stained-glass artist Harry Clarke (1889–1931). These are located in the main coffee and tea room with its high ceilings, chandeliers, paintings and sculptures and the room is named in his honour. The Harry Clarke room is found by walking straight through the front café to the back of the building on the ground floor. Bewley's Grafton Street also comprised a café theatre, located in the 'Oriental Room' of the café, famous for its lunchtime dramas and for cabaret, jazz and comedy in the evening.

Bewley's Café,
Grafton Street,
Dublin, *c.* 1970s.

Unfortunately, over the years Bewley's cafés have had their ups and downs. The one on Westmoreland Street is now a Starbucks and on a visit to Dublin in 2016 I was disappointed to find the Grafton Street café 'closed for refurbishment' and was told by a workman that the 'whole lot' was being taken out and redone.

Teatime at home in Ireland was a homely affair and usually taken around 4 p.m. During the week it might be quite simple fare – bread and butter, perhaps a biscuit or two and a cup of tea. At weekends teatime was more lavish, with sandwiches. Bridget Haggerty in *Memories of Teatime* remembers affectionately her childhood teatimes of the 1950s – her favourite meal and the last one of the day. She remembers Marmite and watercress sandwiches and sandwiches made with Shippam's paste. She also recollects that when times were hard sandwiches might be made with the dripping saved from the Sunday joint. Sometimes her mother

would give her beans on toast or prepare soft-boiled eggs served with 'soldiers' – toasted bread cut into vertical slices. In winter they would sometimes have Welsh rabbit or warm bread and milk sprinkled with sugar. Crumpets were another winter teatime treat, toasted and drizzled with butter.[28]

The famous food writer, chef, hotelier, hostess and teacher of Ballymaloe Myrtle Allen remembers that one of her childhood treats was to picnic at a rocky cove on the coast of Cork on a hot summer's day. After a swim, when wet and shivering, her mother would have a lunch of potatoes served with big pats of butter with cold chicken, ham, brawn and salads ready. She also remembers that at 4.30 p.m. it was time to find a well and bring her mother fresh spring water to boil for tea. While that was boiling they would have the last swim of the day. 'Tea was taken with freshly-buttered slices of barm brack, perhaps biscuits and cake as well.'[29] She also remembers an invitation to one of the big houses when 'tiny scones with fresh homemade jam and thick cream instead of butter and deep soft sponge cakes were served for afternoon tea.'[30]

In some families teatime was at six o'clock. Writer and TV personality Monica Sheridan remembers 'tea' consisting of boiled eggs, bacon and eggs or cold meats and salad but always accompanied by a variety of home-baked breads, buns and cakes.[31] Author of *The Cookin' Woman* Florence Irwin remembers the farm-house teas,

> at which for the first time I ate two eggs at one meal – the bread straight from the oven-pot – the sponge cakes and seed cakes all good – the children after tea singing their little songs learned at school – the large open peat fires – all most vivid still – then the real party teas with their chicken and ham and endless varieties of cakes, hot and cold, eaten from tables covered with the wonderful damask dear to the heart of all Ulster women.[32]

Bread is at the root of the Irish baking tradition and so many different types of bread have evolved in Ireland. As food historian Regina Sexton explains:

> soda bread, soda scones, sweet buttery country cakes, oatcakes, bran loaves, apple tarts, potato cakes, potato apple cakes, maize bread, buttermilk bread, crusty wheaten loaves, gingerbread, caraway cakes, plum cakes, tea bracks, barm bracks, simnel cakes, and pancakes – truly no matter how hard you try, you can't but fall victim to Ireland's impressive baking tradition.[33]

The variety of scones and biscuits is also quite remarkable. Buttermilk, which has always formed an important part of the staple diet of the country folk, north and south, plays an important part in Irish baking, especially bread making. The buttermilk provides the acid; bicarbonate of soda the alkali for raising purposes instead of yeast. (Buttermilk is the milk left over after the butter has been removed from the churn.) Nowadays, since the greater part of the milk is sent to creameries, buttermilk is not so plentiful. The Irish also have a great affection for, and dependence on, potatoes. Potatoes

'Matchmakin' in Ireland', *c.* 1908. Two old women negotiate a match over a cup of tea. The potential bride and groom look on with keen interest.

play an important part in the Irish diet and many ways of cooking them have been devised, including the renowned boxty bread, boxty pancakes, potato farls, dumplings and, of course, champ and colcannon. They are not just for the main meal of the day but important at teatime too.

Italy

WHILE IRELAND IS one of the largest consumers of tea in the world, Italy is one of the lowest, but as far as tearooms are concerned Babingtons tearooms must be mentioned.

Two young women, Isabel Cargill and Anne Marie Babington, introduced the tea habit to coffee-drinking Rome at the end of the nineteenth century. Isabel Cargill, a New Zealander, left Dunedin for England in her late teens, it is said because she had been jilted at the altar, and decided to visit relatives in England and look for work in London. There she met Englishwoman Anne Marie Babington in an employment agency and the two of them decided to set off for Rome with savings of £100 to set up tearooms. Rome was, at that time, a place where the aristocracy of Europe congregated and it was popular with British visitors.

Babingtons, in piazza di Spagna, Rome, since 1893.

In Italy the tearoom opened in 1893, when tea was only available in pharmacies, and was an immediate success. The next year a new branch was opened in the piazza San Pietro and two years later the business was doing so well it was decided to relocate to another premises strategically situated next to the Spanish Steps in the piazza di Spagna. Babingtons has been a successful mix of Italian style and English tradition with silver-plated teapots imported from England and unique Richard Ginori porcelain. The menu is traditional English teatime fare, offering sandwiches, hot buttered scones, muffins, teacakes and toast, plum cake, sponge cake and chocolate cakes.[34] Babingtons has survived two world wars, fascism and various other crises. In the 1960s film stars like Gregory Peck and Audrey Hepburn took tea here. The tearoom continues to flourish as a charming tea oasis in the centre of the coffee-oriented city and today continues to attract writers, actors, artists, politicians, Italians and tourists alike.

Poland

ALTHOUGH THE PEOPLE of Poland are mainly coffee drinkers, they also enjoy drinking black tea, which is unusually called *herbata*, coming from the Latin *herba thea*, meaning tea herb.

Black tea grown in Georgia is the most commonly imported tea. Polish people drink their *herbata* strong, sometimes with lemon if available. To sweeten the tea, sometimes a spoon of honey is taken into the mouth followed by some sips of tea. Syrups are also made to add to the tea for sweetness; the most common is raspberry. The tea is often served in a tea glass and, as the glass is hot to hold, it is usually placed in a Russian-style filigreed metal holder with a handle.[35]

In Poland there are *kawiarnias*, establishments where people go for pastries, coffee and tea. Tea cafés are also meeting places for tea drinkers. The historic city of Kraków has a number of them, including the popular Czajownia, which is close to most of the important sights. The hotel Bristol in Warsaw serves a traditional British afternoon tea with English cakes, scones and sandwiches.

Mary Cassatt, *Lady at the Tea Table*, 1883–5, oil on canvas. The painting shows Mary Dickinson Riddle, Cassatt's mother's first cousin, presiding at tea, a daily ritual among upper-middle-class women. Mrs Riddle's hand rests on the handle of the teapot, part of a gilded blue-and-white Canton porcelain service that her daughter had presented to the artist's family. This painting was done in response to this gift.

Three
United States of America

W E USUALLY ASSOCIATE the United States with coffee drinking but in fact tea, which had been introduced by the Dutch to their trading post, New Amsterdam, in the 1650s, became the favourite beverage in the Thirteen Colonies. The Dutch had brought their own customs of tea drinking. Saffron – which was stored in special saffron pots – or peach leaves were often used to flavour the tea and wealthy ladies gave tea parties using tiny teacups imported from China.

Tea drinking was enjoyed by both men and women. George Washington enjoyed drinking tea. Early records from his Virginia plantation, Mount Vernon, include a December 1757 order of tea from England for 6 lb (2.7 kg) of best Hyson and 6 lb of any other best tea available. Inventories show that he had impressive tea equipment of caddies, tables, cups and saucers, teaspoons and a silver-plated urn.[1] Thomas Jefferson, who is famous for his great passion for food and drink, was also a fan of tea drinking, including during the time he lived in Paris (1784–89). Records show, for example, that he ordered *Chu-chong* (souchong) and Hyson at a high price from a Richmond merchant in 1780. Imperial tea was also one of his favourites.[2]

Impressive tea gardens, named Vauxhall and Ranelagh after their London counterparts, were established in New York and many more were to follow. In the eighteenth century the city had two hundred tea establishments. The tea gardens, like those of London, provided evening entertainments for the public. There were firework displays and concerts, and at Vauxhall Gardens there was also dancing. Tea, coffee and hot rolls could be had in the gardens at any time of the day, including breakfast. The water in New York at that time was notoriously bad, being brackish and with a disagreeable taste. However, in the early 1700s a natural spring of fresh water was found which was said to be particularly suited for

Caddy for Hyson tea made with opaque glass and enamel decorations. Probably made in Bristol, England, in the 1760s–70s.

protest. Tea had become a hated symbol of oppression and tea consumption plummeted. Patriots took to drinking 'liberty tea' made from the leaves of loosestrife (a wild flower) or raspberry leaves, chamomile and sage. Many took to drinking coffee.

Tea consumption revived somewhat after the American War of Independence of 1775–83. George and Martha Washington continued to serve the best quality tea. Others followed suit and, as in Britain in the early days, tea drinking became associated with the elite and gentility. The then British tradition of drinking tea after dinner was followed. Late daytime or evening tea parties were held in the early 1800s, similar to those during the Regency period in England. This was an excessively formal age. High-backed chairs would be arranged in a circle and guests were expected to sit upright and rigid as if sitting for their portraits. Silence was observed until a door swished open and tea and cakes were brought in. Talking was allowed while partaking of the tea and cakes but not above a whisper.

making tea. It became known as the Tea Water Pump. Later the spring and the surrounding area were made into a fashionable resort which became known as the Tea Water Pump Garden. Other springs were found, leading to a thriving trade. Vendors would hawk what was called 'tea water' all over the city.

But tea drinking in the American colonies was not to follow a smooth path. Heavy taxes imposed on this popular drink led to what became the most famous 'tea party' of all – the Boston Tea Party – in 1773 when patriots threw 342 chests of tea into Boston Harbor in

'Boston Tea Party'. Three cargoes of tea destroyed, 16 December 1773. Print published *c.* 1903.

The hostess would then sit down at the piano and play. Everyone would sing along and then went home.[3]

Expensive fine china and silver tea services and implements were usually imported from Britain. The precious tea was stored in tin canisters or caddies. A full tea set at the end of the eighteenth century consisted of a teapot, twelve cups without handles, twelve saucers, a cream jug, a sugar bowl and a slop bowl for pouring out dregs. The booming new silver-plating industry, plus the discovery of new silver deposits in Nevada in the mid-nineteenth century, led to many specialized pieces of teaware being made including elaborate hot-water swing kettles, butter dishes, spoon holders, sugar tongs, cake baskets and much more.

Afternoon tea and high tea had become established by the mid-nineteenth century. Afternoon tea was sometimes called 'low tea' and high tea was often called evening tea, or sometimes supper. These meals followed much the same pattern as in England but had their own character. 'Low tea' was so-called because it was usually served on low tables which were placed near sofas or chairs in a sitting room. 'High tea' on

American mahogany tilt-top pie crust tea table, 1765. These tables, associated with the serving and drinking of tea, were indispensable for fashionable tea parties during the second half of the 18th century. Featuring a single pillar supported by three legs, the table could be placed against a wall when not in use as the top could be tilted to a vertical position.

C. M. McIlhenny, *Five O'Clock Tea*, c. 1888, print. This tea is being taken out of doors in the garden, perhaps because it is summer. There seem to be no teacups on the table but on closer inspection the lady at the back (the hostess?) looks as though she is presiding over a tea service.

the other hand was usually eaten at a high dining table, perhaps out of necessity because of the more substantial food served, often hot. There were also what were called 'five o'clock' teas, which became as much as an institution in the United States as in Britain.

Tea parties

AFTERNOON TEA PARTIES became fashionable in private homes or public halls. They were specifically a middle- or upper-class female event, usually only lasting about two hours, and taken at about four o'clock. Many women organized tea parties to raise funds for their churches or other charities such as the restoration of Mount Vernon and other old buildings. The American Centennial celebration of 1875–7 had an energizing effect on tea drinking and tea parties. Some were fancy events in which guests wore elaborate historical costumes. Others were called 'Martha Washington Tea Parties'. One was announced in the *New York Times* on 23 November 1874:

On tomorrow evening, as already announced in THE TIMES, a 'Martha Washington Tea Party' will take place at the Brooklyn Academy of Music, in aid of the Brooklyn Maternity. The lady patrons of this deserving institution, who belong to the best families in the city, have expressed their determination to make the 'tea party' a complete success. Thus far their efforts have been attended with most gratifying results. More than 1,500 tickets have been sold at $5 a ticket. In Brooklyn the 'tea party' is looked forward to as the great social event of the season . . . It is intended to reproduce as far as possible an exact copy of the Republican court of Washington. General Washington and his lady will be personated by a lady and gentleman well known in Brooklyn society. The costume of the evening will be the court dress of 1778, and it is hoped that as many of the guests as possible will come in that dress . . . Thirteen ladies, dressed in Martha Washington costume will preside at the

Print of a wood engraving of the Centennial Tea Party in the Rotunda of the U.S. Capitol, Washington, DC, December 1875, in Frank Leslie's *Illustrated Newspaper*.

tables. A thousand cups and saucers of elegant antique china, ornamented in gilt and coloring and bearing a photograph of Martha Washington have been secured for the occasion. The tables will seat three hundred people at once and supper will be served from 7 o'clock until 12, when the band (Conterno's) will play 'Home Sweet Home' . . .

Here is the bill of fare:

Tea and Coffee
Fried Oysters   Chicken Salad
Sandwiches   Tea Biscuit
Cakes of various kinds

The Ladies Home Journal, a popular American magazine which first appeared on 16 February 1883, gave advice on how to organize a good tea party. In 1892 the journal described an old-fashioned and grand tea party given by a young New York socialite in honour of her grandmother:

The guests came in old-fashioned costumes, with hair well powdered, carried old-fashioned reticules, wore tiny black patches upon their faces, and, of course, their choicest pieces of lace. Tea was served in the dining-room; a snowy damask tablecloth covered the table, at the head of which was placed a large silver tray, upon which were arranged, in perfect symmetry, the dainty white and gold dinner teacups and saucers. Upon either side was placed the quaint silver tea service of Queen Anne pattern, with its gracefully-curved, fluted handles. Old-fashioned candelabra, with plain white wax candles, and no new-fangled paper shades, stood upon lace mats on either side of a china bowl filled with crimson dahlias. The guests were in number ten. At each place was laid a plate of white and gold, a large damask table napkin folded perfectly square, a knife and two-pronged fork, both with white ivory handles, and a heavy silver dessert spoon. At the foot of the table was a large white and gold platter filled with slices of cold chicken garnished with nasturtium leaves, and upon either side similar dishes, containing daintily-cut slices of ham and tongue. The bread was cut in thin slices and buttered, so that neither butter plates nor butter dishes were needed. At certain equal distances stood little white pots of preserved strawberries and gooseberries, a jar of orange marmalade, and a pretty china dish of honey in the comb. Tiny little dishes in which these dainties were to be served and silver spoons of dessert-size stood near. Low baskets of silver covered with lace held golden sponge and rich, dark fruit-cake, and upon two silver trays, covered with lace, stood little Dresden china cups filled with custard, upon which a generous supply of nutmeg had been grated. The tea was hot and fragrant. There was no ice-water, nor, indeed, ice visible anywhere, yet everything looked cool, attractive and beautiful . . .[4]

Formal tea parties followed strict etiquette but there were also homely, much less formal tea parties. Tea tables could be set up easily in the parlour, on porches or on the lawn. They were also an occasion for gossip and fun. They were sometimes called kettledrums. Marion Harland, writing in 1886, described kettledrums as

Lady Baltimore Cake

IT WAS IN THE *Ladies Home Journal* of 1889 that the first known recipe for Lady Baltimore cake appeared in the letters column. This soft white cake later evolved into a cake of three layers sandwiched together with a meringue-like fluffy frosting, into which chopped nuts and candied fruits are mixed. Who actually invented this cake is a matter of dispute. My favourite story is that it was made by one of Charleston's former belles named Alicia Rhett Mayberry who gave, or served, this cake to Owen Wister, a popular romantic novelist. He liked it so much he wrote about it in his next novel, *Lady Baltimore* (1906), which refers not to a person but to the cake and much of the story revolves around it. The narrator first tries the cake in the Woman's Exchange tearoom after hearing a hapless young man order it for his forthcoming wedding. Whatever the true origins of this cake it was Wister's description that made it famous and readers scrambled around to find the recipe.

The Woman's Exchange in Charleston, run by Florence and Nina Ottolengui, was later named the Lady Baltimore Tearoom to capitalize on the popularity of the novel and the famous cake. They managed the tearoom for over 25 years and are said to have sent a cake to the author in thanks every Christmas. This is the recipe which appeared in the *Ladies Home Journal* in August 1889 – it had no frosting.

Mrs K.J.H. Lady Baltimore Cake

Beat half a cup of butter to a cream, adding gradually one and a half cups of sugar. When very light add three quarter cups of cold water and two cups of flour; beat well, and stir in half the well beaten whites of four eggs. Have ready one cup of English walnuts cut into small pieces, flour them well, stir into the cake, add the remainder of white of the eggs, and a teaspoon of baking powder.

Bake in a moderate oven for fifty minutes.

so much in vogue at this time, – tea being to women, say the cynics, a species of mild intoxicant, of which they are not to be defrauded by evening dinners and their sequitur of black coffee. Others, who cleave to ancient customs, and distrust innovations of all kinds, will have it that the popularity of these feminine carousals has its root in the remorseful hankering after the almost obsolete 'family tea.' 'Since there must be fashionable follies,' growl these critics, 'this is as harmless as any that can be devised, and is, assuredly, less disastrous to purse and health than an evening crush and supper.'

For once, we say 'Amen' to the croakers. The 'kettle-drum' is objectionable in nothing except its absurd name, and marks a promising era in the history of American party-giving.[5]

Advice on how to best prepare tea was also given in cookbooks and household guides. Writer and editor Sarah Josepha Hale recommended the use of 'polished tea urns' rather than 'varnished ones' because they 'may be kept boiling with a much less expense of spirits of wine than such as are varnished'.[6] The successful brewing of tea depended on the water being boiled properly. Another writer and cookbook author, Eliza Leslie, advised that the tea should be strong, not weak. The pot should be scalded twice and not filled with too much water:

The practice of drowning away all the flavor of the tea is strangely prevalent with servants . . . who do not, or will not, remember that the kettle should be boiling hard at the moment the water is poured on the tea – otherwise the infusion will be insipid and tasteless, no matter how liberally the Chinese plant has been afforded.

Leslie also instructed that teacups were not to be filled to the brim, to enable the addition of cream and sugar. Even though she liked the tea to be made strong, she suggested to 'also, send round a small pot of hot water, that those who like their tea weak may conveniently dilute it'.[7] There was much discussion on the benefits or disadvantages of green or black tea, especially regarding tea's stimulating qualities. Fannie Farmer, who became principal of the Boston Cooking School in 1894 and who was famous for *The Boston Cooking-school Cook Book* in 1896, suggested that hostesses should offer both types.

Tea cosies, which originally came from Britain, were sometimes used to keep the tea hot. Marion Harland, in her usual witty style, talks about the necessity of using a cosy:

This is not an article of diet, yet an accessory to good tea-making and enjoyable tea drinking that deserves to be better known in America. It is a wadded cover or bag made of crotcheted worsted, or of silk, velvet or cashmere, stitched or embroidered as the maker may fancy, with

Tea cosy, *c.* 1870. Canvas embroidered with wool, silk thread and beads.

a stout ribbon-elastic drawn loosely in the bottom. This is put over the teapot as soon as the tea is poured into it, and will keep the contents of the pot warm for an hour or more. Those who have known the discomfort, amounting to actual nausea, produced by taking a draught of lukewarm tea into an empty or weary stomach; or whose guests or families are apt to keep them waiting for their appearance at table until the 'cheering' (if hot) 'beverage' lowers in temperature and quality so grievously that it must be remanded to the kitchen, and an order for fresh issued – will at once appreciate the important of this simple contrivance for keeping up the heat of our 'mild intoxicant' and keeping the temper of the priestess at the tea-tray down.[8]

Tea was usually sweetened with sugar. In the nineteenth century, white sugar, in the form of cone or 'loaf' sugar, was preferred, being the most highly refined and sweetest form of sugar. The cone came wrapped in deep blue-purple tinted paper. Women used sugar

Cone (or loaf) of sugar wrapped in purplish-blue paper. This one is on show at Ham House in Richmond, Surrey.

nippers to cut lumps from the cone for the sugar bowl, or pounded the lumps into a fine powder to serve with fruit or sweets. Although it was very expensive, used with thrift, one cone could last a year. For those who could not afford loaf sugar, brown sugar was used, or maple syrup or molasses, which were even cheaper. In the 1890s granulated sugar became available.

There was plenty of guidance on how to arrange the tea table and what food to serve with the tea. Precise instructions for summer and winter tea parties were given by cookbook author Mrs T. J. Crowen in 1847:

SUMMER. Let a pure white cloth be neatly laid; let the tray be covered with a white napkin; and on it, as for breakfast, the sugar, cream, and slop-basin, containing the spoons and the cups and saucers within them . . . Put around the tables as many small plates as may be wanted, with a small knife in front of each, or at its side; at the other end or side, opposite the tray, let the dish of ripe or stewed fruit be set, with a large spoon and a pile of small saucers in front or at the side of it. On either side, at some little distance from it, let there be plates, with bread sliced, about the eighth of an inch in thickness; or let one dish be of hot wigs [small rich buns, often spiced], or rusk, or tea-biscuit. Let a fine mould of butter occupy the centre of the table; let its knife be beside it; and on each side a small plate, the one with cold meat, ham, or tongue, sliced thin, (and a fork to help it); the other with sliced cheese, or a fresh pot-cheese. A pitcher of ice-water, with small tumblers surrounding it, may occupy one corner, and a basket or plate of cake the other. Or a glass-dish of custard may occupy the place mentioned for the fruit, and it (the fruit) be distributed in small saucers, with fine white sugar heaped on the centre of each, and placed upon each plate: this gives the table a very pretty appearance. Or, the custard baked in small cups, may occupy the places of the saucers of fruit. Smoked beef, chopped thin, or Bologna sausages, sliced, may be served at tea; also, cheese; this may be sliced or grated.

FOR WINTER TEA TABLE. The same appurtenances, with the addition of forks, are requisite, with perhaps an urn of coffee, for winter tea-table. Oysters pickled, in the place of cold meat, or stewed in the place of fruit, or instead of the stew, a bit of broiled fish, or ham or fried oysters, with hot tea-biscuits and rusks or wigs, and stewed or preserved fruit, and fancy cakes. Grated cocoanut, with tart preserves, or currant jelly, or cranberry jam, may be served thus: grate the white meat of a cocoanut, and put it in a flat glass dish, then turn a mould of jelly upon the middle of it.[9]

Mrs Crowen's menu suggestions are quite 'high tea'. The monthly magazine *Table Talk* of January 1890 considered 'high tea' to be a pleasant way of entertaining a few friends and assured its readers that the refreshments should be simple and within the means of everyone. The etiquette was also quite simple:

The invitations are oftentimes simply visiting cards with the date and words, 'high Tea' written below; while some are engraved purposely, and still others are informal notes ... Invitations should be sent out at least three or four days in advance, but many successful and pleasant teas have been impromptu, and the invitations sent out the day before.

The magazine suggested menus. In the edition of January 1890 there were four to choose from, and it is interesting that at two of them coffee is on the menu, not tea:

Menu No. 1
Fried Oysters, Chicken Salad, Thin Bread and Butter, Wafers, Macaroons, Tea.

Menu No. 2
Oyster Patties, Cabbage Salad, Chicken Sandwiches, Olives, Salted Almonds, Wafers, Coffee.

Menu No. 3
Chicken Croquettes, Shrimp Salad, Thin Bread and Butter, Sardines, Wafers, Russian Tea.

Menu No. 4
Rolled Sandwiches, Escalloped Oysters, Olives, Veal Croquettes, Coconut Balls, Wafers, Coffee.

Two summer menus are given in the August edition of that year, one for a tennis tea:

Tennis Tea
Sugared Berries, Cold 'Turkish' Tongue, Tomatoes Stuffed with Cress, Rolls, Sweet Sandwiches, Lemonade, Ice Cream.

No. 2
Chilled Raspberries, Crab Croquettes, Cream Sauce, Rolls, Ice Cream, Cake.

Additional tea dishes were also given. There are several lobster and crab dishes such as Lobster Newburgh, Deviled Lobster, Lobster Croquettes, Kromeskies of Crabs and Scalloped Crabs. Other dishes include Caviare Toast, Egg Sandwiches, Canapés, Rolled Ham, Jellied Chicken, Cheese Toast, Cheese Straws and Brandy Cheese Crackers.

Instructions for a stylish bridal tea party are given in the September edition:

After the table is covered with a heavy piece of Canton flannel, and over this a perfectly white damask tablecloth, put in the centre a square of either embroidered or plain white linen, or a piece of China silk. The silk, however, may be folded around a bowl of roses, or a large, handsome glass dish of fruit. The linen could be put on perfectly plain. In the centre arrange a glass dish of fruit and appropriate flowers, with silk twisted around the base. On the two sides, have white or glass candlesticks, double ones, if you have them, with perfectly white candles and white shades. These may also stand in the folds of silk. On the other two sides have pretty little glass or silver dishes of salted almonds. Small corsage bouquets, or appropriate white and delicate flowers, may be placed at each plate and, with the exception of glass and water bottles, do not have any other decorations on the table. As this tea is for a bridal party, try, as nearly as possible, to have a perfectly white tea, in dishes, food and decorations. Menu: Shrimp Cutlets, Cream sauce, Parkerhouse Rolls, Coffee, Chicken à la Creme, French Peas, Tomato Salad, Wafers, Brie, Ice Cream, Angel's Food.

'High tea' was not just an occasion for entertaining; many families had a full evening meal called 'tea' or 'high tea'. It was usually served at about six o'clock and was the final meal of the day. The sort of dishes on the table would be things like scrambled eggs, lobster cutlets, salads of different kinds, crumpets, muffins, toast, Parker House rolls, a cake of some sort and perhaps some fresh or stewed fruit or fruit jelly plus of course tea and perhaps cocoa or coffee.

In *1095 Menus: Breakfast, Dinner, and Tea* (1891) a broad assortment of dishes were suggested. Cold dishes,

including roast beef, ham, mutton, smoked tongue, Bologna sausage, corned beef, spiced beef, potato and beef salad, sweetbreads mayonnaise, or potted fish. As 'hot relish,' it proffered lobster cutlets, baked eggs, fancy roast oyster, broiled smoked salmon, coquilles of grouse, boiled sausages, or omelet. Cakes, biscuits, toast, rolls, griddle cakes, rusks, cookies, crumpets, and wafers, along with fruit, completed its recommendations.[10]

In her book *Breakfast, Luncheon and Tea* (1886) Marion Harland reminisced about an old-fashioned tea:

The evening meal, call it by whatever name we may, is apt to be the most social one of three which are the rule in this land . . . The talk of the six o' clock p.m. dinner, or supper, or tea, makes itself . . . I should be the sorriest of the sorry to see the tea-table swept out of American households . . . Late dinners and late suppers used to be the fashion, seldom altered – in Southern homes. In summer, the latter were always eaten by artificial light. In winter, lamps were brought in with the dessert, at dinner-time. I was almost grown before I was introduced to . . . 'a real old New England tea-table.' During one delicious vacation I learned, and reeled in knowing, what this meant. 'Black tea with cream . . . rounds of brown bread, light, sweet, and fresh; hot short-cake in piles that were very high when we sat down, and very low when we arose; a big glass bowl of raspberries and currants that were grow-ing in the garden under the back windows an hour before; a basket of frosted cake; a plate of pink ham, balanced by one of shaved, *not* chipped beef – and *sage cheese*! I had never eaten it before. I have never tasted it anywhere else than in that wide, cool tea-room, the level sun-rays flickering through the grape-vines shading the west side of the house, and through the open casements opposite, a view of Boston bay – all purple and rose and gold, dotted with hundreds of white sails. This was what we had, when, in that Old New England farm-house, Polly, the faithful – who had startled me, for a time, by saying, 'proper glad,' and 'sweet pretty;' who 'hadn't ought' to do this, and 'should admire' to do that – Polly, whom nobody thought of calling a servant, but was a 'help' in every con-ceivable sense of the word – had 'put the kettle on and we all had tea!'[11]

Advice on how to arrange and plan a tea party for guests continued in the early twentieth century in magazines and cookbooks. The editors of the *Economy Administration Cook Book*, Susie Root Rhodes and Grace Porter Hopkins, declared in 1913 that no 'well-to-do' home should be without its tea service and

'Polly put the kettle on, we'll all have tea' – a popular English nursery rhyme. The illustration is by Kate Greenaway from *Mother Goose* (1881).

that the art of making and pouring tea gracefully was one that every woman should acquire and practice until perfection was reached, if she wished to acquit herself as a finished hostess. Bread should be cut as thin as possible and then cut again in any desired shape – strips, diamonds, triangles and circles. Beaten biscuits, they said, were always in demand. The edi-tors also described the English custom of putting a cluster of their favourite flowers in a tight jar with the butter to be used, thus giving it a delicate flavour suggestive of the type of flower used, such as rose or violet. Chocolate, cocoa or cacao could also be served for those who did not care for tea. Lemon in tea was approved of, the citric acid offsetting the tannic acid of the tea:

All lovers of lemon in tea like this combination: Add to each cup of tea a teaspoon of orange marmalade. Stir it in well; the result is delicious. A slice of pineapple with a bit of lemon is also favoured, while a whole clove dropped into a cup just before the tea is poured is popular and tasty.

Colour-themed tea parties became fashionable. The editors describe a 'Studio tea' with a brown and white colour scheme with 'celery sticks, Date Sandwiches, Stuffed Dates, Devil's Food served with Tea with lemon or Conserved Ginger'.

For a successful afternoon tea party organization was important. Guests would be received in one room, and the tea, cakes and sandwiches would be prepared in an adjoining room. At the right moment the connecting door would swing open and the hostess or maid would bring in the tea service on a mahogany or silver tray. A tea kettle would be on the tray along with other necessary equipment and items such as a tea caddy, teapot, sugar bowl and tongs, a pitcher of cream, a plate of lemon slices, teacups and saucers and teaspoons. Plates covered with doilies containing sandwiches and small cakes and cookies were also de rigueur.[12] Often a tea cart, sometimes called a tea wagon or a curate, would be used. The tea service, perhaps on a tray, would sit on top of the tea wagon with sandwiches, cakes, napkins and plates on the lower shelf.

A curate, or three-tiered basket or stand, sometimes called a muffin or cake stand, was often used for bread or scones (on its top shelf), sandwiches (middle shelf) and cake (bottom shelf), and in this way it could be informally carried round the room and its contents offered to guests. The diligent hostess would pour a cup of tea for each guest, add the sugar, cream or lemon as desired, and pass the cup herself.

One reason for the popularity of the 'five o'clock' tea was its relative simplicity. Dishes were easy to prepare and the guests served themselves. In 1921 *Good Housekeeping* magazine stated that hostesses 'arranged their tables after luncheon was finished, and, as most of the work of preparing the dishes had been completed in the morning, they had a long, restful afternoon to themselves before the arrival of even the earliest guests'. At the same time the magazine described what seems to be a rather more elaborate style of afternoon tea:

With the exception of delicate rolls and hot tea and coffee, the entire menu was composed of cold dishes – white bread, cheese, old time pound or sponge cake, exquisite blanc mange made from arrowroot or sea moss farina and served in small forms, trifles of all sorts, floating island, citron preserves, election cake. These were all popular, and as each hostess usually had some special dish for which she was famed, the menus were never trite or monotonous. In cool weather, oysters in some form were much liked, or fried chicken might be preferred; lobsters or crabs prepared in delectable fashion were high prized.[13]

Lucy G. Allen of the Boston School of Cookery gave much tea party advice in *Table Service*, including that for summer out-of-doors teas, iced tea, iced chocolate or punch were more convenient, as well as more acceptable, than hot tea. Ices could also sometimes be served, 'although frappé [a fruit flavoured mixture that is similar to sherbet] (or some frozen cream, not too rich) is usually preferred, served in frappé glasses from a frappé bowl'.[14]

In 1932 the Coca-Cola Company published the book *When You Entertain: What to Do, and How* by Ida Bailey Allen. Formality still ruled for many tea parties. Recommendations are given on how to arrange and give several different types of tea parties: a formal afternoon tea, a casual afternoon tea, a smart studio tea and tea receptions. In a section entitled 'The Gracious Art of Afternoon Tea', guidance is given for formal tea parties, an opportunity to entertain a large number of guests, perhaps to introduce a daughter to society, or a new daughter-in-law to friends of the family, or to welcome new neighbours or house guests:

Tea, coffee or chocolate may be served. These are poured by an assisting debutante and other debutantes offer sandwiches and relishes, if served, or cakes and candies.

The foods should be comparatively simple. All of them must be of a type that can be held with the fingers.

A cold drink is also provided for those guests who prefer it. Coca-Cola Tropical Punch is new and delicious.

For this type of formal tea, Ida Allen offers two alternative menus:

Tiny Club Salad Sandwiches
Rolled Smoked Salmon Sandwiches
Olives   Salted Brazil Nuts
Lemon Ices   Little Silver Cakes
Tropical Coca-Cola Punchs   Tea
French Butter Creams

Or,

Open Lobster Paste Sandwiches with Olive Garnish
Cucumber sandwiches   Rolled Parsley Butter Sandwiches
Orange Ices   Frosted Lady Fingers
Tea
Mints   Nuts

Even a 'football tea after the game for the smart young set on Thanksgiving' is formal:

A seasonable table may be arranged by using brass candlesticks with candles matching the college colors, and a bowl of brightly colored fruits with laurel leaves for greenery. The cups and saucers should be on the table with a samovar, or a tea service. Ice-cold Coca-Cola, with slender glasses and a bottle opener, arranged on a tray at the opposite end of the table, contributes the sparkle essential to the success of the party.

The sandwiches may be cut in football shape, and the cakes decorated with little chocolate eggs striped to look like footballs. The favors may be miniature leather footballs, or paper cups covered with brown paper may be used, with a tiny pennant stuck on the side of each. In this case fill them with round chocolate candies.

The menu:

Football Sandwiches
Open Egg and Pimiento Sandwiches
Variety Tea Cakes
Ice-cold Coca-Cola
Small Chocolates

Tea out: tearooms, department stores, hotels and the tea dance

IN THE EARLY twentieth century teatime spread to tearooms, department stores and hotels. Restaurants were the domain of men; tearooms provided a place for women to meet, exchange gossip and refresh themselves after shopping.

Iced tea

Oh, there are drinks and drinks and drinks,
Enough to drown the sea;
But of the multitude, methinks,
The best is iced tea . . .
Then cool it nicely, add your ice,
And churn it in a shaker;
'Twil show a broth of creamy froth,
And be a blessed slaker . . .
Squeeze o'er the ice a tiny slice
Of lemon till it's tart,
And handle well your sugar shell –
Be still, my pulsing heart! . . .
Daily Picayune, 1897

ICED TEA recipes began appearing in American cookbooks in the early 1800s, initially in the form of alcoholic punches. Ice by this time was becoming available to many households. These early punches were made with green tea, rather than the black tea mostly used today, and laced with wine or liquor such as rum or brandy. In 1860 Solon Robinson, writer, agriculturist and founder of the Lake County (Indiana) Temperance Society and author of *How to Live*, commented: 'Last summer we got in the habit of taking the tea iced, and really thought it better than when hot.' It is often thought that the first recipe in a cookbook for iced tea is in the book *Housekeeping in Old Virginia* from 1879. Green tea was boiled and steeped all day, then the preparer should 'fill the goblets with ice, put two teaspoonfuls of granulated sugar in each, and pour the tea over the ice and sugar.' The recipe also called for a lemon garnish. The first iced teas, however, were medicinal. In 1869 the *Medical Times and Gazette* claimed that 'The most delicious and sustaining beverage that can be drunk in hot weather is good strong tea, cooled down with lumps of ice. It should be only slightly sweetened, without milk, and flavoured with a few slices of lemon, which are infused at the time the tea is first made.'

By the 1870s it was being served in hotels and on railroads. Russian tea (tea à la Russe) became popular and Marion Harland gave a recipe for iced tea à la Russe in her book *The Cottage Kitchen* in 1883:

Make tea in the usual way; let it get cold on the leaves; then strain off into a pitcher, and slice two or three peeled lemons into each quart. The slices should be thin. Put sugar and ice into tumblers and fill up with the tea.

Great bowls of this, ice-cold and well sweetened, are popular at fairs, church receptions, and picnics, and have become a fashion at evening parties where wines and punch are not served.

In *Breakfast, Luncheon and Tea*, Harland suggests adding a glass of champagne to the iced tea, thus making Russian punch.

Iced tea was popularized at the St Louis World's Trade Fair in 1904 when English tea merchant Richard Blechynden, who was in charge of the fair's East India pavilion, was finding it difficult to sell hot cups of tea to the fairgoers in the sweltering heat. He decided to pour the hot tea over ice in cups and customers were soon crowding round to drink the cooling and refreshing beverage. The popularity of iced tea rose and spread quickly across the entire United States. During Prohibition in the 1920s iced tea consumption rose as people began looking for alternatives to wine, beer and other alcoholic drinks.

Today iced tea accounts for about 80 per cent of tea consumed in the U.S. It is particularly favoured in the South where it is sweetened before being iced. Southerners drink it by the gallon and it is not just a summertime drink, but is served all year round with most meals. In the movie *Steel Magnolias* (1989) Dolly Parton's character refers to sweet tea as 'the house wine of the South'. Southern culture also refined the practice of serving iced tea by pouring it into special tall glasses. Long spoons and lemon forks also became customary. The custom spread and by the end of the First World War the entire country was drinking out of tall crystal goblets or glasses.

When people order tea in a Southern restaurant the chances are they will be served sweet iced tea. In other parts of the U.S. if you order 'tea' you will automatically be served iced tea, usually unsweetened. What is called 'hot tea' is often prepared by heating up iced tea. Iced tea today is also sold in cans and bottles.

For the tea-loving British people who travel to the United States, getting a good cup of strong tea can be a bit of an ordeal. The tea is often made with a tea bag and served in paper cups. It is usually very weak and is often served with hot rather than cold milk.

Iced tea.

Tearooms

THE TEAROOM CRAZE in America was sparked by three social phenomena: the rise of the automobile, Prohibition and the women's suffrage movement. Women had for a long time been restricted and wished to be independent, travel freely and lead a more adventurous life. The automobile offered the chance to drive a car – and go to places such as a tearoom; they could even own or run one. Most tearooms were run by women for women. Many hotels and restaurants had closed down as they had been dependent on the income from selling alcohol; tea provided an alternative.

Tearooms in America developed along different lines from those in Britain. Many early tearooms began when women opened up their homes at weekends and provided inexpensive, simple home-cooked meals for passing travellers. Tearooms also opened up in cities across America from the bohemian Greenwich Village in New York to the high society tearooms of Chicago. The main attraction of the tearoom was the quaint, homely atmosphere, especially for women when many restaurants or eating places were the domain of men. Many people, especially the young, preferred a tasty snack in an informal atmosphere to an expensive five-star meal in a hotel. Instead of the typical English-style afternoon tea of hot tea, dainty sandwiches, scones and jam, coffee or iced tea was often preferred and the type of fare offered was more likely to be wholesome savoury dishes, such as the chicken pie on the menu at the Miss Ellis Tea Shop in Chicago. This chicken pie, according to Chicago journalist John Drury in *Dining in Chicago* (1931), was 'something you shouldn't miss'. He observed that the tea shop was 'Patronized by smartly-gowned women and by women who come here to look at the gowns. The cuisine was commendable and the numerous old family recipes used in this place make the menu

inviting'. He described the Southern Tea Shop on East Oak Street, where specialities such as Southern fried chicken, date torte and hot Southern biscuits were on the menu, as 'a quiet and charming tearoom . . . where prices are very reasonable'.[15]

In the 1920s Americans fell in love with colour, especially bright colours. Everything that had been black, white or drab became colourful: clothing, furniture, cars and the decor, tableware and uniforms of tearooms. There was lots of mixing and matching of bright colours. Food historian Jan Whitaker in her illuminating book *Tea at the Blue Lantern Inn* (2002) shares 'Tearoom', a poem of the early 1920s, which describes a possible colour palette like this:

Of course the dishes are not mates:
The cups are yellow, and the plates
Are green like grass; cut lemons gleam
On lacquer red; the yellow cream
Is in a black jug, squat and droll;
The sugar in an orange bowl.[16]

Colour also governed many tearoom names. The most popular seems to have been blue, as in the Blue Lantern and the Blue Teapot. The fictitious Indigo Tea Shop in Charleston is the setting of a series of tea shop mysteries written by Laura Childs; the heroine Theodosia Browning even has a dog called Earl Grey.

Colour played an important part in the unconventional tearooms of bohemian Greenwich Village. They were often run in tandem – some even inside the tearoom – with gift shops selling colourful batik clothing, hand-painted bead necklaces, scarves, hats, bags, carvings, pottery and art prints.

Before the First World War many professional women lived in the Village working as social workers,

Women's suffrage

TEA PLAYED an important part in the American women's suffrage movement. The Boston Tea Party is perhaps the most well known story of
tea's role in rebellion, but a simple tea party of five key members of the
American women's suffrage movement, held in Waterloo, New York, on
9 July 1848, turned out to be very important in the movement's history.
Over tea the women discussed their revolutionary ideas, which triggered
the Seneca Falls Convention – the first women's rights conference in
the Western world. Just over half a century later one of the legendary
hostesses of the day, Alva Vanderbilt Belmont, built a Chinese tea house
in the grounds of her mansion where she could hold fundraising tea
parties to benefit her new passion, women's suffrage. At two events
guests received Votes for Women teacups and saucers as favours. With
the Seneca Falls Convention, and thanks to the commitment of many
women who worked tirelessly, the movement achieved its goal – votes
for women, the Nineteenth Amendment – in 1920.

'Afternoon Tea', a caricature by Albert Levering in *Puck*, 1910. The
illustration shows a socialite, prisoner 'no. 500', in prison as a martyr for
the cause of women's suffrage, having a tea party with her society friends
outside her cell, labelled 'Cell no. 500 Our Noble Martyress'.

teachers and reformers. They were also social rebels trying to break loose from the restrictions of Victorian living. They were joined, around 1910, by artists, both male and female, who were taking advantage of the low rents and liked the atmosphere. Tearooms became a place where they could meet and chat over a cup of tea or coffee and some simple food. One tearoom which attracted artists and actors with its homely decor was the Crumperie, run by Mary Alletta 'Crumpie' Crump and her elderly mother. They opened their first Crumperie in 1917 and moved several times over the years as rents went up. Customers would come to enjoy a bowl of pea soup, crumpets, 'crumpled' eggs, peanut sandwiches and a cup of tea or coffee and perhaps play a game of chess or chat with friends.

At the same time (1910s) Greenwich Village also attracted migrants arriving from Paris who had escaped the threatened war in Europe. This mix of people, many of them writers, radicals and feminists, resulted in a lively, unconventional culture and tearooms, many of which were modelled on Paris's Latin Quarter, were an ideal place to go and hang out.

Romany Marie's was another well known tearoom-cum-tavern in Greenwich Village. It was opened in 1912 by Marie Marchand, who had come to the U.S. from Romania as a teenager in 1901. She said she patterned her taverns (so-called, though she served no alcoholic drinks) after the inn her mother ran for gypsies in the old country. Marie frequently dressed as a gypsy and did a bit of fortune-telling by reading tea leaves.

Gypsy became a popular name for many tearooms, some of which, like Romany Marie's, provided the added attraction of fortune-telling. In the mid-nineteenth century Roma gypsies had emigrated to the United States from England and later from Serbia, Russia and

Austria-Hungary. Roma women practised their fortune-telling in the cities although it was frowned upon and attempts were made to restrict it by banning payment. However, tearooms got round the difficulties by offering the service free of charge, but the fortune-tellers could receive tips from their customers. These tearooms may not have been renowned for their food but they flourished in cities such as New York, Boston, Cleveland, Kansas City, Los Angeles and Chicago, where the Gypsy Tea Shop on West Monroe Street was the city's first fortune-telling tearoom. Some of the tearooms hinted of the exotic East with names like Persian Tearoom and the Garden of Zanzibar in Chicago. During the Depression prices fell and many tearooms advertised free tea-leaf readings to attract business, as described in Bob Crosby's lyrics to 'In a Little Gypsy Tea Room' (1935):

It was in a little Gypsy tearoom
When I was feeling blue,
It was in a little Gypsy tea room
I first laid eyes on you;

When the Gypsy came to read the tea leaves
It made me feel quite gay,
When she said that someone in the tea room
Would steal my heart away.

Some tearooms, such as El Harem in Chicago, held tea dances. The hubble-bubble pipes, the ornate hanging Turkish lamps and the Turkish dishes served gave the exotic atmosphere of a Sultan's harem. Clarence Jones and his orchestra provided the music for dancing.

Despite tearooms struggling to keep going, one brave woman took a risk; Frances Virginia Whitaker opened the Frances Virginia Tea Room during the depths of

'In a Little Gypsy Tea Room'. Sheet music cover,
New York, 1935.

the Depression in Atlanta, the centre of the agrarian
Deep South. It prospered and became *the* place to meet
friends and enjoy delicious food, including sweet dishes
such as sherry chiffon pie, gingerbread with fluffy wine
sauce, and pumpkin pie with sherry whipped cream.
The Frances Virginia continued to thrive during the
Second World War, serving more than two thousand
meals a day.[17]

Department stores

TEAROOMS WERE ALSO set up in department stores
but were quite different from the cosy, homely tearooms, the bohemian dens of Greenwich Village or the
exotic fortune-telling at gypsy tearooms. Here ladies,

often wearing hats and gloves, held up a high standard
of decorum and good manners. In 1890 the first tearoom in a department store opened at Marshall Field's
in Chicago. Harry Gordon Selfridge, the manager
(later the founder of Selfridge's in London), had taken
the unusual decision of asking a middle-class woman
to help create a 'tearoom' at the store. Her name was
Sarah Haring and her job was to recruit 'gentlewomen'
who knew how to cook 'dainty dishes' which they were
willing to prepare and deliver to the store each day.
Although the tearoom was tucked away in a corner of
the fur department with only fifteen tables and the
menu was limited, it flourished and became the place
to go for the wives and daughters of the rich and pow-
erful. On the day of its opening about sixty people
ordered from hand-embroidered menus. Orange punch
was served in orange shells garnished with smilax.[18]
There was also rose punch as well as ice cream with a
sauce served on a plate with a rose. Sandwiches were
arranged in baskets tied with ribbons.[19] One of the
team, Harriet Tilden Brainard, initially supplied gingerbread and chicken salad, and it was she who introduced
Cleveland Creamed Chicken, which became one of
the tearoom's best-loved dishes. Other women prepared codfish cakes and Boston baked beans. Corned
beef hash also became an all-time favourite. The venture was very successful and more tearooms were added
within the department store.[20]

In 1907 the South Tearoom was opened. It became
known as the Walnut Room because of its beautiful
Circassian walnut panelling and by 1937 this had
become the official name. The popular chicken pot pie
is still a standout on the menu today. By the 1920s
Marshall Field's had seven tearooms, serving about five
thousand meals a day. In the Narcissus Fountain Room
customers could partake of triangular pieces of

cinnamon toast and an assortment of bread rounds spread with cream cheese, variously combined with pepper, chopped nuts, pineapple and pimiento. A 1922 tea menu listed fourteen kinds of tea sandwiches, eleven kinds of pickle, 37 salads and 72 ready-to-serve hot dishes. Orange punch was still on the menu but not the rose punch. Potato flour muffins, which had been introduced as a wartime substitution and had become a hit, remained.[21]

A later description of Marshall Field's tearooms comes from John Drury. He reports that the most widely known and most elegant of the tearooms was the Narcissus Fountain Room on the seventh floor whose decor, atmosphere, service and food were on a par with any dining room of a first-class Michigan Avenue or Gold Coast hotel. Between 3 and 5 p.m. tired shoppers could enjoy a special menu of sandwiches, salads, beverages and desserts while listening to chamber music: 'half an hour spent in such surroundings, and with the stimulation of a light and most carefully prepared snack, and you are refreshed and ready again for another round of shopping.' He had special praise for the famed potato flour muffin: 'Nowhere else can you get a muffin like this; it is an epicurean thrill of the highest order.'[22]

Tearooms were opened in department stores all over the country. In New York, for example, Macy's introduced a Japanese tearoom in 1904. Around 1910 free tea and cakes were served in a Japanese tea garden decorated with ferns, wisteria and lanterns in the Yamato Bazaar in Los Angeles.

Tearooms in department stores had their own specialities on the menu, the managers always on the lookout for new dishes and combinations to entice customers. In Philadelphia at Strawbridge & Clothier, the chicken in their club sandwich was replaced with fried oysters and the resultant dish christened the Rockaway Club Sandwich. Chicken pie was a very popular dish at many department stores. The pie made at the Miller & Paine tearoom in Lincoln, Nebraska, was memorable for having a double crust. Favourites at Filene's in Boston were chicken à la king, chop suey and maple layer pie. Some department stores offered expensive varieties of tea. Lasalle & Koch's 1920 menu had a pot of Ming Cha tea ('The most Expensive Tea Grown') for 20 cents and at about the same time Mandel Brothers in Chicago offered tea drinkers a choice of oolong, English breakfast, uncoloured Japan, Young Hyson, Ceylon orange pekoe and gunpowder.[23]

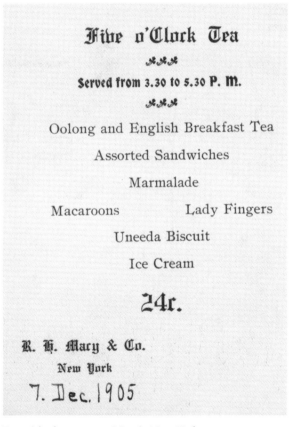

Five o'clock tea menu, Macy's, New York, 1905. Uneeda biscuits were a kind of cracker.

Hotels and the tea dance

AT THE BEGINNING of the twentieth century many new grand and luxurious hotels opened in the big cities such as the Fairmont in San Francisco in 1906, New York's Plaza Hotel in 1907, the Drake in Chicago in 1920 and Boston's Ritz-Carlton in 1927. Catering for royalty, the rich, celebrities and well-travelled people, they served elegant and stylish 'teas' in surroundings with plenty of veined marbled columns and glittering glass chandeliers, often accompanied by the dulcet strains of an orchestra. In these glamorous settings people could enjoy the latest craze that had come from Europe – the tea dance, or *thé dansant*, as it was often called.

'Mme X' wrote about this new craze as a 'Pleasing Diversion for Afternoons' in the *Chicago Daily Tribune* on 1 June 1913:

Chicago must 'look alive!' New York is getting far ahead of us as a merry metropolis. 'Thé dansant' of which I have written several times in the column is a firmly established institution there and under very decent and respectable auspices.

Nothing within the memory of the present and passing generation has been more extraordinary and worthy of note than the growing passion for dancing which has taken possession of people in many walks of life . . .

That this passion can be ministered to in a proper and orderly fashion is shown in the 'dancing teas' at one hotel in New York this last winter. The tearoom concession has been let to a southern woman. She maintains it daily in this ballroom from half past 4 to 7 o'clock. The room is pillared on both sides. Between the pillars and the windows the tea tables are set. At one end

is a stage for the orchestra. The center of the hall is cleared for dancing . . .

At the entrance the proprietress sits at a little desk and sells tickets at $1 a head. These tickets include tea, cake, and sandwiches and the privilege of dancing with your acquaintances . . . No intoxicating liquor of any kind is sold or permitted . . . no alcoholic beverages keep out the undesirable element who might otherwise spoil the tone of the place.

Tea dances, like the tea gardens of earlier years, provided an opportunity for young men and women to socialize without damaging their reputations. They were often given for debutantes or to raise money for charity. But some people were not so sure; the tea dance did not seem so innocent. On 5 April 1913 the *New York Times* in an article titled 'Slandering the Tea Dance' reported:

The tea dance is a comparatively new diversion in New York, a custom of not more than two seasons' growth. It began, informally, in some artist's studio. Friends were invited to tea, and a few musicians were hidden behind ferns and palms. A waltz was played and some of the guests were impelled to dance. Then followed other teas with dancing, and after a while the hotels and restaurants where shoppers and others drop in for tea took up the thé dansant. So far as is known there have been no deplorable goings on at the public tea dances. Even in the restaurants where they have the so-called cabarets at night, the afternoon dancing has been orderly, if informal. Of course, if girls dance in these places with strange men they are not nice girls, but thus far there is no widely proclaimed evidence that the tea dance is one of the lures of Satan . . . As for the whisky and cocktails; they have nothing whatever to do with the tea dance. Where they abide there is assuredly no thé dansant.

Many people, including Lillian Russell, suggested there might be other reasons for women wanting to go to tea dances. In the *Chicago Daily Tribune* of 13 February 1914 Russell wrote the following, fortunately ending on a positive note:

What is this new craze which has cast a spell over the universe? What is the attraction of the afternoon tea? Is it just the mad craze of dancing? I wish it were only that for one and all, but I fear many of the women of the present day use it only as a blind to hide their real motive for frequenting the thé dansant or afternoon dancing restaurant . . .

Of course in many ways this afternoon dancing craze has its good points . . . Some people have the erroneous idea that women and girls who go to these dancing places consume highballs, cocktails etc., and smoke cigarets. Some do unfortunately . . . but the finest of tea, chocolate, or any of the refreshing so-called soft drinks are available.

. . .

How much better for a woman to spend the afternoon in dancing than in leaning over the bridge table gambling, when perhaps she cannot afford it . . . Now she can join her friends at the thé dansant, and after her husband leaves his office he meets her there, and after one or two dances they speed homeward together after a day pleasantly and satisfactorily spent.

The tea dance continued to flourish, particularly during Prohibition, including new dance crazes such as the turkey trot, the maxie, the suggestive bunny hug and the Charleston. One was called the shimmy; Bert Williams, a star with the Ziegfield Follies, did not approve of tea as an alternative to alcohol and is famous for protesting in song 'You can't make your shimmy shake on tea.' But the tea dancers could and did!

During the Depression and the end of Prohibition in the 1930s tearooms and tea dances declined. Suburbanization, national chain ownership and a faster pace of life also played their part in the decline. All the qualities of tearooms, so much enjoyed at the beginning of the century, were now considered to be old fashioned. In the department stores moneymaking was the name of the game and floor space was devoted to food service at a fast pace. The furnishings were no longer homely and, as one department store executive put it in 1949,

There is a subtle relationship, in any food operation, between profit and uncomfortable chairs. Put a customer on a stool and he will eat his sandwich and get out to make room for another customer; but give him nice surroundings and an easy chair and he will dawdle the afternoon away.[24]

Menus were reduced too, and afternoon tea eliminated, replaced by quick lunch specials. The Greenwich Village bohemian tearooms were replaced in the beatnik coffee house movement of the 1950s and '60s.

However, in recent years the tearoom has been enjoying a revival. Some consider tea a healthy alternative to coffee or soda and there is also a lot of interest in the myriad types of teas now available. Many cities boast tearooms and many have menus which include enticing and exotic dishes from all over the world. One tea house can be found at the famous Japanese Tea Garden in San Francisco. The Garden provides visitors with a chance to experience the natural beauty, tranquillity and harmony of a Japanese-style garden at the heart of San Francisco's Golden Gate Park. The garden was originally created as a Japanese Village exhibit for the California Midwinter International Exposition of 1894. When the fair closed, Mr Makoto Hagiwara was allowed to create and maintain a permanent Japanese-style garden.

The Garden features classic elements such as an arched drum bridge, pagodas, stone lanterns, stepping stone paths, native Japanese plants, serene koi ponds and a zen garden. In March and April people can admire the cherry blossom trees in bloom. At the tea house visitors can choose from a selection of teas: sencha, genmaicha, hoji cha, jasmine and iced green tea. Tea sandwiches are available as well as soup, green-tea cheesecake, *dorayaki* (red-bean pancake, two small pancake-like patties made from castella wrapped around a filling of sweet Azuki red bean paste), sweet rice cakes and *arare* tea house cookies (fortune cookies). (*Arare* is a type of bite-sized Japanese cracker made from glutinous rice and flavoured with soy sauce.) The first evidence of fortune cookies in the United States is in connection with this tea garden and the descendants of Makoto Hagiwara claim that he introduced this special biscuit to the United States from Japan (where they originated as early as 1878) in the 1890s. At first the biscuits were made on site by hand using a special

The tranquil and beautiful Japanese Tea Garden, in the heart of Golden Gate Park, San Francisco.

iron mold or *kata*. Demand grew and Mr Hagiwara hired San Francisco confectioner Benkyodo to produce the fortune cookies in large quantities. The original fortune cookies made in Japan were savoury rather than sweet and it is believed that Benkyodo developed a recipe using vanilla as a flavouring. This made them even more appealing to Western tastes and is the flavour now popular across the U.S. Today the tradition of serving fortune cookies at the Tea Garden continues, with one tucked inside every bowl of Japanese rice crackers or *arare* sold at the tea house.

A more traditional tea house in San Francisco is the Secret Garden. They serve salads, all kinds of sandwiches including 'tea' sandwiches, tea scones and a good selection of pastries and sweets. They also have a number of 'afternoon teas' to suit different tastes: the Bedford's Delight; Earl's Favourite; Afternoon Delight; Garden Escape; a Prince and Princess Tea for the under-twelves and a Lord's and Lady's Cream Tea.

The legendary Palm Court of New York Plaza provides music while people enjoy one of a number of afternoon teas: the 'New Yorker Holiday Tea' with sandwiches and sweet classics such as Key lime tart and New York-style cheesecake; the Champagne Tea boasts savouries such as Peekytoe crab salad, foie gras torchon and lobster roll with daikon sprouts and buttered brioche roll. Sweets include a chocolate and hazelnut plaisir and a Tahitian vanilla éclair, served with a choice of exotic teas; and for children the 'Eloise Sugar and Spice Tea' has favourites such as organic peanut butter and jelly, and peppermint cotton candy. Thirst can be quenched with a 'hot' tea such as rooibos or a cold drink of pink lemonade or vanilla iced tea.

The Drake Hotel in Chicago continues to be the quintessential social hotspot. Princess Diana, Queen Elizabeth and the Empress of Japan have all been seen in its Palm Court, where customers can still be delighted with afternoon tea and music still plays its part with a harpist filling the room with enchanting melodies.

Four

Canada, Australia, New Zealand and South Africa

THE TRADITION OF teatimes spread to Britain's colonies such as Canada, Australia, New Zealand and South Africa. Early British settlers to these new and challenging lands were anxious to keep links with their past and also brought with them many customs and foodways, including baking skills and teatime traditions. Immigrants from Asia brought with them their own food traditions.

Tea in Canada

CANADA IS THE FOREMOST tea drinking country of the Western Hemisphere. Tea drinking and teatime traditions in Canada reflect the diverse origins of its inhabitants. The indigenous population has its own traditions, such as those of the Inuit and their herbal teas of the north. Teatime traditions were brought to Canada by British, Irish and French settlers, as reflected in the varied baking traditions: the English-style tearooms of Victoria, British Columbia, and the *salon de thé* tradition of Montreal, Quebec. New immigrants to Canada are also bringing their own tea cultures with them, including dim sum. There are around 1.5 million people of Chinese origin in Canada – 4.5 per cent of the total population – with large populations in Toronto, Vancouver and Montreal. Traditional Chinatowns in these cities date back to the nineteenth century. The majority are Cantonese-speaking people from Hong Kong or Guandong where dim sum is a way of life and there are many dim sum restaurants in these cities.

Although there are many coffee drinkers in Canada, tea drinkers drink tea at breakfast and several times during the day. 'Hot' tea is favoured over iced tea, which is the most popular way of serving tea across the border in the United

States. Tea bags are much in use, especially in tearooms and restaurants. A massive national advertising campaign was introduced around 2007 for steeped tea by Canadian Tim Horton's chain of 'donut' and coffee shops letting Canadians know that the chain now uses 'loose' tea leaves and that the tea is steeped in the time-honoured fashion. Green, white, flavoured or herbal teas have also become popular.

The first shipment of tea to Canada was made, according to Hudson's Bay Company records, on 7 June 1715, when '3 cannisters of Bohea tea' were shipped aboard the frigate *Hudson's Bay*, under the command of Captain Joseph Davis.[1] Unfortunately, owing to bad weather, the ship could not reach the bay and had to return to England. The unlucky Captain Davis was dismissed and it was not until the next year that the same three canisters finally reached their destination under the command of another captain.[2]

It seems that the Bohea tea was far from the best tea in the world, described as 'the poorest kind of black tea, mixed with dust and large flat brown and brownish-green leaves. The liquor was a dark brownish-red, and always left a black sediment in the cup.'[3] Even so, tea became popular not just with trappers but with First Nations. The Inuit still drink their tea strong and without milk or sugar and regard it as a precious drink.

Prior to the 1950s the Labrador Innu bands were migratory. When the Innu people of Sheshatsiu, Labrador, travelled to the hunting grounds, everyone was expected to carry his or her share of the load. The children carried theirs by bringing along a doll that held a reserve of around 2 lb (900 g) of loose tea stuffed in its body. When the camp was set up and the tea was needed to provide a warm drink, it was removed. The doll could be restuffed with grass or leaves.

The early immigrants, who looked forward to the arrival of all provisions, including tea, had to make do with the tea whatever its quality. Winter blizzards, ocean storms and poor inland transportation all conspired against healthy stocks of tea. Prior to the mid-1800s most of the settlers had a pioneering lifestyle and would make do with an old iron pot in which to brew their tea. The tea leaves were topped up with boiling water as the day went along and the resulting tea became very strong, its taste leaving much to be desired. In these days, with distances so vast and travelling difficult, visits became important – either with friends or strangers. Many people lived in isolation and would welcome any opportunity to socialize. Tea came to represent warmth and hospitality. Writer Frances Hoffman in her book *Steeped in Tradition* recounts a story:

Explorer Charles Francis Hall, while at Northumberland Inlet during the 1860s, was pleasantly surprised when his hostess offered him a cup of tea. 'Before I was aware of it, Tookoolito had the "tea-kettle" over the friendly fire-lamp, and the water boiling. She asked me if I drank tea. Imagine my surprise at this, the question coming from an Esquimause in an Esquimaux tent! I replied, "I do; but you have not tea here, have you?" Drawing her hand from a little tin box, she displayed it full of fine-flavoured black tea, saying, "Do you like your tea strong?" Thinking to spare her the use of much of this precious article away up here, far from the land of civilisation, I replied, "I'll take it weak, if you please." A cup of hot tea was soon before me – capital tea, and capitally made. Taking from my pocket a sea-biscuit which I had brought from the vessel for my dinner, I shared it with my hostess. Seeing she had but one cup, I induced her to share with me its contents. There, amid the snows of the North, under an Esquimaux's hospitable tent, in the company with Esquimaux, for the first time I shared with them in that soothing, cheering, invigorating emblem of civilization – TEA.'[4]

Gradually the number of shipments of tea increased and tea rations became more stable. Some of the early settlers brought their fancy tea services and china with them. As shipments of tea increased so did the importation of tea accoutrements.

Saint John in New Brunswick has a rich tea heritage. It was here that Canada's well-known tea brands, Red Rose and King Cole, were developed. The King Cole blend was created by the G. E. Barbour Company, founded in Saint John in 1867. The Red Rose blend was created by Theodore Harding Estabrooks and was a special blend of Indian and Ceylon teas. The blend was launched under the name Red Rose in 1899. The tea has been popular in Canada ever since. It was also Theodore who came up with the idea of producing a pack of quality blended tea that was consistent from cup to cup; tea until this time had been sold loose from chests and the quality varied a great deal. Initially, Red Rose was sold mainly in the Atlantic provinces of Canada but soon distribution expanded into other parts of Canada and into the United States. Red Rose also introduced tea bags for the first time in 1929.

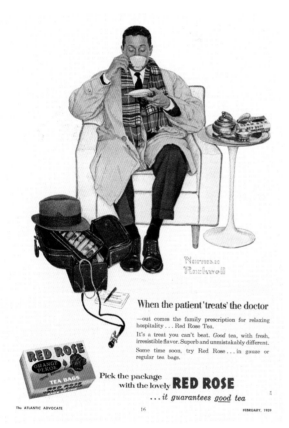

Magazine advertisement for Red Rose tea bags, 1959, artwork by Norman Rockwell.

Afternoon tea, 'at homes' and high tea

IN THE 1860s the tradition of entertaining for afternoon tea was becoming established in Ontario. The visiting or the receiving of visitors was quite formal at this time and was linked with the serving of tea, often with all the rituals of social etiquette and having the right tea set, kettle and so on. For example, it was not considered appropriate to invite anyone for tea if one owed any social calls. A good hostess would make sure she had done all the visiting required of her before she herself gave a tea. Once her tea had taken place, with all of her guests having left their calling cards, she would then owe them all a visit.

As in Britain there was also the problem of what to wear for these occasions. Those women from affluent backgrounds paid close attention to the fashion of the day. These society women had the choice of a carriage dress (but only if they were arriving by horse and carriage), or a morning dress, walking dress or visiting dress (if arriving on foot). An 'ordinary' woman might wear an 'afternoon tea frock' – a simple but elegant dress for day visits.

Servants too caused problems. It was essential to have enough on hand and they must be competent. When they were not, problems could arise. But tea parties became firmly entrenched into the social network and many hostesses held 'at homes' which were designed to invite many visitors and to provide elaborate food. Often the daughters of the hostess were enlisted to help pour the tea, coffee or cocoa or to help serve food. If no daughters were available then perhaps a 'charming' married woman would pour. Someone was responsible for welcoming the guests and somebody was in charge of replenishing sandwiches, cakes and the teapots.

Advice for hostesses and guests could be found in *The Home Cook Book* of 1877. This book was the most successful Canadian cookbook of the nineteenth century and was Canada's first community cookbook, with one in six households having a copy. It was a collection of recipes and remedies compiled by the ladies of Toronto and other cities and towns in Canada. It provided a model for women in English-speaking Canada to use their own recipes and support good causes such as hospital and church charities and organizations like the Women's Institute, a tradition which continues to the present day. The book gave this advice for afternoon tea in the home:

> Guests arrive in the five minutes before the hour, or five minutes after. The tea is brought in punctually and placed on the hostess' table in the corner, where are the urns of black, green and Russian tea for those who like each, a basket of wafers, delicate sandwiches of chicken or thin sliced meats, and a basket of fancy cake. If the English style is followed, the cups of tea are carried to guests on a tray, and a tiny table to rest the cups on placed in the reach of the group.

Tea parties of one kind or another became fashionable from the 1860s to the 1960s. During the Victorian era the Victoria sandwich cake became popular and scones were also a favourite. Fundraising teas were organized by church committees. 'Temperance' teas provided 'respectable' venues for women during the Victorian era. 'Thimble' teas were often held in rural areas where communal quilting or sewing projects were undertaken. Noreen Howard, who lives in Calgary, told me that she still gives and attends this sort of tea party and said that it gives a chance to get out the best tea set.[5]

In contrast to these industrious and sedate teas, there were 'kettledrum' teas with much gossip, noise and laughter. 'Trousseau' teas were often organized by a bride's mother either on the married couple's return from honeymoon or sometimes before the wedding. In these simple but elegant affairs, thin bread and butter, tiny sandwiches and a few simple cakes or a plate of cut cake would be displayed in one room and wedding presents in another. There were also 'mother and daughter teas' sponsored by churches, Women's Institutes and schools with home economics departments.

By the 1920s many homes boasted an elegant tea cart or wagon. The tea wagon usually had small side leaves which, when in use, were opened to make a table which was then covered with a small but pretty tablecloth. On the top tier the teapot, cups, saucers, sugar, cream teaspoons and slop bowl were placed. The lower tier held plates and serviettes as well as plates of dainty sandwiches and cakes. One confection which often appeared on tea carts or the tea table at this time were Chinese chews, alongside Empire cookies, melting moments and pecan snowballs. How this chewy confection got its name is a bit of a mystery but it was at this time that the Chinese were settling in Canada, after a lot of the men had come earlier to help build the trans-Canadian railways and their families had joined them. They started little Chinese restaurants in small towns and some of their dishes were concoctions of Chinese cooking with Canadian additions. The use of quite exotic ingredients in Chinese chews (such as walnuts and dates) provided a link with the Orient. A recipe first appeared in the June issue of *Good Housekeeping* in 1917 and was widely reprinted in newspapers:

Chinese Chews 2600 Calories
1 cupful dates, chopped
1 cupful English walnuts, chopped
1 cupful sugar
¾ cupful pastry flour
1 teaspoonful baking-powder
2 eggs
¼ teaspoonful salt

Mix all dry ingredients together, put in the dates and nuts, and stir in the eggs after beating them light. Bake in as thin a sheet as can be spread and when done cut in small squares and roll into balls. Then roll them in granulated sugar.
Mrs L. G. Platt, North Bend, Ore

[N.B. no oven temperature or timing has been given but I suggest baking at 160°C (325°F), for about 25 minutes]

Later recipes varied; some included candied ginger and pecans instead of walnuts. The popularity of 'Chinese chews' has waned somewhat although there are modern versions containing coconut and chocolate chips.

Although teatimes continued to be an important ritual for women to get together for mutual support, the two world wars changed the way people lived. Women were now going out to work and there was less time and less demand for organizing tea parties. More and more young people were switching to drinking 'trendy' coffee, as in the United States. But despite all the social changes many people in Canada still clung on to taking tea in the afternoons. Edna McCann, who lives in southern Ontario, reminisces in her book *The Canadian Heritage Cookbook* about how she prepared an elegant tea in about the 1930s:

When I was a young bride, George and I moved to a parish in a farming community. To greet the new parishioners, we gave a small reception in the church basement (known as the meeting room). Hoping to make a good impression, I made dozens of 'tea' sandwiches – small triangles or squares of bread with egg salad decorated with an olive 'flower', or ham salad on tiny strips of bread rolled around a pickle. At the time these were considered to be the last word in elegance in the gracious homes of east coast cities. I was so proud of my trays of little sandwiches until I heard one of the farmers talking to his wife. 'Sakes alive, Martha, maybe we'd best have a meeting about the new minister's salary. Will you look at the size of the sandwiches his poor young wife has made!' I learned pretty quickly that large quantities of good food were what was expected by these hardworking men of the community. Elegance was unnecessary.

Mystery novel writer Gail Bowen kindly sent me her reminiscences of teatime in Toronto in the late 1940s:

We lived on Prescott Avenue in the west end. It was a British enclave at that time. We had a pork store (that sold great blood pudding and amazing pork pies) and we had two bakeries that made selections for afternoon tea – all kinds of lovely things, but I remember my Nana favoured Parisian tarts and eccles cakes. After school, she and I would go down to St. Clair Avenue and choose what delicacy we'd have for tea. Once a week, my Nana would have all her friends in for tea. They always kept their hats on as they had tea and although they had known each other for decades, they always called one another Mrs. Ollerenshaw, Mrs. Bartholomew, Mrs. Exton etc. when they had tea.

Still quite formal, then. However, Gail goes on to say that on other occasions when they met, they called one another by their first names: Ness, Hilda, Edna. She also describes that her family had an evening meal at 6 p.m. which they called supper, not high tea or tea. Perhaps no tea but 'high tea' type dishes were served, such as bubble and squeak, fish, liver, fish and chips and so on.[6]

Noreen Howard remembers teatimes at her husband's parents' home in Montreal in 1965. Every afternoon at four o'clock tea would be made and served with some cookies or squares such as Nanaimo bars, one of Canada's favourite teatime treats.[7] Cookies and squares and a full tin were the pride of Canadian housewives. Canadians have a love of baking. Catharine Parr Traill wrote in her book *The Female Emigrant's Guide* in 1854 that 'Canada is the land of cakes.'

Recipes could be found in the cookbooks of the day. *The Home Cook Book* (mentioned earlier) was not just a good source of advice but gave numerous

Nanaimo bars, a favourite teatime snack to be found in the well-filled tins of many Canadian homes.

bread, biscuit and cake recipes such as 'rye cakes for tea', teacakes, gingerbreads, doughnuts, muffins and cupcakes, shortcakes, mountain cake, white mountain jelly cake and velvet cake. Many recipes called for 'the cook's friend', meaning baking powder, which was a relatively new 'aid' for cooks and bakers at that time. Another best-selling book was *The New Galt Cook Book: A Book of Tried and Test Recipes* (revd edn 1898). Included are recipes for breads, rolls, muffins, buns, biscuits (such as gems, tea biscuits and ginger biscuits) and scones. There are lots of cakes including some less well known ones (to me anyway) such as Minnehaha cake, jelly cakes, Princess May chocolate cake, Spanish bun and huckleberry cakes. There is also a section on sandwiches, some of which are made with slightly unusual ingredients such as mincemeat, dates or nasturtium (described as a novelty with a piquant flavour) and Devonshire cream.

The Five Roses Cookbook was first published in 1913, and the 1915 edition had sales of 950,000 copies, enough for one in every second Canadian home. The recipes were almost exclusively for sweet baked goods and breads, favouring cakes over puddings, pies and biscuits using Five Roses flour. Among the book's prized recipes is one for Butter Tarts, which many people consider as one of only a few recipes of genuinely Canadian origin.

Baking is important in Newfoundland and Labrador. Many immigrants claim English, Scottish or Irish ancestry and have a long tradition of baking. Tea buns (or teacakes) are popular. They are a sort of cross between a teacake and a scone. There are many variations, every family having their own 'secret' recipe. They were often given to children to eat when they came home hungry from school, or served for high tea. When raisins (often soaked in rum first) are added, they are called raisin buns. The rum came to Newfoundland from the Caribbean. When merchants shipped their salt cod and traded it down to the Caribbean, they got rum back in exchange. It is said that the best raisin buns are made with evaporated milk but fresh milk can be used and many Newfoundlanders like to serve them with Fussell's canned thick cream.

Salt cod was also traded for molasses. Many traditional Newfoundland and Labrador recipes trace their roots back to molasses as an ingredient. It became a kitchen staple used for spreading on bread, as a sauce for puddings and a syrup over pancakes. Molasses became the sweetener of choice for tea breads, gingerbreads, biscuits, fruit cakes, puddings and buns, such as the distinctly flavoured, sweet and often spicy Lassy buns (sometimes called tarts). As with tea buns, raisins can also be added. All are good just as they are but some add a little bit of butter or a spoonful of jam. Soft drop cookies called Cry Babies, or others rolled thick and cut, such as Fat Archies (known as moose hunters in Cape Breton), also have molasses as an ingredient and are good with a cup of tea.

Molasses accompanies another Newfoundland speciality, toutons, which are sometimes described as pancakes. Bread dough (traditionally leftover bread dough) is fried in a pan with butter or pork fat, then often served with more butter and either dark molasses, maple syrup or golden syrup. Although toutons are usually served for breakfast or brunch they are sometimes served at teatime.

High tea was, as in Britain, a meal taken in the early evening instead of dinner later on. Suggestions and recipes for tea were given in cookbooks. *The Home Cook Book* (1877) gives two bills of fare for tea:

Tea No. 1:
Tea   Coffee   Chocolate Biscuits
Oyster sandwiches   Chicken salad
Cold tongue
Cake and preserves
Ice Cream and cake later in the evening

Tea No. 2:
Tea   Coffee   Chocolate
Escalloped or Fried Oysters
Muffins
Sliced Turkey and Ham
Cold Biscuits
Sardines and Sliced Lemons
Thin slices of bread rolled
Sliced Pressed Meat
Cake in variety

Another book published in 1904 by Sara Lovell was called *Meals of the Day: A Guide to the Young Housekeeper*. She gives a number of recipes for tea. Savoury dishes include egg dishes such as omelettes, poached, fried, scrambled or stuffed. There is macaroni with fish or meat or with tomatoes or gravy or creamed with cheese, potato dishes such as potato cake, timbales with chicken, oyster or fish, salads with fish, chicken and lobster. Sandwiches include ham, tongue, lettuce and one called Queen's.

Queen's Sandwiches

Sixteen sardines, four hard boiled eggs, thin slices brown bread and butter, cut lettuce.

Bone the sardines and divide them in half, cut thin slices of brown bread and butter. Chop the eggs and put first layer on the bread the sardines next, and lettuce next. Trim nicely, and cut in rounds or in strips.

There is also bread fried in egg or bread pancakes and cold meats garnished with sliced tomato or aspic jelly, pickled salmon or white fish and smoked herrings 'dressed and heated', cheese on toast, Welsh rabbit and one dish with an unusual name – English monkey:

English Monkey

One cup of stale bread crumbs, one cup milk, one teaspoon butter, half a cup of milk cheese cut in small pieces, one egg, half a teaspoon of salt and a speck of cayenne.

Soak the crumbs fifteen minutes in milk, melt the butter, add the cheese when melted and soaked crumbs, eggs slightly beaten and seasonings.

Cook three minutes and pour on toasted crackers.

Sweet dishes include fruits, canned or preserved or stewed, sometimes served with shortcake, or fresh currants covered with sugar and water, or junket and cream.

In the third edition of a book entitled *Culinary Landmarks; or, Half-hours with Sault Ste Marie Housewives* (1909), first published in 1898, there are some interesting recipes for tea in the chapter 'Breakfast, Luncheon and Tea'. The preface, written by Annie M. Reid, President of the Women's Auxiliary, makes clear that the recipes are not a 'haphazard collection gathered at random', but are made up of 'the choicest bits of the best experience of the members of St Luke's Woman's Auxiliary and their friends'.

Recipes include omelettes (plain, shrimp and with oysters), curried eggs, devilled eggs on toast, egg patties, eggs on foam and jumbled eggs. There are cheese dishes such as macaroni cheese, soufflé, fondue, custard, scallops, Welsh rabbit, cheese puff and cheese straws. Croquettes are made with potatoes, ham or rice. There are pancakes, savoury and sweet. Sweet dishes include apple fritters, rice fritters, snow fritters and bell fritters, which we are told are nice served with Yankee honey (made by beating up one egg quite thick with granulated sugar and flavoured with vanilla) for tea. There are four shortcake recipes – two with strawberry, one peach and one orange. The bread recipes include one called 'Twist' which we are told is a 'delicious and beautiful bread for tea'.

Garden parties

THE GARDEN TEA PARTY became popular in Ontario. The setting for these grand occasions was provided by Government House in Toronto, the home of the early Lieutenant Governors of Ontario. Prominent Canadians and Toronto society folk were invited to mingle with visiting royalty and dignitaries on the spacious terrace and manicured lawns. Many were attended by up to five hundred people and capably directed by Thomas Lymer, who served as butler and chief steward to eleven of Ontario's Lieutenant Governors. One of his rules for a successful tea party was that the food should not be too sticky or crumbly: 'People who are holding a tea cup in their hands do not want a sticky cake that crumbles, they prefer the light firm sponge cakes and assorted sandwiches, mainly of chicken, tomatoes or cress.' He felt that guests should feel as elegant at the close of the function as they had at the opening.[8]

One of the most splendid garden parties at Government House was held in 1901 when the Duke and Duchess of Cornwall and York (later to become King George V and Queen Mary) visited. A whole list of 'who's who' in Ontario attended and the weather was perfect, making it a legendary occasion.[9]

Of course there were much less grand garden tea parties. Many Canadian families loved a relaxed outdoor tea in their own garden when the weather was favourable. In late Victorian times an informal tea might consist of sandwiches, fancy cakes, bonbons and, of course, tea. For a more formal tea the beverages might include bouillon (hot or cold), coffee, chocolate, Russian tea or iced tea punch. Ices and frappés were also popular.[10]

Tea out

AFTER QUEEN VICTORIA died in 1901 the flamboyant Edward VII and his beautiful wife Queen Alexandra came to the throne and with them a new age dawned, with new trends and fashions in Britain and the Commonwealth. Canada had grown from a pioneering nation to one of industry and commerce. The population had increased and people were more prosperous. There was more gaiety and entertaining became less formal. People would go out for 'five o'clock tea' to one of the fashionable hotels. The expansion of the railways had ensured that people could travel more easily to cities and many railway hotels were built. Ontario's first grand railway hotel, the Chateau Laurier, was completed in

1912 in Ottawa and at once became a huge success with people enjoying tea out in elegance and comfort. By the 1920s and '30s just about everyone had acquired the habit of 'taking tea' out. The wealthy held lavish tea parties in these luxurious hotels. Glamorous tea dances become popular, usually held between four and six o'clock. Tea was sipped and dainty sandwiches were nibbled to the accompaniment of a band. They were generally not formal affairs; women wore afternoon frocks and coats and gloves were laid aside. However, hats continued to be worn. The dances were fun and a place where people could meet – a perfect setting for mixing with the opposite sex.

In the late nineteenth and early twentieth centuries the development of department stores in North America gave birth to a new kind of restaurant where ladies could lunch or relax over tea after a busy afternoon shopping in elegant surroundings. Across Canada, Eaton's opened restaurants in several of their department stores including the Grill Room in Winnipeg in 1905 and the Georgian Room in Toronto in 1924.

The dynamic Lady Eaton oversaw the architecture, decor, staffing and menus for more than a dozen Eaton's restaurants. Women flocked to them, with their glamorous decor, high quality food and affordable prices, some of them serving as many as five thousand customers a day. A number of the dishes served at the Georgian Room gained fame over time. The red velvet cake – a chocolate layer cake with either a dark red, bright red or red-brown colour (beetroot or red food colouring were used), filled and topped with a cream cheese or cooked roux icing – became synonymous with Eaton's restaurants. Promoted as an exclusive Eaton's recipe, with employees who knew the recipe sworn to silence, many mistakenly believed the cake was the invention of Lady Eaton herself.

The Georgian Room, Eaton's, Toronto, in 1939. Eaton's became famous for its red velvet cake and Queen Elizabeth cake.

Another cake popular at Eaton's was the Queen Elizabeth cake. Although known more as a dessert cake it is equally good served at teatime. There is some debate over its origins. Some accounts assert that it was invented for the 1937 coronation of King George VI and Queen Elizabeth. Others say it originated in 1953 for the coronation of Queen Elizabeth II. Still other accounts state that the recipe was sold, for 15 cents a copy, as a fundraiser during the Second World War, and as Queen Elizabeth, the Queen Mother, was very popular in Canada it may have been named in her honour. Apparently recipes that appeared in wartime cookbooks during the 1940s reappeared in Canadian cookbooks in 1953 for the coronation of Queen Elizabeth II. Whatever the origins, this is a moist cake made rich by the generous addition of dates and nuts. The top is frosted with a mix of butter, sugar, coconut and cream and then put back into the oven to lightly brown the frosting.[11]

In Victoria, British Columbia, tea culture has been engrained in its history for as long as the city has been around. When the British immigrated to Victoria they brought the practice of afternoon tea with them. It has been an honoured tradition since and is still thriving in many of the city's tearooms. The most famous tearoom for many decades is the Victoria Room in the Empress Hotel (named for Queen Victoria, Empress of India), which started serving teas in 1908. It is the very epitome of Victorian class and is reported to serve more afternoon teas than most hotels in London, with eight hundred to a thousand people a day coming to enjoy the tradition. In elegant surroundings (throughout its history the Empress has played host to kings, queens and celebrities), their traditional English afternoon tea starts off with fresh seasonal berries and cream followed by finger sandwiches, scones, toasted crumpets, pastries and tarts, and is still served today. The tea (sadly today, I am told, in the form of tea bags) is the Empress's own special blend, a blend of China black, Ceylon and Darjeeling made by Murchie's, a hundred-year-old British Columbia company famous for its teas.[12]

Murchie's, apart from being famous for their teas, is another favourite place for afternoon tea with a good selection of savouries, cakes and pastries to eat. Murchie's has been operating as a shop selling tea since it was founded in 1894 by John Murchie, an immigrant to Canada from Scotland. As a young lad John worked for Melrose's of Scotland, a prestigious tea import merchant in Britain, and one of his jobs was to deliver tea to Queen Victoria while she was in residence at Balmoral Castle.

Also in Victoria is the Abkhazi Garden and Tearoom. The Abkhazi estate also has a royal connection with a romantic story that began in the 1940s when Prince and Princess Abkhazi, originally from Georgia, came to Victoria to settle down after many years apart. In their garden they created a magical oasis. After their deaths the home and garden was purchased by the Land Conservancy and now there is a lovely tearoom overlooking the beautiful garden. They often hold special events such as an annual Mad Hatter's Tea and a Prince and Princess Tea to celebrate the anniversary of the Prince and Princess.

Another favourite tearoom is the White Heather Tearoom which caters for all appetites, providing three sizes of tea: the 'Wee Tea' with an assortment of sweets and scones, the 'Not So Wee Tea' and the 'Big Muckle

Empress Hotel
VICTORIA, B.C.

Afternoon Tea
85¢

English Crumpets or
Toasted Mohawk Cake
Salmon, Celery Spread Sandwich
Pimento Cheese Sandwich
Almond Tartlet
Tea

$1.00

English Crumpets or
Toasted Mohawk Cake
Tomato Stuffed with Crabmeat
Thin Buttered Bread
Almond Tartlet
Tea

An Empress Hotel afternoon tea menu, *c.* 1920.

Tea' with tiered trays of finger sandwiches, sweet and savoury tarts, fresh fruits, tiny cakes and cookies plus, of course, the traditional scones with jam and Devonshire cream.

Some new trends in tearooms are also appearing with a distinct west coast contemporary eco flair, with honey produced locally, seaweed-infused teas and Asian-influenced menus.

Although Victoria is the most renowned place in Canada for afternoon tea, tearooms are mushrooming everywhere. Many hotels all over Canada now cater for afternoon tea, including within the Fairmont chain. At the company's Vancouver hotel children can have a special bubblegum tea with peanut butter and jelly finger sandwiches and are encouraged to dress up like their favourite fairy tale characters. In Edmonton at the Fairmont Hotel Macdonald, where the Queen stayed in 2005, they serve a 'royal tea' which includes a glass of sherry or champagne and a tour of the royal suite.

Many hotels across Canada from the Pacific to the Atlantic coasts were established during the development of the Canadian Pacific Railway. The railway company realized passengers were in need of places to stop and rest during their long journey. One was the Chateau Lake Louise hotel, which was constructed in 1890 in the Rocky Mountains of Alberta. Afternoon tea can be taken here while enjoying spectacular views of Lake Louise and the Victoria

Glacier. Meanwhile children can have a Teddy Bear Picnic, first creating their own teddy bear then picnicking (with teddy) on iced tea and finger sandwiches and receiving a special visit by Bow the Bear.

Situated near Lake Louise is Lake Agnes, named for Lady Agnes MacDonald, the wife of Canada's first prime minister. In 1886 she visited Lake Agnes and loved the beauty of this idyllic lake and the hanging valley it sits in. Located in this valley on the shores of the crystal clear waters of the lake, the Lake Agnes Tea House was built by the Canadian Pacific Railway eleven years after the Chateau Lake Louise and started serving tea in 1905. It was built as a rest stop for visitors and hikers around this remote area. The original log building was replaced in 1981 but to preserve the Tea House's rustic charm the original windows, tables and chairs were kept. It is a family run teahouse offering home-made soup, sandwiches on freshly baked bread and pastries, with a selection of more than a hundred loose-leaf teas from around the world.

Other notable places for afternoon tea include the King Edward Hotel in Toronto, which has hosted numerous celebrities and dignitaries in its one-hundred-years-plus history and serves 'the best tea in Toronto'. Reflecting Toronto's cultural diversity, the menus are varied and so are the teas, with various exotic blended teas such as jasmine snow dragon, bergamot rose and Marrakesh mint. The 'Duchess of Bedford' tea offers chai spiced carrot cake and sugar shack maple tartlet with bourbon plumped raisins and candied pecans – a far cry from the Duchess's original toast, fine bread and butter and little cakes. 'The Earl of Sandwich' tea caters for those with a savoury tooth with finger sandwiches such as beef wellington and five-spice chicken with spring scallion. There is also a 'Spring Tea', a 'Garden Tea' and, for children, a 'Jester's Tea' which includes a jelly roll lollipop, banana bread building blocks and a sugar-dusted cookie crown. There is no tea but a choice of hot cocoa with marshmallows, apple cider or milk.

Charlottetown, a port city on Prince Edward Island, has an important tea culture. Tea was in the past imported and distributed from here. Sadly, none of the original tea businesses have survived. One such was Milton's Tearoom which was advertised in *Mrs Flynn's*

Lake Agnes tea house, across from its namesake lake in the Canadian Rockies.

Cookbook, originally published in 1930. The book also advertised the Brahmin tea which was locally blended and sold by Higgs and Company.

Prince Edward Island was the home province of Lucy Maud Montgomery, author of *Anne of Green Gables*. This novel, written in 1908, recounts the adventures of Anne Shirley, an eleven-year-old orphan girl who is mistakenly sent to Matthew and Marilla Cuthbert, a middle-aged brother and sister who had intended to adopt a boy to help them on their farm in Prince Edward Island. The story tells of Anne's life with the Cuthberts, in school and within the town. One day when Marilla is going out she tells Anne that she can invite her friend Diana to tea. Anne exclaims that 'it will be so nice and grown uppish' and begs to be allowed to use the best rosebud spray tea-set:

'No, indeed! The rosebud tea-set! You know I never use that except for the minister or the Aids. You'll put down the old brown tea-set. But you can use the little yellow crock of cherry preserves. It's time it was being used anyway – I believe it's beginning to work. And you can cut some fruitcake and have some of the cookies and snaps.'

'I can just imagine myself sitting down at the head of the table and pouring out the tea,' said Anne, shutting her eyes ecstatically. 'And asking Diana if she takes sugar! I know she doesn't but of course I'll ask her just as if I didn't know. And pressing her to take another piece of fruitcake and another helping of preserves.'

Anne is even more delighted when Marilla tells her:

'There's a bottle half full of raspberry cordial left over from the church social the other night. It's on the second shelf of the sitting-room closet and you and Diana can have it if you like, and a cooky to eat with it along in the afternoon.'

Diana arrives and when the time comes for the cordial Anne finds the bottle on the top shelf, not the second. Diana finds it delicious and compliments it saying 'That's awfully nice raspberry cordial, Anne.' Being the perfect little hostess, Anne replies, 'I am so glad you like it. Take as much as you want.' Three tumblers later, Diana is feeling sick and unable to eat anything. She totters away unsteadily. The next day it is found out that the raspberry cordial was in fact currant wine – definitely disapproved of by the church ladies of the temperance society, including Diana's mother. Later in the story Anne does much better when she goes to tea at her Sunday school teacher's house and declares: 'We had an elegant tea, and I think I kept all the rules of etiquette pretty well.' She says to Marilla, 'I believe I could be a model child if I were just invited out to tea every day!'

Today at the Delta Prince Edward Hotel in Charlottetown visitors can enjoy an 'Anne of Green Gables' tea party with raspberry cordial, slices of pound cake and an assortment of tea-party-style sweets. There is a live musical performance by an Anne impersonator and at the end of the tea there is a period costume dress-up photo opportunity with Anne, or as Anne if you put on the wig and hat. It is also possible while on the island to participate in 'Anne's Perfectly Scrumptious Wild Rose Tea Party', which includes a museum tour, making a floral decked hat and afternoon tea served on Montgomery family china.[13]

In recent years Charlottetown's colonial tea history has also been supplemented by a number of tea shops reflecting tea traditions from other cultures. One is the

Formosa Tea House, serving teas and authentic snacks from Taiwan. Several other Asian-style tea houses have also emerged in the city.[14]

The French influence on tea drinking is reflected in the *salons de thé* in Quebec and Montreal. They seem to concentrate more on selling or serving a large selection of exotic teas and blends than on tea served with exquisite patisserie as in France, although the Camellia Sinensis tearoom does serve a small assortment of exotic desserts with tea.

Many of Canada's tearooms, as south of the border in the United States, are homely places and, while many offer a choice from one to two hundred varieties of tea, many specialize in lunches and dinners with savoury dishes and desserts rather than tea and cakes. Some tearooms double up as a gift or craft shop.

Australia

ALTHOUGH AUSTRALIA has recently become a nation of coffee drinkers, tea has been the traditional hot beverage since British settlement. When the First Fleet arrived on Australian shores from England in 1788 they were carrying food staples and medical supplies founded on naval victualling standards for the times, dominated by salted meat, flour, rice and dried peas.[15] Tea and sugar were not included in the government ration despite the fact that at this time tea had become entrenched in British culture and rather than being considered a luxury item was now regarded by many as a necessity. In fact some of the more privileged individuals did bring their own luxuries and 'necessaries', including tea, with them.

One substitute for tea was found in the form of the native sarsaparilla, *Smilax glyciphylla*, which the colonists called 'sweet tea'. This alternative not only provided a necessary 'comfort' but was regarded as a health-giving restorative. It was drunk universally and because of its sweet taste it served as both tea and sugar.[16]

Tea was on sale in Sydney from at least 1792. A variety of both green and black teas were being imported from China, such as Hyson, a green tea, and Bohea, a black tea. Both were probably not the best quality teas but were strong bodied and would have been quite economical and quenched the settlers' thirst for tea. These teas were regularly advertised for sale in *The Sydney Gazette and the New South Wales Advertiser* from its first issue in 1803.

In the second half of the nineteenth century the commercial growing of tea in India developed rapidly and in the 1880s Indian black tea was being imported. Fresh milk in tea, when available, had always been popular and with the expansion of the dairy industry tea with milk and sugar became the national beverage.

By the early twentieth century Australia was a major market for Indian and Ceylon teas. For much of the twentieth century up to today, Australian tea brands such as Bushells – 'Our cuppa since 1883' – and Liptons were household names. Although there is now a niche market for green tea again and many Australians are keen coffee drinkers, strong tea with milk, and often sugar, is still a popular beverage among many Australians.[17]

Tea drinking had its own ritual in the rough and challenging life of the outback. An iconic image is of a drover or swagman sitting around a campfire with a 'billy' on the boil for tea and perhaps some damper (a simple bread) being cooked in the embers of the fire. The billy is a kind of simple tin with a metal wire handle. A fire was lit usually using eucalyptus branches and a tripod constructed to hang the billy from. The billy was boiled, tea added and traditionally a eucalyptus leaf was included. The smoke from the fire had a lovely scent and the added leaf gave the tea a special flavour. The tea was made strong and, after steeping, in order to settle the tea leaves to the bottom, the billy was swung back and forth at arm's length or swung round the head three times. This required some level of caution. The tea was then poured into tin mugs and sweetened condensed milk (which became available from the 1890s) was added in place of fresh milk.

An adventurous traveller to Australia in 1870, G. Earnest, wrote about his outback experiences. He describes damper with relish:

> I suppose everyone knows what dampers are but I do not think any, who have not tasted them, red hot from the wood ashes, can have the faintest idea how nice they are, especially when they happen to be the first thing you have eaten for ten or twelve hours.[18]

Damper is fairly easy to make. It is made with wheat flour and water, perhaps a pinch of salt and baking soda for leavening and is baked primitively in the embers of an open fire. Damper was originally developed by stockmen who travelled in remote areas for long periods with only basic rations of flour, sugar and tea, sometimes supplemented by whatever meat (dried or cooked) was available or perhaps some golden syrup, which was known as 'cocky's joy'.

Francis Lancelott, a mineralogical surveyor who visited Australia in the mid-1800s, wittily describes in a poem the monotonous weekly menu of a shepherd in the outback:

> You may talk of the dishes of Paris renown,
> Or for plenty though London may range,
> If variety's pleasing, oh, leave either town,
> And come to the bush for a change.
> On Monday we've mutton, with damper
>   and tea;
> On Tuesday, tea, damper and mutton,
> Such dishes I'm certain all men must agree
> Are fit for peer, peasant, or glutton.
> On Wednesday we've damper, with mutton
>   and tea;
> On Thursday tea, mutton and damper,
> On Friday we've mutton, tea, damper while we
> With our flocks over hill and dale scamper.
> Our Saturday feast may seem rather strange,
> 'Tis of damper with tea and fine mutton;
> Now surely I've shown you that plenty of
>   change
> In the bush, is the friendly board put on.
> But no, rest assured that another fine treat
> Is ready for all men on one day,
> For every bushman is sure that he'll meet
> With the whole of the dishes on Sunday.[19]

Another early settlers' snack was the delightfully named puftaloon, which was somewhere between a damper and a scone. Like damper it could be easily made by those camping in the outback. The puftaloon belongs to the large family of makeshift breads which sustained explorers, travellers, shepherds and pioneer settlers in the early years of colonization when 'proper' bread made at the baker's was a luxury of the cities. Yet unlike damper, puftaloons were equally accepted by housewives as well as those camping out in the bush. Made with flour, salt, butter and milk and traditionally fried in dripping, puftaloons are good savoury or sweet, served warm with butter and jam, honey or golden syrup, or with grilled tomatoes, bacon and brown gravy.

Tea and Damper, print of a wood engraving by A. M. Ebsworth, 1883.
Four men gather round a campfire in the bush, eating and drinking.

Here is a recipe given in the *Manilla Express*, New South Wales, on 15 October 1904:

Puftaloons
Ingredients: ½ lb. of good self-raising flour, 1½ gills of milk, salt.

Method: Sift the flour and salt, make into a moist dough with the milk, turn out on to a floured board; knead slightly and roll out half an inch thick; stamp out small rounds with a cutter, and fry in plenty of hot fat till golden brown, being so light they must be turned. Drain on paper. Serve hot with jam, treacle, honey, or sugar.[20]

The outback was very much a man's world and men needed their meat to sustain them during the long, hard working days. Few women went with them and while the men might have been enjoying their damper (or puftaloons), mutton and tea over a campfire in the outback, in the home teatime with cakes and biscuits (which were not considered by men as 'real food') was very much the domain of women. Australian women, just like their British counterparts on the other side of the world, were swift to adapt to afternoon tea in the late nineteenth century. Teas allowed a hostess to show off not just her best china but her baking skills and great pride was taken in baking such items as Balmoral tartlets (which enjoyed a brief popularity in Australia in the 1950s) and Banbury cakes. Other treats included scones, London buns, oat cakes, rock cakes, cream puffs and brandy snaps, seed cake, spice cake and sponge cake, all originally from Britain. Food historian Barbara Santich suggests that the sponge cake became more Australian than the rest, even saying that the art of the sponge reached its apogee in Australia. That may be so, for she goes on to describe in detail the many different variations on the sponge which the Australian housewife made to impress her family or guests, such as the 'blowaway sponge', which was so light and airy it could presumably be blown away. There was the 'never-fail sponge' (how many of us would go for that one?) with eggs and sugar beaten for a very long time. Tips and hints were given in cookbooks: use duck eggs, day-old eggs, sift the flour three times and so on. It was all a test of the housewife's skill. What made the sponge so special to Australia were the fillings and toppings. Jam, with or without whipped cream or butter cream, was the standard with a light dusting of icing sugar on the top, often using a doily to produce a pretty pattern. Chocolate or passion fruit icing might top the cake. Santich goes on to explain that by the 1930s the flavour was in the sponge itself: 'chocolate, coffee, cinnamon, ginger, and lemon were all popular.' The sponge was sometimes baked in a long sheet, spread with jam and rolled up, dusted with sugar, like a Swiss roll.[21]

However, two of the best known Australian teatime treats are lamingtons and Anzac biscuits, which were invented in Australia at the turn of the century. Lamingtons, which are said to have been named after Lord Lamington, governor of Queensland from 1895–1901 (although some believe they were invented in the Queensland Government House kitchen and named after his wife), are popularly supposed to have been invented as a way of using up stale sponge cake.[22] However, as Santich points out, 'one of the earliest recipes, in 1902, instructs the cook to begin by making a plain butter sponge.' Lamingtons are made by splitting the sponge and sandwiching it together with butter cream. The cake is cut into cubes, which are then dipped in a chocolate mixture and rolled in coconut. Lamingtons became very popular and are a quintessential part of every Australian's childhood. Although lamingtons have gone out of fashion somewhat they are still made for fundraising events, and lamington drives are organized by schools, youth groups and churches. Orders for the cakes are taken within the community and on the day of the drive vast slabs of sponge cake that are supplied by commercial bakeries are cut, dipped in chocolate and rolled in coconut, packed into trays by teams of volunteers. Handsome profits are made all in a good cause.[23]

Anzac biscuits also serve a charitable purpose as they were, and still are, made for fundraising events to help soldiers and war veterans. The origin of Anzac biscuits is complicated. They have for long been associated with the Australian and New Zealand Army Corps (ANZAC) established in the First World War. The original Anzac biscuits were hard and tough (tooth breakers) with good keeping qualities. They were a kind of bread substitute, like a ship's biscuit, made with flour, water and salt. They were so hard they had to be dunked in tea or other liquids to soften them. Other names for them were Anzac tiles or Anzac wafers.

The Anzac biscuit we know today is a sweet biscuit made with rolled oats, flour, sugar, butter, golden syrup, baking soda, boiling water and optionally desiccated coconut. It has been claimed that the biscuits were sent by wives to soldiers serving abroad but contrary to popular belief there were no Anzac biscuits at Gallipoli, although some evidence suggests a rolled oats biscuit was sent to troops on the Western Front, but this was not widespread. The exact historic details of Anzac biscuits are yet to be uncovered.

The majority of rolled-oats biscuits were in fact sold and consumed at fetes, galas, parades and other public events at home to raise funds for the war effort, and it was this connection that led to them being referred to as 'soldiers' biscuits'. As the war drew on many groups like the Country Women's Association, church committees, schools and other women's organizations devoted a great deal of time to making them.

According to Barbara Santich recipes probably date from just after the war. In 1919 a reader wrote to the *Weekly Times*, asking: 'Anzac Crispies – will someone kindly supply me with the recipe of Anzac Crispies which is evidently a new kind of biscuit.' In 1920 a recipe for Anzac biscuits, or crispies, was published in the *Argus* and specified John Bull oats. The other ingredients were flour, golden syrup, sugar, carbonate of soda, a pinch of salt, boiling water and melted

Anzac biscuits for Anzac Day – 'Lest we forget'.

butter. No coconut; that was added later.[24] However, food historian Janet Clarkson suggests that it may have been the women of Dunedin in New Zealand who were responsible for the Anzac biscuit as we know it today. Oat biscuits are a Scottish tradition and Dunedin is a city with strong Scottish roots. The style of biscuit had been around for a long time and they were often called 'golden crunch biscuits' or 'golden syrup biscuits'. Someone, sometime during the war, made a batch, and they became known as Anzac biscuits.[25]

Recipes were fiercely guarded, especially for baking competitions at the local church fete or agricultural show where competition was stiff for the best and lightest sponge cake or the richest and moistest fruitcake. Commercial baking powder only became available from 1852 and self-raising flour from 1953. Before then cooks had to devise their own raising agents by combining bicarbonate of soda with cream of tartar, or by using vinegar, sour milk or lemon juice. The flour, especially for light sponges, had to be finely sieved and eggs laboriously whipped up by hand.[26]

Dried fruits such as sultanas, raisins and currants were a prominent addition to many baked goods and even savoury dishes for teatime. In the 1930s a promotional booklet entitled *The New Sunshine Cookery*

Lamingtons.

Book was published to encourage greater consumption of dried fruit. (It was the successor to the first *Sunshine Cookery Book* published in 1886.) It aimed to provide the Australian housewife with recipes, household hints and new ways to use nutritious dried fruits.[27] It contains many recipes and suggestions for afternoon tea including quantities for entertaining. Recipes for cakes include cinnamon coffee cake, sultana teacake, five o'clock fruitcake and sultana baskets. Celebration fruitcakes for birthdays and Christmas are also included. An intriguing recipe for 'stuffed monkeys', a sort of pastry turnover with a stuffing made of mixed dried fruit and peel, is given in the biscuit section alongside raisin shorts, iced currant fingers and others. Savoury sandwich recipes are also given, such as egg and lettuce, egg and curry, and cheese and celery, as well as for elaborate rainbow sandwiches and some more unusual sweet ones filled with minced or chopped dried fruits.

There are also recipes for gem scones (not really a scone but a light little cake traditionally baked in a gem iron) and raisin scones but no recipe for pumpkin scones, perhaps the most famous scones in Australia. Although invented in the early twentieth century, pumpkin scones became legendary during the premiership in Queensland of Sir Joh Bjelke-Petersen from 1968 to 1987, thanks to his wife, affectionately known as Lady Flo. Although a politician in her own right – she was National Party Senator for Queensland for twelve years until 1993 – Lady Flo is best known for the homemade pumpkin scones that she generously offered to guests at their Kingaroy property.

The scones contain cold mashed pumpkin to add texture and flavour and, although always more popular in Queensland than in other states, perhaps because pumpkins were in abundance on the north coast, the

Front cover of *The New Sunshine Cookery Book, c.* 1938.

love of pumpkin scones spread rapidly in the 1920s and they were soon being entered into cookery competitions at country shows. Eager to make the most of this prolific yet under-estimated vegetable, cooks embraced the pumpkin scone and in the decades that followed up until the 1950s, almost every cookbook included a recipe.

Here is a recipe which appeared in *The Chronicle and North Coast Advertiser* on 28 July 1916:

Pumpkin Scones

Owing to the praise expressed by Mr Forsyth M.L.A. at Caboalture Show we sought the recipe and have to thank Mrs Bell, wife of Cr. A Bell,

Saturday was usually baking day in Australia, although many did their baking on Sundays when the oven was on for cooking the roast dinner, saving fuel. Hal Porter, in *The Watcher on the Cast-iron Balcony* (1963), remembers baking days and Sunday teas from the 1920s:

Saturday afternoon is for baking. This is a labour of double nature: to provide a week's supply of those more solid delicacies Australian mothers of those days regard as being as nutritiously necessary as meat twice daily, four vegetables at dinner, porridge and eggs and toast for breakfast, and constant cups of tea. Empty biscuit-barrels and cake-tins being as unthinkable as beds not made before eleven a.m., Mother, therefore, constructs a great fruit cake, and a score or more each of rock cakes, Banburies, queen cakes, date rolls and ginger nuts. These conventional solidities done, she exercises her talent for ritual fantasy, for the more costly and ephemeral dainties that are to adorn as fleetingly as day-lilies the altar of the Sunday tea-table. Now appear three-storeyed sponge cakes mortared together with scented cream and in whose seductive icing are embedded walnuts, silver *cachous*, *glacé* cherries, strawberries, segments of orange and strips of angelica. Now appear cream puffs and éclairs, creations of the most momentary existence, deliberately designed neither for hoarding against a rainy day nor for social showing-off. Sunday tea is the frivolous and glittering crown of the week; there is the impression given of throwing away money like delicious dirt; there is the atmosphere rather than the fact of luxury; Sunday tea, is above all, my parents' statement to each other and their

Back cover of *The New Sunshine Cookery Book* showing fruit cake, sultana baskets, Eccles cakes, sweet mince roly, raisin pie and sago and currant mould.

for the following, which has been successfully tested by our editor's own youngsters, who agree in a decided dislike for the vegetable, yet relish the scone:–

Half a cup of sugar, 2¾ cups of flour, 1 tablespoonful butter, 1 egg well beaten, 1 cup boiled mashed pumpkin, 1 teaspoon soda, 2 teaspoons cream of tartar. Beat sugar and butter to a cream, add egg, then pumpkin, then flour with cream of tartar, soda, salt, sifted together, lastly a little milk. Bake in a quick oven.

children that life is being lived on a plane of hard-earned and justifiable abundance. I watch abundance which means that I watch Mother, its actual as well as its symbolic impulse.[28]

Australians, like some people in Britain, call their evening meal 'tea', a tradition started in the early days of the settlers. The basic foods were bread, beef, mutton, pork, milk, eggs, fruit and vegetables, consumed with tea and alcohol. Breakfast for the working man might consist of chops or steak and the midday meal might be taken at a café (also called a sixpenny restaurant). At six o'clock the working man had a substantial tea with cold or hot meat. Two or three cups of tea would be drunk at every meal.[29] The meal often started with a soup or broth, followed by dishes such as meat pies, rissoles, casseroles, curries, stews and roasts with vegetables. A pudding such as sago, tapioca, bread and butter, roly poly or fruit pie, often served with custard, rounded the meal off. Nowadays this meal is often called dinner rather than tea and is taken a little later owing to social changes and working patterns.

The meaning of 'tea' could cause misunderstandings when guests were invited to (afternoon) tea but turned up late expecting a more substantial meal. The embarrassed guests would be able to guess their mistake quickly when they glanced at the table. Afternoon tea is an elegant affair, with the best china on the table and sandwiches and cakes served with delicate teas, whereas high tea is usually more homely, with substantial food served with strong tea poured from a large pot.

By the beginning of the twentieth century Australians were the greatest black tea drinkers in the world, drinking tea – usually strong black tea with milk – several times a day, including 'morning tea' and 'afternoon tea'. During the working day a 'tea break' or just 'tea' might refer to either 'morning tea' or 'afternoon tea'. Afternoon tea is sometimes called 'arvo tea' – arvo being Australian slang for afternoon. It is also still sometimes referred to as a morning or afternoon 'smoko' or just 'smoko', a term which was commonly used by tradesmen and in the building industry for a tea break. This meant a cup of tea and a cigarette with perhaps a sweet or savoury snack or biscuit. During the Second World War rationing severely curtailed tea consumption, much to the displeasure of avid tea drinkers.

Afternoon tea at home is less common nowadays, except perhaps for a cup of tea with a biscuit such as Australia's most popular one, the Tim Tam. They are made by the Australian food company Arnott's and went on the market in 1964. Similar to the British Penguin, Tim Tams are composed of two layers of chocolate malted biscuit separated by a light chocolate cream filling and coated in a thin layer of textured chocolate. The biscuits have spawned their own teatime dunking tradition, the Tim Tam Slam. Opposite corners of the Tim Tam are bitten off, one end is submerged in the tea and the tea is then sucked through the biscuit – as though the Tim Tam were a straw. The crisp interior of the biscuit softens, the chocolate coating begins to melt and the entire Tim Tam has to be swallowed quickly before it completely collapses. Some people make Tim Tam cake with these biscuits – a gooey, chocolatey affair.

Picnic teas

AUSTRALIANS HAVE A LOVE of the outdoors and have raised the picnic to a new level. For early nineteenth-century travellers in the bush, picnicking became a necessity because of the lack of facilities. At the same time picnics were enjoyed by the masses – an outing to take a break from work and have a change of air and surroundings. Picnics were also a form of social entertainment for the upper classes and were often quite lavish affairs, the tablecloth laid out and laden with all kinds of food, not just sandwiches but cold meats, pies, fruits and so on, and lots to drink. There are many different kinds of picnics: lunch picnics, holiday picnics, beach picnics and, of course, picnic teas.

At popular picnic spots tearooms advertised sandwiches, pastries, fruit and tea as the basic necessities of a picnic. Sandwiches in the nineteenth century were mainly filled with meat but sardines, egg and salad were also popular. Later, in the twentieth century, sandwiches became more adventurous with more varied fillings such as salmon, celery and mayonnaise, apple and cucumber, olives and cream cheese, and eggs and green chillies. Other foods were also taken which could easily be eaten with the fingers. Lady Bonython recalled her childhood picnics around the turn of the century where

> There would be masses of buttered French bread, and we would crack and peel hard-boiled eggs, and take chicken legs or wings in our fingers and nibble the delicious cold meat. For drink we would have lemon squash or, if preferred a cup of tea.

She also remembered her mother taking a 'Chinese teapot packed ingeniously in a specially padded Chinese basket having spaces for the spout and handle' which 'kept the tea piping hot'.[30]

Tea was undoubtedly the favoured beverage on picnics although often alcoholic beverages or soft drinks would be taken too. The tea was usually made in the traditional 'billy':

> The girls spread a snow-white tablecloth on the grass, and placed thereon some bracken and green palm-leaves to serve for plates and dishes; with little piles of rosy apples, gold oranges and fresh bananas, small home-made cakes and daintily-cut sandwiches. Then Helen distributed the dainty napery she had brought, and set the tea cups out.
>
> 'Light a fire, boys, and fill the billy with fresh water for the tea. Bring the milk here, Alison; you'll find two bottles in the boat.'[31]

Picnic fare became even more elaborate and by the end of the 1930s foods like mutton pies, Cornish pasties, jellied tongue, sausage rolls, Scotch eggs, egg and bacon pies and little salmon balls, to be eaten on a toothpick, might be taken.[32]

Tearooms

IN APRIL 1895 THE *Australian Star* reported: 'there is no more popular resort among business men for lunch or among ladies in town shopping for afternoon tea. In the middle of the day always and frequently in the evening the place is crowded with city men, merchants, agents and many members of Parliament.' The *Star* was referring to the Loong Shan Tea House at 137 King Street, the largest and most spectacular establishment in the chain of tearooms run by Chinese immigrant and self-made entrepreneur Quong Tart.

These tearooms were quite the rage in Victorian Sydney and were lavishly decorated with hand-painted Japanese art, Chinese wood carvings, elegant golden mirrors and marble ponds with plump golden carp. Sydney's social set stopped by to rub shoulders at Quong Tart's tearooms while savouring fine teas imported from China. Ladies rested their weary feet, dusty from the streets, in the ladies' reading room on the first floor where they flicked through magazines while sampling pastries, scones and pies. For the gentlemen, with their hearty appetites, more substantial dishes like hare in port wine sauce or shoulder of mutton were on the menu.

An account of Quong Tart's extraordinary life was written by his widow. Margaret Scarlett of Liverpool, England, married him in 1886 and together they had six children. Quong Tart had arrived in Australia from Canton in 1859 at the age of nine. He was raised by the Simpsons, a Scottish family in Braidwood, New South Wales, and converted to Christianity. Thanks to Mr Simpson giving him an interest in gold claims he became wealthy and made up his mind to establish himself as an importer of tea and silk in Sydney.

In 1881 he visited China to see his family and on returning to Australia started business as a tea merchant in Sydney. He sold his imported tea in the Sydney Arcade and, as an advertisement, handed out sample cups; it became so popular he had to find larger premises and started charging for tea and scones, for which his tearooms became famous. By 1885 he had opened four tearooms and then extended his business into the Royal Arcade in King Street – where one lady asked him for a 'cup of tea and a Quong Tart'! He also opened a tearoom at the bamboo pavilion at the Zoological Gardens called the 'Han Pan', and a year later the refreshments rooms at 777 George Street.[33] In 1889 he opened Loong Shan Tea House in King Street. It soon became famous and was frequented by governors and premiers. This was followed in 1898 by the luxurious tea house and restaurant the Elite Hall, in the Queen Victoria Building, which could hold five hundred people.

Quong Tart was best known for his selection of teas – many imported from China – which he served in delicate china cups from decorative Chinese porcelain teapots. The tearooms offered substantial meals, mainly solid English fare like pork sausages, corned beef and carrots, lamb cutlets, plum pudding and apple pie. Curry was also on the menu, as were oysters and lobster. However the tearooms were best known for their scones, made with butter, sugar and extra baking powder and served warm with lashings of butter.

The Quong Tart tearooms also played a part in the feminist movement. Formerly, the city had no respectable gathering place for ladies (and no public toilets). The tearooms provided a suitable meeting place (and powder rooms). Women flocked to the new establishments; Maybanke Anderson and her fellow suffragettes would regularly meet at the Loong Shan Tea House in King Street. Louisa Lawson, mother of the poet Henry Lawson, sipped tea in the Loong Shan while she organized the campaign for female suffrage in Australia.

The popularity of these tearooms was due not only to the quality of the tea, the excellent food and the rich, exotic furnishings, but to Quong Tart himself. He dressed as a European; he treated workmen and politicians equally; he was a great philanthropist, holding many benefits for charity; and he was a generous employer. He had great enthusiasm for self-made men and this extended to 'always having a kindly word for the newsboys of Sydney'. Michael Symons tells of one occasion when he invited 250 newsboys of Sydney to his tearooms one Saturday afternoon in December 1893:

The youngsters first paraded the streets of the city, headed by the Croydon School Cadet Band, and carrying bannerettes indicating the names of the newspapers. They ended up seated at five long tables, and as fast as the good things vanished, the waitresses replaced them, until the boys had

Oil painting portrait of Quong Tart, *c.* 1880s.

women went shopping or wanted to meet friends they needed refreshments. Buckley's Tearooms in the department store of Buckley & Nunn in Melbourne provided this. They became a fashionable meeting place for ladies in the 1920s. In 1919 the *Argus Melbourne* advertised the tearooms:

> The attractions of Buckley Tearooms are those that appeal to refined tastes. We cater exceedingly well for luncheons (Hot or Cold) and Morning or Afternoon Tea, prices for which are very reasonable. Seats may be reserved without extra charge by phone or letter.
>
> Tearoom – Second Floor
> Buckley's
> Buckley & Nunn Ltd
> Bourke Street Melbourne

to confess that their efforts to clear the tables had failed. Afterwards, leading men of the city gave instructive addresses, the boys leaving better for the tea and advice tendered.[34]

Sadly Quong Tart's successful career and life came to a tragic end. In 1902 he was savagely beaten during a botched robbery at his Queen Victoria Market shop and died the following year from pleurisy.

There were other tearooms in other Australian cities. In the late nineteenth and early twentieth century Housewives' Associations and various Country Women's Associations were being formed. When these

Another tearoom at that time in Melbourne was the Hopetoun Tearooms of the Block Arcade. The tearooms were first opened in 1892. The tearooms were first opened in 1892 at 6 Block Arcade, moving to shops 12 and 13 in 1893. A teetotal ladies' domain, it was a fashionable place for lady shoppers to have lunch or afternoon tea. Until 1907 they were run by the Victorian Ladies' Work Association. The tearooms then moved to their present location, shops 1 and 2, and were named the Hopetoun Tearooms after the Association's founder, Lady Hopetoun, wife of Victoria's first Governor, Lord Hopetoun. They continue to flourish, yet have still retained a quaint atmosphere of Old World charm. The tearooms still serve what they call 'high tea' which is served on an 'afternoon tea style' three-tier stand with savouries at the top, an assortment of petit fours on the second tier and fresh seasonal and tropical fruit on the

Window displaying a wonderful array of cakes and
patisserie at Hopetoun tearooms in Melbourne.

third. The teas on offer are organic and varied such as Buddha's finger, a dark rich oolong and 'cha cha chai' with spices.

New Zealand

THE PEOPLE OF NEW ZEALAND, like the Australians, are avid tea drinkers. Tea is served after every meal – breakfast, lunch and dinner (often known as tea and the main meal of the day). There are also tea breaks in the morning and afternoon (called 'smokos', as in Australia). Until recent times, tea, an essential part of 'smoko' for manual labourers, with biscuits or scones, was vital, keeping them energized during their working day. New Zealand shares many traditions of tea drinking with Australia, including many of the cakes and biscuits served with afternoon tea.

New Zealand's foremost supplier of tea is Sri Lanka and it is predominantly black tea. Sometimes ordinary black tea is called 'gumboot tea', which is the equivalent of the UK's 'builder's tea'. The term is fairly recent (the first citation is from 1997) and probably arose when more exotic blends of tea started to become popular.

Early days

THE SETTLERS arriving in the nineteenth century tried as much as possible to keep the traditions and foods of their homeland, particularly the English and Scottish. Tea was one of the staple food items brought to New Zealand and it became a national drink. Tea was also used as one of the items of payment, along with rum and sugar, for sealing and whaling gangs. When tea was in short supply the leaves of the manuka tree were used as a substitute. Captain James Cook, the British explorer, and his crewmen were the first Europeans to drink manuka tea.[35]

When tea (from *Camellia sinensis*) became cheaper in the nineteenth century and the population of New Zealand grew, the drink became universally popular with both rich and poor, from society ladies to bushmen. Tea drinking was also endorsed by the local temperance movement followers.

Tea gardens, more usually known as pleasure gardens, became popular in the mid- to late nineteenth century and were modelled on those in England. Dunedin's Vauxhall Gardens were opened in 1862, some 130 years later than the Vauxhall Gardens in London. The entertainment was similar, with fireworks, tournaments and so on. And, as with the pleasure gardens of London, while the concept of sipping tea in a tea garden seems genteel enough, the Vauxhall Gardens of Dunedin also quickly developed a racy reputation and the good citizens of Dunedin were murmuring that much more than tea was being served.[36]

Dunedin's Vauxhall Gardens were only one of many tea gardens that opened throughout New Zealand, and they were embraced with enthusiasm by the outdoor-loving New Zealanders. The types of entertainment varied. The Wilkinson Tea Garden in Wellington, for example, was a place to admire the trees and rose gardens and enjoy a cup of tea, along with 'curds and cream, ginger beer, fancy bread, Burns' cakes and fruit in season'. The Bellevue Gardens in the Hutt Valley had farm, kitchen and show gardens and also served tea with hot scones, home-made butter and jam, fruitcake and seed cake. Picnics could be enjoyed at Donald's Tea Gardens where produce could also be bought from the market garden. Bligh's Tea Garden in New Brighton provided hot water for visitors to brew their own tea while they enjoyed the aviary, fernery, walks, flowers, trees and an impressively long vinery. Cricket, tennis, archery, shooting and fishing also took place. Christchurch had

Tea on the Lawn, taken by Leslie Adkin in 1912.

a number of tea gardens with varying entertainments and had mixed success.[37]

By the 1920s, however, the tea garden fashion was mainly over. Women's emancipation was partly to blame and entertainment was changing with the rise of the cinema.

Afternoon tea and 'at homes'

IN THE LATE nineteenth and early twentieth century afternoon tea parties were often very formal occasions, retaining the social rules of the Victorian period. There were etiquette books to help. The degree of formality depended on the size of the gathering. The 1920 guide *Etiquette for Women* states that if there are fewer than ten guests, tea should be served in the drawing room:

> This can either be done by having tea set out on a table at one end of the room, over which a maid presides and pours out tea, bringing round a cup to each guest as they arrive, on a tray, with milk and sugar, to which they help themselves, while cakes, bread & butter, &c., are handed afterwards, or else the hostess presides at her own tea-table, which is brought in and set immediately in front of her for her to pour out tea, the guests helping themselves to cakes, &c., which are displayed on plates and silver cake dishes arranged on the tea-table or on three or four-tier cake stands specially designed for this purpose.[38]

Food historian Helen Leach relates a letter written to her by Noeline Thomson describing the formal visiting cards for afternoon teas. She wrote the letter in 1998 (her ninetieth year) reminding Leach that in those days (the 1930s) it was still common for visiting cards to be presented as the guests arrived:

> Referring to NZ afternoon-teas . . . my early memories of these included elegant visiting cards sometimes carried in a special card-case

– copperplate style printing with 'curly' capitals. My mother had a special bowl on the hall stand where the cards were left. If the visitor was married she left 2 of her husband's cards (one paying his respects to the husband of the one being visited and one for the hostess herself) and one of the visitor's own cards for the hostess. If the hostess was unmarried there would be 2 cards, one from the visitor and one from her husband. I'm not sure what happened when unmarried ladies visited an unmarried lady but that would have been in the book of 'etiquette' on our bookshelf.

Noeline went on to describe the items that were necessary for a proper afternoon tea:

Mother had very elegant cake forks with initial T on the handle – a silver tea service, cream jug, sugar basin and silver tongs for the lump sugar, embroidered (and often lace edged) tablecloth and small serviettes, a three tiered silver cake stand (sandwiches on the top layer, small cakes in centre and cream sponge or other large cake on bottom layer) and a silver hot water kettle on a silver stand which contained a little lamp (methylated spirits) to keep the water hot. She also had a silver hot water jug. I also remember an Oamaru friend in the 1930s who had a beautiful large silver tea urn (a family heirloom) which had a tap at the front bottom area. It stood on the tea wagon and it was quite a little ceremony as cups and saucers were held in turn under the tap! Another friend had a beautiful tea caddy (I think it was Japanned) which had compartments for different teas and had a lock and key; so it must have been pretty old. I have a feeling that

for some reason the 3 tiered cake stand was called a 'curate' . . .[39]

Garden parties

NEW ZEALANDERS enjoyed outdoor garden parties. The custom came from those introduced in England around 1868 by Queen Victoria when she began giving afternoon receptions in the gardens of Buckingham Palace. In New Zealand, Governors General, as representatives of the Crown, invited guests to tea parties at Government House in Wellington. The most memorable one was in 1954 when Queen Elizabeth II and Prince Philip paid a state visit to New Zealand, the first visit by a reigning sovereign. Four thousand guests were invited for afternoon tea. It was reported that Queen Elizabeth and Prince Philip 'took tea in the flower-decked Royal pavilion' and there was a brief mention of 'ices with strawberries and raspberries, cool drinks and tea and cakes'.[40] To cope with the extra hungry crowds of well-wishers, an additional 20,000 dozen eggs and 25,000 lb (11,300 kgs) of butter were ordered for the city. A huge cafeteria was set up on Taranaki Street that remained open from 9 a.m. until 11 p.m. The estimated ten thousand visitors to the cafeteria were expected to consume twenty thousand sandwiches, thirty thousand cakes, ten thousand pies and at least ten thousand cups of tea.[41] Smaller tea parties were held in other cities in their honour: one at Auckland's Government House, one in Christchurch and one at Dunedin. Reports give few details of what anyone actually ate or drank on these occasions; it was more about the occasion, dressing up and seeing and being seen.

Baking skills and cookbooks

HOSPITALITY AND BAKING culture in New Zealand has deep roots in the colonial past. Housewives took great pride in the cakes and biscuits they produced. Afternoon tea was an opportunity to show off their baking skills. Early recipes can be found in Mrs Murdoch's book *Dainties; or, How to Please Our Lords and Masters* (1888), which provided recipes for 21 assorted cakes (large and small), two sorts of biscuits, three buns and two gingerbreads. By 1921 the ninth edition of Dunedin's *St Andrew's Cookery Book* contained recipes for 56 large cakes, 26 small cakes, 24 scones and breads, thirteen eggless cakes and 22 different sorts of biscuits.[42] Housewives liked to be renowned for their 'well-filled tins':

> I've just filled my tins. My husband likes it but I try to avoid it because I think I've put on a bit of weight since we came to [this place] . . . but he'll make himself a cup of tea, he always does, and mostly he'll go and get himself a bun, and have a look in the tins.[43]

Almost every Kiwi household has a battered copy of the *Edmonds Cookery Book*, first produced in 1908 and still selling over twenty thousand copies a year. The recipes are wide ranging but the focus is on baking, usually using Edmonds baking powder. This cooking bible is the first place people turn to for a recipe for cakes, biscuits and desserts, and contains many recipes for New Zealand's top teatime favourites such as banana cake, ginger crunch, Afghans, Neenish tarts, Louise cake (made with a thin layer of cake or biscuit which is spread with jam, usually raspberry, topped with a coconut meringue and then baked), pikelets, Anzac biscuits, scones, santé biscuits, yoyos, peanut brownies, lemon meringue pie, marshmallow shortcake, Belgian biscuits and hokey pokey biscuits. Also popular are date loaf (or cake), made with preserved

dates and often thickly spread with butter, ginger kisses (two ginger biscuits sandwiched together with a cream filling), lamingtons and tennis biscuits.

Neenish tarts, which are also popular in Australia, are individual pastry cases filled with sweet gelatin-set cream and covered with icing in two colours, half and half. Typically the colours are white and brown, white and pink, or pink and brown. The name of the tart is something of a mystery and has various spellings, including *nenische* and *nienich*, which suggest a German origin. The most popular theory is that they were first made by a Ruby Neenish in the Australian town of Grong Grong, New South Wales, in around 1913. She supposedly ran low on cocoa and made do with half-chocolate, half-white icing. The origin of 'Afghans' is also a mystery despite lots of speculation.

Tennis cakes do not feature in the *Edmonds Cookery Book* but seem to have been particularly popular in the early twentieth century. Tennis cake is a Victorian light fruitcake made to accompany the newly invented game of lawn tennis, which became a popular sport particularly among women in the late nineteenth century. At first the cake was round but it evolved into

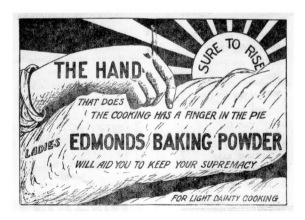

Edmonds Baking Powder advertisement from a theatre programme, *c.* 1907, featuring the famous slogan 'Sure to rise' and the brand image of a rising sun.

'Afghans' with their typical chocolate frosting and walnut on top.

Tennis and tea are inseparable, and a good cake is appreciated by all. The following recipe . . . will please the patrons of the courts:– One pound of butter, one pound and a quarter of caster sugar, twelve eggs, one pound and a-quarter of flour, three-quarters of a pound of ground almonds, half a pound of sultanas, four ounces of currants, four ounces of peel, four ounces of cut cherries, Vanilla essence. Beat up the butter and sugar, add the eggs two at a time, and with the last add the essence, then stir in the flour, and last of all the fruit, peel cut fine and the cherries; mix all to a nice cake batter, put into a papered tin, bake in a moderate oven, and when done and cold lay a piece of almond paste on top, and ice with fondant icing any colour desired. A nice tea to serve with this cake is the Empire Company's 'Dragon' Blend . . .

an oblong, resembling the shape of a tennis court. Decorations evolved too, becoming very elaborate, like miniature tennis courts. An early recipe appeared in the *Wairarapa Daily Times* on 30 December 1910:

Afternoon Tea, photograph of Maud Herd and her husband Leslie Adkin taking tea on the lawn in March 1917. The small table is elegantly set with a starched white tablecloth with edged with lace. Maud is pouring tea from a silver teapot into a delicate china cup as her husband looks on expectantly. Griddle scones are to be served with the tea.

War times

TEA AND BISCUITS sustained soldiers at war. A New Zealand soldier called Norman Gray, who fought on the Western Front in 1916–17, wrote a journal and in one entry he evoked the welcome relief that a cup of tea and biscuits gave to exhausted soldiers:

It had been raining for two and a half days and was still pouring. The walk up the hill was just about the finish for most of us. We were drenched to the bone, utterly fagged after sixty hours of almost continuous work, and it required a series of supreme efforts to keep from flopping into the mud – anywhere – and letting things rip. Just on the ridge, before we reached our site, we were greeted by the Y.M.C.A. canteen, a cup of tea and two packets of biscuits ready for every man.[44]

During the Second World War and for some time after there was rationing. Tea was rationed (2 oz., or 57 g, per person, per week) and so were a number of other ingredients essential for baking such as eggs, butter and sugar. Cream was officially unobtainable. Baking for teatime became a challenge for the cook and many cookbooks of the time offered recipes for eggless cakes and puddings.

Between the wars and after

TIMES WERE ALSO hard during the depression of the 1930s but many cakes were still made, especially sponge cakes. Helen Leach explains that during the Depression, those families whose salaries and wages were not reduced benefited from lower food prices and it was also still common for households to have a henhouse at the bottom of the garden providing eggs. She goes on to say that the Women's Division of the New Zealand Farmers' Union opened the second edition of the national cookbook with 'Cakes' and in this section there were an amazing number of recipes from which the afternoon tea cook could choose: thirty fruit cakes, thirteen cakes described as sponges and 33 assorted cakes ranging from old favourites such as Seed Cake, Khaki Cake, Ladysmith Cake, Marble Cake and Madiera [sic] Cake to Pink Cocoanut sandwich, Pineapple Cake and Potato Caramel Cake. There were also six chocolate cakes. However, for some people eggs were not readily available so there were some recipes for cakes without eggs such as a gingerbread, walnut and date cake and three fruit cakes.[45]

The year 1950 marked the start of a new and much more prosperous half-century for New Zealanders. Rationing finally came to an end and new appliances such as Neeco electric ranges and Kenwood food mixers were in the shops. Home baking with these new appliances made baking easier and 'tin fillers' continued. However, times were changing with more and more women taking on paid jobs, and with the variety of commercially manufactured biscuits available there was to some extent a decline in home baking. Formal afternoon teas, with all their silverware, fine china and white linen, were on the way out and dinner parties and buffet suppers became the modern way to entertain.

For some New Zealanders, however, the pride in baking continued. Sybille Ecroyd fondly remembers teatimes at her mother-in-law's home in Auckland in the 1980s, and that the cake and biscuit tins were rarely empty:

there are lots of things that are served with Edglets or Bell – you were either an Edglets person or a Bell person – both sorts thinking they were drinking something of better quality[46] . . . But what went with the tea in John's mother's house was a pound or two or three of butter not to mention sugar in cake, biscuits, and slices every week! Homemade possibilities included Santé (santy) biscuits, scones (date scones, made with dried dates . . . were a favorite), endless slices (e.g. ginger crunch, Louise cake) . . . Barbara made an incredible assortment of such things and the tin was never empty and we rarely had store bought biscuits.

Apart from lots of butter and sugar, golden syrup and sweetened condensed milk featured in many of the teatime treats. She remembers Russian fudge, caramel biscuits, caramel fingers, chocolate caramel squares, as well as sultana loaf and carrot cake.[47]

Tearooms

NOT ALL WOMEN wanted to bake and not everyone excelled at baking. Some preferred to go out to tearooms and, for the women of the nineteenth century, tearooms meant freedom, offering a place where they could socialize in public and take refreshments after a tiring day of shopping. For the less affluent an outing to a tearoom was ideal for a birthday treat. Tearooms were often located at the top of a department store and were accessed by cage-like elevators with white-gloved attendants, calling out the type of merchandise on each floor en route – 'going up, maids', misses' and ladies clothing' and so on. The tearooms were stylish and quite formal. A typical image was of high ceilings, cane furniture, palm trees, silverware, white tablecloths and waitresses in crisp black-and-white uniforms. Tea was served with sandwiches, scones and cakes arranged on silver tiered stands.

One of the most stylish tearooms was in New Zealand's oldest department store, Kirkcaldie & Stains, which was established in Lambton Quay, Wellington, in 1863 by two young immigrants, one Scottish, one English. The store flourished and in 1898 the premises were extended, including an ornate facade, elegant fittings, restrooms for ladies and the largest tearooms in the capital. The tearooms were on the first floor and customers could admire the Gothic arches, imposing glass double doors and the sophisticated sound of a grand piano. The waitresses wore black dresses with white collars, caps and aprons. The tearooms attracted many customers, who not only came for refreshments of tea and cakes, but perhaps more importantly to spend liberally in the store.

Not long after the tearooms had opened there was a dramatic and unexpected incident. It was late in the afternoon and the tearooms were busy with customers taking afternoon tea. The manager, Ellen Dick, came out of the kitchen and a customer, Annie McWilliam, drew out a .45 calibre six-chamber revolver and fired three shots at her. Ellen turned and collapsed through the door into the kitchen. Miraculously two of the bullets missed and the other deflected off her whalebone corset. She suffered only minor bruising and shock. Her corset had saved her. Customers fled the tearoom. Mrs McWilliam apparently calmly walked down the stairs where she was disarmed by the store manager and Mr Sid Kirkcaldie. She reportedly said, 'Oh give me a cup of tea, that's what I came here for.'[48] The popularity of the tearooms did not suffer from this incident; rather they went on to become a great success and were busier than ever. (Sadly, however, they closed for business in January 2016.)

There were many department store tearooms. Tea authority William Ukers wrote in 1935 that 'Every drapery establishment of any consequence has a tea-room.' He cites J. Ballantyne & Co.'s tearoom and the Tudor Tearoom on the top floor of Auckland's Milne & Choyce department store as worthy examples. The Tudor not only served tea to customers in individual one-, two-, or four-person nickel-plated teapots, but had a measuring machine dispensing the correct amount of tea. They also had a special hot-water boiler to ensure the leaves for each brew were steeped in water at the correct temperature.[49]

Another department store, Beath & Co. in Christ-church, boasted a roof garden and a tearoom with an orchestra dais with a parquet floor, viridian green walls with gold mouldings and bronze grills. John Court's department store in Auckland had spacious rooftop tearooms and a roof garden overlooking the children's playground with breathtaking views of the City of Auckland and the Waitemata Harbour. The tearoom established a particularly fine reputation, especially for its morning teas, and over the years 'meet me at John Court's' became the store's advertising slogan.

The tearooms of the D.I.C. store in Wellington were considered to be the best and smartest in the city. Queen Elizabeth and the Duke of Edinburgh attended a banquet there during their 1954 tour of New Zealand.

Not every woman had time to relax over a cup of tea and cakes in a tearoom. Many women were employed in shops or worked in factories or as servants. Some went into business. In 1906 a Miss Meddings is listed as the successful tenderer for the Cherry Tearooms on the ground floor of the New Zealand International Exhibition in Christchurch. The tearooms served tea with small cakes, block cakes, scones, buns, pies and ice cream. The power behind Miss Meddings was a formidable lawyer who negotiated the deal, Ethel Benja-min, New Zealand's first woman lawyer. The deal stated

that 'every effort will be made to make the tearooms attractive, and expense will not be spared to induce custom.' 'Best butter' was ordered and one hundred walnut-coloured Austrian cane chairs were hired. 'Best tea' was bought from Fletcher Humphreys & Co. Ltd, wholesale tea importers and pioneer tea packers in Christchurch. The six-month Exhibition was an impres-sive affair and all the while Miss Meddings and Ethel Benjamin served their customers with tea and cakes and at Christmas time gave them wedges of honey-comb toffee wrapped in messages of goodwill. At the end of the Exhibition the Cherry Tearoom closed.[50]

Another equally hardworking and resilient woman in the early tearoom trade was Ann Cleland. In 1900 she took the lease of the Coffee Palace, a tearoom, oyster and dining saloon and bakehouse. She changed its name to the ACM Company. The business was suc-cessful and in 1911 she added the lease of the Federal Tearoom with its shop and function room. Both tea-rooms with the shop, bakery and grill rooms continued to boom. When some ingredients became scarce during the First World War and resourcefulness was called for, ACM began baking a small tea loaf. The local bread makers retaliated by refusing to supply sandwich bread for the tearooms. Undeterred, ACM started their own bread making industry and it became very successful.[51]

The Blue Baths Tearoom in Rotorua was another classic tearoom in New Zealand. It was upstairs above the ornate main entrance to the Rotorua Blue Baths and overlooked the baths on one side and the Government Gardens with croquet and bowling greens on the other. The Blue Baths were part of a complex opened as part of a national tourism development programme. The first stage of the Blue Baths was opened in 1931, the final stage in 1933. They were designed by John Mair, the government architect, who with his American training and European experience had a reputation for departing from tradition in style. For the Blue Baths, by combining the symmetrical layout of a Roman bath house with an exotic palette of Art Moderne, Spanish Mission and Mediterranean styles, he created a glamorous building of chic 1930s style.[52]

The Baths were very popular and soon became the 'place to be' for a dip in the swimming pool with afternoon tea upstairs afterwards. The tearoom was elegant with potted plants, high-backed chairs and square wooden tables that had starched doilies arranged beneath a sparkling glass top. Tea was served by a waitress (there were four altogether) in a floral and belted princess line dress and white shoes. Two of the waitresses were responsible for making the tea and setting up the three-tiered wooden cake stands, with sandwiches at the top, scones with jam and cream in the middle and pikelets at the bottom. The other two waitresses served the afternoon teas to guests – who were mostly tourists – from trolleys, with the cake stands on the upper level and cups, saucers and teapots below. Tea was served from chrome teapots with chrome sugar bowls. Tea and a cream cake, a cheesecake and a jam tart cost ninepence and tea with sandwiches cost one shilling.[53]

During the Second World War in 1940 the tearoom was commandeered by the dental section of the Royal New Zealand Air Force and one of the pools was closed. When the Air Force left, Ivy Dawson got the tearoom up and running again and in 1946 Connie and Roy Haggart took over. The war was over, everyone was celebrating and it was the heyday of the tearoom. The tables were still there, and the potted palms; even the deep blue curtains. The little chrome-plated teapots were joined by large china ones for bigger orders. The tearoom seated eighty and it was often full. In the summer thirteen waitresses were employed and now wore white aprons, not uniforms. Two cooks were employed producing plain, chocolate and coffee sponges, lamingtons, cream puffs and chocolate éclairs. Connie Haggart

The elegant 1930s Spanish-inspired Art Deco building of the Blue Baths, Rotorua.

herself became famous for her lemon tarts; she made hundreds of them in the five years she and her husband ran the tearooms.[54]

Times change and at the end of the 1960s the famous Baths were recording losses and they closed along with the tearooms in 1982. The Blue Baths fell into disrepair. However, in 1999 under a joint partnership the buildings were restored to their former glory, except for the main pool which was transformed into a lawn. The tearoom was reopened. Customers could once more admire the terrazzo staircase, the view and the 1930s ambience, and enjoy afternoon tea.[55]

For a special occasion a top-class afternoon tea can still also be had at the Savoy in Dunedin. In its prime, the Savoy was the centre of social life in the town. Many can remember how exciting it was as a child to take tea there, to sit near the stained-glass windows and enjoy eating their way through the various tiers of the cake stand, especially the butterfly cakes. Thanks to the Southern Heritage Trust, the rituals of afternoon tea have been restored. The original china from the old Savoy has gone but a few of the silver teapots, milk jugs and sugar bowls were found in dusty cartons in the basement and have been restored. Afternoon tea can once again be taken complete with formal tableware, piano accompaniment and occasionally a tea dance with a jazz band.[56]

A recent development in New Zealand is the emergence of a café culture, with coffee being preferred to tea. Many tearooms, so popular before the 1990s, offering traditional cream teas with scones and cream, cucumber sandwiches, muffins and custard squares, are disappearing. However, many new cafés are reinventing some teatime Kiwi classics such as Afghans, Anzac biscuits, carrot cake and lamingtons.

Railway Teas

NEW ZEALAND Railways has been a staunch supporter of the tearoom (called a refreshment room by the Railways). In the heyday of steam trains the earliest refreshment rooms were opened in spaces leased in railway stations. The engines needed regular stops for watering and so did the passengers. The stops were once an essential feature of customer service, including toilet facilities.[57] David Burton, in his book *200 Years of New Zealand Food and Cookery* (1982), remembers from the 1960s the 'reinforced concrete teacups' in which the tea was served and that 'the mad rush to the tearooms for cakes, sandwiches and pies continued unabated.'

Dining cars on the trains were introduced in 1899. They provided meals, including morning and afternoon teas with bread and butter, biscuits, sandwiches and tea, but they proved too costly to run and were withdrawn in 1917.[58]

High tea

THE MAIN MEAL of the day in New Zealand is still often known as tea, although many nowadays refer to it as dinner. It is usually taken in the early evening although this is also changing and becoming later. The formality and structure of this meal varies from family to family but it is basically the same as what is known as 'high tea' in Britain. Meat pies of various kinds are particularly favoured. Sausage rolls are also popular. Although meals may be cooked from scratch many home cooks rely to some extent on pre-made ingredients (such as packet soup and sauce mixes). Takeaways such as fish and chips, Chinese food or pizza are becoming more popular. Cakes, however, are still usually home-made.

South Africa

SOUTH AFRICA IS OFTEN referred to as the 'Rainbow nation' and this is because of its colourful and ethnic diversity resulting from several waves of colonization and immigration. In the seventeenth century the Dutch East India Company established a settlement at the Cape and began trading with the indigenous people. Farmers from Europe (Dutch, French Huguenot and Germans) were allowed to establish permanent settlements. It was these people and their successors, later to become known as Afrikaners, who brought in slave labour from Southeast Asia to work on the farms and in the kitchens. These people became known as Cape Malays and they and their descendants laid the foundation for Cape Malay cuisine. In the early nineteenth century the British seized control of the Cape and added to the ethnic mix by bringing in indentured labourers from various parts of India to work on the sugar, banana, tea and coffee plantations. In the late nineteenth century there was another wave of Indian immigrants, mainly traders and businessmen, many coming from Gujarat. All this mix has led to a colourful and interesting cuisine. Apart from spicy *kerries* (curries) and kebabs influenced by the Cape Malays and Indians, the earlier European settlers brought with them their baking skills and this is evident in the variety of baked goods served at teatime.

Hildagonda Duckitt was the first collector of typical South African recipes. She was well known at church bazaars, not just for her preserves and chutney but for the 'light cakes' she baked. She also invited Boer War invalids and nurses to tea with scones and cakes.[59] Her book, *Hilda's 'Where is it?' of Recipes*, was first published in 1891 and went through many editions. The recipes reflect the diversity of baking and include, for example, tea biscuits of various kinds, shortbread, scones for 'five o'clock tea', a number of tarts with Dutch or German origin, teacakes including 'Hilda's', Jumbles and *Soetkoekies*, a traditional Africaans spicy and chewy biscuit – her recipe described as being a 'Very old Dutch Recipe. Mrs. Van der Riet's.'

A good number of cakes and biscuits for teatime are to be found in a book compiled by another Hilda, Hilda Gerber, called *Traditional Cookery of the Cape Malays* (1957). She states that all of them, except one, originated with European settlers: 'Puff pastry, short crust, sponge mixtures are made by the Cape Malays as they are made by housewives all over Europe.' Recipes include apple tart (to be served hot for dessert but cold for tea) and apple tartlets, coconut tartlets, coconut tart, coconut biscuits called *coconutscraps* ('scraps' seems to have been corrupted from crepes, formerly used to denote thin batter or biscuits crisply fried or baked), cardamom biscuits, butter biscuits and sugar biscuits. There is also raisin bread, raisin tartlets and sweet potato cake. Sweet pastry crusts with a creamy filling flavoured with cinnamon called *melktert* (milk tarts) are popular. Light cream cakes (*ligte creams*) are baked in two layers and put together with jam, butter icing or whipped cream and, as Malays are fond of colouring their food brightly, they are iced gaudily – the top section might be red, the lower one mauve and the icing green. *Donker creams* are dark cream cakes – sponge mixtures to which cocoa is added. They are filled with jam, butter icing or whipped cream and usually iced white or bright pink then covered with a generous amount of desiccated coconut.

Hilda gives three recipes for *koesisters*. A *koe'sister* (or *koeksister*) derives from the Dutch word *koekje* (cookie). They are a type of deep fried fritter, a bit like a doughnut. Dipped into a syrup they are crunchy and sticky on the outside and moist and syrupy in the inside, and make a delicious teatime snack. There are two popular versions: an Afrikaner version which is plaited and a Cape Malay version which is twisted, less sweet and spicier and coated with a sprinkling of coconut.

Hilda Gerber advises that if a number of people are to be served tea then instead of being served in a teapot, the tea is customarily made in a white bucket:

TO MAKE TEA IN A WIT EMMER
(in a white bucket)

Put the tea into a bag and pour as much boiling water over as you will need. Add some sugar to the tea and withdraw the bag after the infusion has become dark enough. Add some pounded cardamom seeds, and if you like, a little dry ginger as well. Add the milk after the bag has been taken out. Serve the tea in cups.

The Indians who settled in South Africa had a huge influence on the food and culture, including teatime. In *Indian Delights: A Book of Recipes by the Women's Cultural Group* (1961), edited by Zuleikha Mayat, there is a whole section of 'Sweets served with tea' including *banana puri* (flaky fried wafers and nothing to do with bananas); *goolab jamboo* (Indian doughnuts); *mithais* (various kinds of sweetmeats, such as *burfee*, *mitha samosas*, *cocoanut paak*, *ladoo*, *rassogolas in ras malai*); *nan khataay* (shortbread); and many other sweet snacks, including ice creams. A suggested menu for a 'Buffet Tea' is also given and includes savoury dishes: *Chana chutputti* with *aamli*

(tamarind) sauce is made with *chana* (split chickpeas) and small white beans, tomato, onion, coconut and spiced with turmeric, cumin, ginger and garlic; mince pies (samosas); fish cutlets (flavoured with herbs, garlic, chillies) and *puri pattas*, a kind of spicy patty served with *puri*. In South Africa the patty is commonly made with the broad leaves of the yam plant. A mixture of chickpea flour, spices and tamarind are blended together then spread over the leaves which are rolled up into a cylinder shape. The roll is steamed. When cool the *patta* is sliced, fried and served with *puri*. Other suggestions for the 'Buffet Tea' are *achars* (pickles), chutneys and lemons; *chevda* (a spicy mix of rice flakes, puffed rice, chana dal, split peas, peanuts, sliced onion, green chillies, fresh coconut, sliced thin, cashew nuts and spices, described as 'a must at Tea Parties'); assorted *mithais* (sweetmeats), ice cream and *sookh mookh* (a savoury made with fresh coconut, almonds, coriander seeds, sesame seeds and fennel). Fresh fruit drinks and soft drinks, and, of course, tea are also served.

Hertzoggies.

South Africa is also famous for its Hertzoggies. Named after General Hertzog, who was South Africa's prime minister between 1924 and 1939, these light pastry tartlets filled with apricot jam and topped with coconut meringue were, it is claimed, his favourite teatime treat. General Hertzog was a direct opponent to General Jan Smuts, whose supporters immediately developed their own little tarts called Smutsies, which have an apricot filling but instead of coconut meringue the topping is a cake-like mixture.

Another teatime favourite which originated in South Africa are Tennis Biscuits, which are made by leading South African manufacturer Bakers. They are square in shape, light and crispy with a little coconut added. Incorporated into an early design was a large embossing of the head of a tennis racquet. It was the custom of children to nibble round the edges of the biscuit until only the racquet head was left. Sadly in about 1952 the embossed tennis racquet head was removed.

Tea out in South Africa follows much the same pattern as in other parts of the world. In cities such as Cape Town, Durban, Pretoria and Johannesburg there are a number of hotels and tearooms serving a variety of interesting afternoon teas or high teas. In Cape Town at the Belmond Mount Nelson Hotel one can have South African treats such as *melktert*, or scones, lemon tarts, quiches and sandwiches served with a choice of teas. For an Indian flavour, Jeera in Durban serves Bombay or masala chai with rose *macarons*, burfee shortbread and cinnamon éclairs or savouries such as smoked salmon bagels with paneer and cucumber and cumin sandwiches, while the Silver Teaspoon in Johannesburg serves teas in a Victorian setting. At the Contessa, also in Johannesburg, one can have a tea tasting or just enjoy a high tea with a variety of teas to choose from, including flavoured teas such as coconut snow, tropical breeze and masala chai.

Five
India and the Subcontinent

T EA HAD BEEN KNOWN to the British in India in the early seventeenth century when they had trading posts at Surat and Bombay, even before tea had arrived in England. Dutch merchants first brought green tea from China to Surat and at that time tea was considered a medicinal drink. Albert Mandelslo, a gentleman of the court of Holstein who visited Surat in 1638, noted that 'At our ordinary meetings every day we took only *Thé*, which is commonly used all over the *Indies* . . . as a drug that cleanses the stomach and digests the superfluous humours.'[1]

In 1689 a chaplain at Surat, the Reverend John Ovington, who was an early enthusiast of tea, recorded in his account of his travels in India, *A Voyage to Surat in the Year 1689*, that the Dutch traders in India used it 'as such a standing entertainment, that the Teapot's seldome off the Fire or unimploy'd'. At this time the tea was drunk without milk although sugar was sometimes added as well as a variety of spices.

The tea, however, was expensive and as early as 1774 the British were looking for ways to break the Chinese monopoly and explored the possibilities of growing teas in India. They discovered tea growing wild in the northeast. Here they also found that the hill tribes were making a kind of pickled or fermented tea called *miang* or *lephet*.

It was not, however, until the mid-nineteenth century that tea drinking by the British in India really got under way with the development of tea plantations in Assam in the 1830s. Later, in the 1860s, tea cultivation spread to the Darjeeling area in the Himalayas, the Nilgiri Hills in the south and Ceylon (Sri Lanka). But it was not until the 1870s that the tea industry in India stabilized and finally began producing good-quality tea.

The Raj

UNTIL THE LATE EIGHTEENTH CENTURY very few British women ventured to India. It was a male-dominated society where ladies played only a subsidiary role. At this time there was a great deal of interaction between the British and those they ruled. A surprising number of company men adopted Indian ways and clothing. They ate spicy local dishes and wore Indian dress, and many went into business partnerships with Indian merchants. Some had relationships with the local women, even marrying and having children.

This intermingling did not last. Not only were strict Victorian values imported to India but two important events changed everything. One was the uprising of 1857, often referred to as the Indian Mutiny, the First War of Indian Independence or the Great Rebellion. In 1858 British Crown rule was established in India, ending a century of control by the East India Company. This became known as the Raj (*rāj* meaning 'rule' in Hindi). In the years that followed there was little friendship or marriage across strictly policed racial and religious boundaries.

The second event was the opening of the Suez Canal in 1869. The journey time was cut from three or

An elaborately decorated Indian silver teapot, 19th century.

four months by steamship round the Cape to as many weeks. Not only could visits be made back to Britain but wives and their families could join their menfolk in India. Sisters, aunts and single ladies could also travel out to India.

When the Raj was at its height, many bright young men went out to India to work as administrators, soldiers and businessmen. With the lack of eligible men in Britain, young women could now follow them in the hope of finding a husband. Many were daughters returning after finishing their English education, or invited to stay with relatives or friends. This social phenomenon was known as the Fishing Fleet and the young ladies could expect to have a good time with a hectic social life of dances or tea dances, parties, picnics, afternoon teas, tennis tournaments, gymkhanas and so on.[2] Romances were often conducted speedily and many did find husbands. (Those unfortunate enough not to sailed disconsolately back to England, and were unkindly referred to as 'returned empties'.) However, after the honeymoon, life could change dramatically for the Fishing Fleet girls who were often whisked off to remote outposts where there were few Europeans for company. It was quite a different life from what they expected. The heat often became unbearable and many became bored and lethargic, reclining on sofas in darkened rooms all day. Many had to return home to Britain to recover their health. In *Woman in India*, published in 1895, Mary Frances Billington wrote that it was only a strong character 'that does not become demoralized into flabbiness and inertia under the combined influences of heat, laziness, and servants at command ... The first sign of deterioration is when a woman omits her corsets from her toilette, and begins lolling about in a sloppy and tumbled tea-gown.'

Many household and cookery books were published locally, aimed at helping newly arrived memsahibs cope with the complexities of life in India with its legions of domestic servants, their horror at the squalor and limitations of the outside kitchens and the unfamiliar foodstuffs. The books also explained the rules of hospitality and entertaining with its intricate social rules not only for formal dinners but for afternoon tea, since many young ladies brought with them this tradition which became popular and embedded in colonial life.

Afternoon tea was usually served late afternoon after tiffin (tiffin is an Anglo-Indian term used in parts of India for lunch, but it can also mean a light snack in the middle of the day or in the afternoon but before the evening meal).[3] Tea was drunk in the same way as it is today in Britain, with milk and sugar. (In India the sugar might be in the form of jaggery or date palm sugar.) Some enjoyed their tea with spices. Sometimes other ingredients were added, as in Beatrice Vieyra's recipe for Cutchee Tea, which includes not only milk and sugar but almonds, sago, cardamom pods and rosewater.[4]

As far as entertaining went, tea parties were seen as an economical alternative to lavish dinner parties. Afternoon tea parties were held in the gardens of hill stations during the summer social season, and in winter down on the plains. Sandwiches might be traditional British-style such as egg, chicken, tomato, cress or cucumber (perhaps with a sprinkling of chilli pepper) but this traditional fare was often fused with local Indian dishes, producing hybrid concoctions such as Delhi sandwiches, a sort of curry sandwich made with anchovies and sardines, and chutney. The ever-efficient Colonel Kenney-Herbert advises on sandwiches:

Ladies and gentlemen taking afternoon tea in India from a drawing originally published in *The Graphic* weekly newspaper in London in 1880.

Spread the bread with green or any fancy butter, and fill the sandwich with chopped sardines, and some bits of pickle here and there; or with mixed chicken and tongue, a lettuce leaf and some *mayonnaise* sauce.

Any potted meat worked up with butter, pepper, a touch of mustard, and a little chutney.

Ham and beef sandwiches should make your nose tingle with mustard: be easy with the butter if you can dot in some nice pieces of fat.

Pound a slice of cheese well, with a little fresh butter, a tea-spoonful of made mustard, a little black pepper, and salt, add an anchovy, wiped

free from oil, and passed through the sieve with a little butter if too thick, mix thoroughly, give it a dust of Nepaul pepper, spread it on your bread. And complete the sandwich.

. . .

Fillets of anchovy with slices of olive, embedded in pounded hard-boiled egg and butter and lightly dusted with Nepaul pepper compose a very eatable sandwich.[5]

Some Raj-era cakes are interesting for the Indian influence too. Fruit cakes, taking advantage of local fruits and spices, were popular, as was Indian gingerbread. Mrs Bartley's recipe for Saucer Cake (Saucy Kate) in her book *Indian Cookery General* (1946) is also a good example:

Mix together a pound of fine flour, three ounces of powdered sugar, a little salt, and three ounces of melted butter, make it into a dough with milk. Scrape the white part of two cocoanuts into flakes, which mix with a tablespoon of sliced almonds, two tablespoons of white plums, the same amount of currants, half a pound of sugar and the seeds of six cardamoms pounded. Roll your pastry very thin, put a layer in a tin plate, sprinkle some of the sweetmeat over the pastry, repeat the process, pastry and sweetmeat alternately, until there are seven layers. With a knife cut the paste in cross lines, two inches apart, not quite through. Put lumps of butter all over the surface, using about four ounces more. Bake a light brown.

Baking cakes or biscuits in British India was a challenge for the cook. Ovens were primitive and there was a shortage of fine flour, good butter and yeast. Good quality tinned butter and other cooking ingredients often had to be ordered from the Army and Navy Stores. Cookery books of the Raj are filled with recipes for home-made yeast, using ingredients as diverse as potatoes, hops, bananas, barley, toddy (palm sap) and a fruit flower known as *mowha*.[6] Baking at high altitudes was another problem. Despite all these difficulties there was keen rivalry among hostesses and many memsahibs tried their hand at baking. Help was also at hand, for many of the Indian cooks became very adept at baking cakes, as Isobel Abbott relates in her book *Indian Interval* (1960):

Bashir was in his glory whenever we had a tea party and his variety of cakes, scones, buns, puffs and sweets were a revelation.

His oven was a kerosene tin placed on an open wood fire, with a few of the burning embers on top of the tin to produce an even heat. One had to be a past master to keep the fire at just the right temperature. His kitchen, on party days, had to be seen to be believed. Dough, slowly rising, swelling and spilling over one corner of the rough table, fudge cooling on another, a mountainous pile of newspaper quills under the table and a blot of pink icing decorating the ceiling. But a beautifully iced and decorated layer

The Cook's Room, one of Captain G. F. Atkinson's illustrations
to his 1859 memoir of social life at 'Our Station' in India.

cake always serenely reposed on the kitchen stool. Crushed egg shells lay, like the may petals, on the mud floor and it was a gymnastic feat to avoid the mixing bowls, the plates of washed, dried fruit, and the large hookah in the centre of the floor. At first I was appalled by the confusion, but I realized I could do no better with an open wood fire, a kitchen table and a stool. Indeed I could have done nothing at all, except mop my eyes and cough, for the wood was always new and damp.[7]

Cakes served for afternoon tea were given Indian-style names such as gymkhana cake and tiffin cake. Some were named after a place, such as Tirhoot teacake and Ferozepore cake, named for the ancient town in the Punjab. It contained almonds, pistachios and green citron (lime). Nurmahal cake (Nurmahal was famous for its cakes) is described by food historian David Burton as 'a wondrously ghastly multi-tiered creation stuck together with three different flavours of jam, with a custard filled well in the centre and a frosting of egg white and sugar'.[8]

For those of who are intrepid enough to try this cake, here is a recipe from *'What' and 'How'* by E.S.P. (E. S. Poynter, 1904):

Nurmahal Cake

Cut four slices of sponge cake about an inch thick, of an oval shape, each slice smaller than the others, spread a thick layer of apricot jam upon the largest slice, and lay the next sized upon it, spread it with another kind of jam, then cover with the next size which spread with a third jam, and cover with the smallest size. Press the top lightly with the hand, and with a sharp knife cut away the centre part to leave a well, mash up the part removed from the centre with good rich custard flavoured, then put it into the centre of the cake, whip the whites of 2 eggs into a stiff froth, and pour over the whole, heaping it up in the centre, and shake sifted sugar thickly on. Then place in the oven till the frosting is set. A few pieces of any preserve placed round the bottom of the dish gives a finish. This cake may be iced or frosted, and ornamented.

Other favourites for afternoon tea included *kul kuls* (sometimes called *kullah kulla*), which are curl-shaped sweetmeats. There are many recipes but they are usually made with semolina (or with rice or wheat flour), coconut milk and eggs. The shape is made by taking a small marble of dough and rolling it onto a buttered fork. The curls are deep fried and then coated in sugar syrup.

Mrs Bartley gives recipes for other sweetmeats including the diamond-shaped almond rock (or cordeal) made with almonds and sugar syrup flavoured with rosewater and coloured pink with a few drops of cochineal. She gives another almond sweetmeat recipe (marzipan) called *mass pow*.

Factory-made biscuits were available. Colonel Kenney-Herbert wrote in *Sweet Dishes* (1884) 'that thanks to Messrs. Peak, Frean and Co., Huntley and Palmer &c., tinned biscuits of undeniable quality are to be got without difficulty', but he went on to say that some biscuits were better home-made if possible and provided a number of biscuit recipes such as convent biscuits, coconut rock biscuits and ginger biscuits, plus several recipes for gingerbread.[9]

Many memsahibs would consult *The Complete Indian Housekeeper and Cook* for advice. The book, first written by Flora Annie Steel and her co-author

Trade card advertising Huntley & Palmer biscuits in India, *c.* 1880s,
showing a supply of the favourite biscuits of the British being delivered by
elephants at a fort on the Indus. On closer inspection the cargo of biscuits
includes boudoir, club, Albert and Swiss biscuits.

Grace Gardiner in 1888, went through many editions. Both were intrepid ladies who had travelled out to India, were married to members of the Indian Civil Service and lived and travelled in India with their families for more than two decades. The book became invaluable for British women living in India, providing practical advice and instructing on all aspects of housekeeping and colonial life, such as coping with the responsibility for the supervision of the kitchen or giving parties.

Tennis parties were very popular and Mrs Steel 'gives a few hints' about how to organize them:

Afternoon teas are, as it were, outclassed by tennis parties, and as these latter are a form of entertainment suitable to the limited purses of most people, a few hints may be given as to the refreshments required, though, nowadays, when everything in India is assimilating itself so rapidly to things Western, most large stations will produce some catering firm (often Swiss) who send out teas, suppers, &c., at a fixed price per head.

The thrifty Mrs Steel, however, advises that this is just a 'saving of trouble, not of expense' and further advises that

It will be found best to have at least two teapots, and not to put more than three teaspoonfuls of tea in each. Anything more tasteless or injurious than tea which has been 'stood strong' and then watered down cannot be imagined. Lump sugar and cream should invariably be given; for the latter the milk must not be boiled; even in hot weather milk will stand for twelve hours in a wide-mouthed jar placed in an earthen vessel of water, especially if a pinch of carbonate of soda or boracic acid be dissolved in it.

Coffee was also served. In hot weather cold cups or punches were popular, such as claret cup, hock cup and cider cup. To quench thirst granitos and sorbets were much liked, made simply by freezing to a semi-liquid-state claret and hock, or sauterne cups made with water. Mrs Steel advises:

it is unkind to have them too strong. Indeed, if once people try it, they will find that a quarter of a tumbler of hard-iced milk with a bottle of soda poured over it is about the best tennis drink in the world. In cold weather ginger wine, cherry brandy, milk punch, and other liqueurs may be given.

She adds:

In regard to eatables, plain bread and butter should invariably be a standing dish. Many people do not care for cakes, and yet find a cup of tea or coffee better for something to eat with it. Brown bread and Devonshire cream is a great favourite, and so are freshly made and buttered scones enriched with an egg or a little cream. Cakes and bonbons suitable for tennis parties are legion, and, as a rule, the one thing to be observed in selecting them is to avoid stickiness or surprises. It is not pleasant to find the first bite of a firm-looking cake result in a dribble of liqueur or cream down your best dress.

. . .

The refreshment tables should be very neatly laid and adorned with flowers. The trays give an opportunity for many little daintinesses in the shape of embroidered cloths, and there should always be a sprinkling of small tables covered with tea-cloths for the convenience of the guests. In ordinary tennis parties in small stations it is infinitely more convenient and pleasant to have two Sutherland tables with trays on them – one for coffee and the other for tea – whence the lady of the house, or, in her absence, the guests them-selves, can supply a cup of tea or coffee without calling for the khitmutgar. There should be room on the table for a plate of bread and butter, and one of cakes.

Mrs Steel, it seems, was not in favour of sandwiches for she ends her guidance with the words, 'in England, the fashion of having various kinds of sandwiches at afternoon tea has of late gained ground, but as it means a necessary disregard of dinner it is not to be encour-aged by anyone who sets up for being a gourmet.'

'Abbas Khan, the *khidmatgor*' (table servant) bringing in the tea things on a tray. Postcard from Ambala, India, *c.* 1905.

The *khitmutgar*

KHITMUTGAR WAS the Anglo-Indian word for a servant, usually a Muslim. All servants wore elaborate liveries. The *khitmutgar* was truly impressive in his red cummerbund and high turban. He often had a number of assistants and was meticulous in the laying of the table for meals, including for afternoon tea. He served at table and was in charge of tea, coffee, eggs, milk, toast, butter, and so on. He was supposed to not leave the house between lunch and afternoon teatime (the time of which was often irregular) and, according to Flora Annie Steel, could occupy himself with the spare silver,

which cannot have too much elbow-grease. The *khit* will thus be at hand to bring tea at any time, should the advent of visitors require it to be brought either earlier or later than usual; if the kettle is boiling, which it should be, on a charcoal brazier in the verandah, a sharp servant will appear with the tray, toast, cakes, &c., less than five minutes after it has been ordered. Yet how often has not every Indian visitor been kept wearisomely waiting or the tea, the offer of which he was unwise enough to accept.

Mildred Worth Pinkham, in her book *Bungalow in India* (1928), describes a party held under a mango tree on the front lawn, at which an uninvited guest eyes the delicacies:

Most tempting pastry appeared – concoctions which Joan had not had the imagination to order. Everything progressed serenely until something happened that the Boy had not anticipated. While the Memsahib and her guests were sipping tea, a huge vulture swung down upon the table, and grabbing an inviting cocoanut frosted tart, made off with it to a distant tree.

'Chota Sahib', in his *Camp Recipes for Camp People* (1890), gives a recipe for these tarts, which were called Presidency Cakes:

Grate a fair sized cocoanut down to the rind and dissolve a cup of sugar in a little water; then add the cocoanut and keep on stirring till it boils; turn this out and let it cool; then add the yolks of 4 eggs well beaten up and place in the oven in small pans lined with a thin layer of good paste. These are good either hot or cold.

There were also teas at other sporting events such as gymkhanas and at charity fetes (these became numerous during both world wars), the tea tents often featuring strawberries and cream.

When the weather became unbearably hot, too hot to play any games or take exercise in comfort, many escaped the cruel heat and went up to the cooler hill stations such as Mahabaleshwar where one could play golf all day and enjoy strawberries and cream for tea, as described in this poem:

The Ladies of Mahableshswar
Have strawberries for tea,
And as for cream and sugar
They add them lavishly;
But Poona! Oh in Poona,
Their hearts are like to break
For while the butter's melting
The flies eat up the cake.[10]

Picnic parties were also popular and quite elaborate, as can be seen on this list of items for a picnic tea for twelve.

Food writer Jennifer Brennan in her book *Curries and Bugles* (1992) reminisced about the elegant teatimes as a child in India in the 1940s:

The late afternoon sun paints broad bars across the pillars of the veranda and stripes the rush mats on the cement floor. It glints on the silver tea pot and hot-water jug on the lace-covered tea trolley. From the garden comes the scent of newly watered grass and the heady perfume of carnations . . . Sandwiches have been arranged in precise, geometric stacks on the doily-covered plates by the bearer. The cakes and scones are elevated in tiers on the silver cake stand. Little blue-glass beads edge the net cap over the milk jug and tinkle gently as my mother removes it to pour a measured amount into the cups.[11]

Pat Chapman, in *Taste of the Raj* (1997), gives us an insight into his grandmother's cookbook. He gives a recipe for Fancy Nancy (who Nancy was, he does not say), a sort of savoury biscuit which was an age-old standby in case the fresh bread man, the *roti wallah*, did not show up. He describes how the *roti wallah* used to

Picnic tea basket list from Constance Eveline Gordon's
Khana Kitab: The Anglo-Indian Cuisine (1904).

carry a large tin box on his head, and inside were fresh, hot English loaves and biscuits. 'One particular treat was especially popular. The twice-daily milk supply was always boiled before it was consumed. When it cooled, a thick cream formed. The kids used to take it in turn at teatimes to spread the cream on their bread, and eat it with lashings of jam.' Also spread with jam or butter sprinkled with sugar were the local *chupattis*. Chapman also gives a recipe for Brown George (a spicy biscuit to be eaten hot or cold with butter) and one for cinnamon toast, a common Raj afternoon tea offering.[12]

Club teas

IN THE EARLY YEARS of the nineteenth century the habit of paying casual visits at all hours of the night and day died out, and around this time taverns and coffee houses became equally unfashionable. For a time after 1835 the advent of imported ice from American ships revived their flagging trade and ices and sherry cobblers (a sweetened iced drink flavoured with fruit) served at the coffee houses became all the rage. By this time, however, gentlemen's clubs were on the rise. In Calcutta, Bombay and Delhi and up at the hill stations, exclusive clubs were established by the British, duplicating institutions started in the mid-nineteenth century in England. The Bengal Club, India's first, was established in Calcutta in 1827. The Madras Club in Madras, the second oldest surviving club, opened in 1832 and the Byculla Club opened in Bombay in 1833. It was not until after the Indian Mutiny that clubs appeared in the remoter stations. Delhi's Gymkhana Club, which opened in 1913, was a relative latecomer. Tea planters established clubs too, like the Darjeeling Club in Darjeeling and High Range Club in Munnar. Clubs were the gathering places for the British ruling elite and at first merchants and Indians were barred. They provided comfort and recreation for men in service, as well as congenial settings for their families. They became the focal point of social life. Despite the fact that women had no official standing and did not appear on the official lists of members, they benefited most from the establishment of the clubs, as previously their own public meeting place had been the local band rotunda, where performances were given in the evening.

Afternoon tea was served in wood-panelled rooms, on shady verandas or out on manicured lawns accompanied by typical Anglo-Indian fare such as club sandwiches, toasts grilled with toppings of garlic, green chillies and grated cheese, and, always, spicy pakoras, samosas and English cakes.[13]

The clubs centred on sports (such as cricket, tent pegging, gymkhanas, tennis and so on), the bar and the dining room. The club became the venue for many of the parties held after sporting events. Jennifer Brennan explains that 'unless the affair was very large or important, in which case catering would be handled by Nedous, Filettis or Larangs from Lahore, the regular refreshments were provided on a member-pitch-in basis with the various cooks of the households showing off their skills.' These refreshments ranged from 'petit bridge-tournament sandwiches to full-bodied buffets, together with the accompanying fruit cups and punches'.[14] Some of the punches, for example the Sarghoda Club tennis cup, contained strong Indian tea.

Anglo-Indian teatimes

IN THE EARLY TO MID-NINETEENTH century the term 'Anglo-Indian' referred to British residents of India, but it later came to mean the descendants of official or unofficial unions between British men and Indian women. Most Anglo-Indians were Christians of various denominations, spoke English, wore European clothes and married within their community. They also had a distinctive cuisine which incorporated dishes from all over the subcontinent as well as British and Portuguese foods. Some came to call it the first pan-Indian cuisine. Afternoon tea became an important part of their tradition, borrowing from the tea drinking rituals of the memsahibs of the Raj and characteristically enjoying the best of both worlds, serving cakes such as seed cake, telegram cake (which may have been so-called because it was a quick cake to bake), coconut cake, treacle buns,

teacakes, hot scones, lemon cake and sandwiches, alongside spicy Indian treats such as samosas, pakoras and *sev ghatia* (a savoury snack made from besan flour). Christmas time is very important in the Anglo-India calendar and a time when special cakes and biscuits are made such as Christmas cake, *kul kuls* and rose (rosa) cookies which are delicate, crisp and sweet fritters.

Tea in the post-British era

TEA DRINKING was strongly associated with the British in India but it took a long time for the Indian population to follow suit. In the early days it was too expensive. Marketing campaigns were set up but it wasn't until the First World War that they showed some signs of success. Tea stalls were set up in factories, coal mines and cotton mills and, perhaps more importantly, workers were allowed tea breaks. On the Indian Railways, the Tea Association equipped small contractors with kettles, cups and packets of tea and set them to work at the major railway junctions. Tea shops were set up in large towns and cities too but it was not until the 1950s that tea became the drink of the masses. Today tea is a normal part of everyday life of India. It is brewed at railway stations, bus stations, bazaars and offices and sold by *chai wallahs* who typically boil the tea with milk and sugar and serve in 'disposable' clay cups called *kullarhs* which are thrown away after use.

This 'railway tea' is the most common tea in India. Masala chai has spices added and is particularly popular in the Punjab, Haryana and elsewhere in northern and central India; the people in eastern India (West Bengal and Assam) generally drink tea without spices. Tasty street food fried snacks such as samosas or *bhel poori* are often bought to have with the tea. In Kolkata a must-have teatime snack called *jhal muri* (sometimes called *Bengali bhel*) can be purchased from the *muri wallah*. *Jhal* means 'hot' and *muri* is puffed rice, one of the ingredients of this tasty snack, along with tomato, cucumber, chickpeas and boiled sliced potato, spiced with coriander, coconut chips, green chillies, spices, salt, mustard oil and tamarind water, all mixed together in a metal pot, then wrapped in newspaper until time to eat.

Tea is also consumed in the home. The British in India had the custom of what was called *chota hazri*, meaning 'little breakfast'. Servants brought an early morning cup of tea with milk and sugar and perhaps some fruit or a biscuit for their employers who liked to work in the cool early morning. The main breakfast was served at about nine or ten o'clock. *Chota hazri* has survived and been anglicized as 'bed tea' for many

Chai wallah at his stall in Kolkata (Calcutta).

Indians, and a late afternoon snack or afternoon tea also thrives in many parts of India as children return from school and workers from the office. This might consist of a light meal of fried snacks with tea (or a glass of milk for children), or something more elaborate with English-style tea sandwiches, fried savoury snacks such as pakoras and samosas, with Western-style cakes and pastries and/or Indian sweets which are usually purchased from an outside vendor. It became an important meal, especially in West Bengal and in other places such as in Tamil Nadu, Uttar Pradesh and Gujarat.

In West Bengal the remnants of the British Raj include afternoon teas, complete with cucumber sandwiches, cakes, savoury snacks and tea prepared English style (without spices). Bengalis are renowned for their love of sweets and teatime is an opportunity to enjoy a wide range. Sweets, which can be complicated to make, are usually bought from the local *moira* (professional sweet-maker). Most sweets are made of sugar and curds (*chhana*), including *sandesh*, *rosogullah*, *pantua* and *rosomalai*. *Ladikanee* is another sweet. Made with flour, sugar and curds, it is rolled tightly into a small ball and fried in hot syrup. It was created in the mid-nineteenth century by Bhim Chandra Nag, a prominent *moira*, for Lady Canning, the then vice-reine of India, for her birthday.[15]

Although tea took second place to coffee for a long time in south India, a light snack with tea known as 'tiffin' is especially popular in Andhra Pradesh and Tamil Nadu. What started as tiffin in British India – a light meal taken in between meals – has become very popular all over India, especially in Mumbai where a south Indian tiffin is available just about everywhere and at any time of the day (or night). 'No day is complete without tiffin, an afternoon snack, to fill the gap between lunch and dinner. There are mobile carts, coffee

Stall selling sweets in Vrindavan, Uttar Pradesh.

shops, sweetshops and cafés on every street in Madras, selling sweets and savouries with coffee and tea.'[16]

It is customary to be offered tiffin as a courtesy when you visit a Tamil resident. Hospitality is taken very seriously and to refuse tiffin may be considered an insult, suggesting that you think the host's hospitality is inadequate, so guests should make sure to leave room for a small snack when visiting a household and sample the offerings. These may include the south Indian specialities *dosa* (or *thosa*), a fermented pancake made with rice batter and black lentils; *upma* (a savoury semolina and pulse snack); *murukku* (a fried crunchy snack made with gram and rice flour, its name deriving from the Tamil word for twisted, referring to its shape. There

are many versions including *chakali* or *chakli*, which is popular in Gujarat); and of course the ever popular samosas and pakoras. However, one should not eat all of the food on offer as the host may feel obliged to make more.

In Gujarat and Maharashtra afternoon tea is an occasion for enjoying delicious snacks called *farsans*. Some are bought from street vendors or shops, although many are made at home. There are many different types: some are fried and then dried and stored, while others are fresh or steamed. *Dhokla*, an emblematic Gujarati dish, is, for example, a steamed dish made with fermented rice and chickpeas. There is also *chevda* (known as Bombay mix in the UK), *ganthiya* (crisp, deep-fried snack made from spiced chickpea paste), *fafda* (a traditional crispy spicy snack made with gram flour), *khandvi* (a tightly rolled snack made with chickpea flour, curds and spices, served in bite-sized pieces), *ragda* (garnished fried potato patties), *vada* (a common term for different types of savoury fritter-type snacks), *mathris* (a speciality of Rajasthan, a kind of savoury flaky biscuit), *khakhras* (thin crackers made with mat or moth bean, wheat flour, oil and spices) and *bakarwadi* (dough spread with a spicy filling, rolled up and fried) and the well-known and popular samosas and bhajis, to name just a few. Gujarat is renowned for its sweets (*mithai*) and they are popular at teatime too. Some are milk-based, such as *barfi*; others are made from pulses such as a sweet lentil-stuffed *puri* and *halwa* made from chickpea flour.

Indian snacks, *chivada* (or *chevda*), served with tea.

Parsi Teatimes

THE PARSIS ARE descendants of Zoroastrians who migrated from Persia to India between the eighth and tenth centuries CE to escape religious persecution by Muslim invaders to Persia, settling in Gujarat. They quickly assimilated themselves into Indian life, combining their own culture with that of the Indians, and a distinctive cuisine emerged with elements of Persian, Indian and Anglo-Indian cuisine.

Parsi teatime snacks are a delightful mixture of Gujarati, Maharashtrian and European dishes, as well as their own traditional ones, both sweet and savoury. Baking and selling cakes is a flourishing business among Parsi ladies, especially in Mumbai. *Nankhatai*, which are like rich shortbread biscuits, are particularly popular in Mumbai for teatime and many are eaten by dunking in sweet, spicy hot tea (garam masala chai).[17]

The cities of Surat, Navsari and Pune are famous for their biscuits. In Surat there is the *khari pur ni biscot*, a light, flaky, salty biscuit, and the crisp round *batasa* biscuits which can be sweet or salty and flavoured with cumin. According to Bhicoo Manekshaw in *Parsi Food and Customs* (1996) a visit to Pune is incomplete without buying the famous Shrewsbury ginger and butter biscuits, or the salty, spicy snack called *batata chevda* (or *chivda*) made with fried potato sticks, dried coconut and nuts, to take home. Another version of *chevda* is made with pressed rice. Other favourite snacks enjoyed with a cup of tea include *ghatia* (also known as *ganthia*), the chickpea flour snack which is so typical of Gujarat and Maharashtra. *Bhel puri*, thin crisp fried rounds of dough mixed with puffed rice, fried lentils and chopped onions, are a favourite snack of every Parsi, especially at teatime. Another typical Parsi teatime savoury is *topli na paneer* – small soft cheeses made in baskets.

Confections and sweet pastries are often served at teatime. Many Parsis have a supply of sweet offerings to hand so that they can welcome visitors at any time of day, including teatime. Many Indian sweetmeats are time-consuming to prepare and throughout the country there are specialist sweet-makers known as *halvais* (or *moiras* in Bengal) from whom households will often purchase sweetmeats rather than preparing them at home. Typical Parsi sweet snacks include the lovely crisp, small, round macaroons made with almonds and cashew nuts and *malai na khaja*, a sort of baklava, reflecting Persian origins, but instead of ground nuts for the filling they are filled with rose-flavoured cream, deep fried and then dipped in sugar syrup.

Some teatime snacks are made at home. *Patrel* is made from taro leaf stuffed with a hot, sweet and sour paste, rolled up then fried or steamed. Different kinds of fritters are made, such as *popatjis* made with yeast or toddy batter,[18] *kervai* (*karvai*) made with bananas and *kerkeria* made with semolina or sweet potatoes. There is *chapat*, which is a nutty pancake, and *bhakras*, which are small round cakes made with almonds and pistachios, lightly spiced with cardamom, nutmeg and caraway seeds and often made with toddy. *Sadhnas* are another speciality made with rice flour and toddy. Sweet pastries include *meethi papdi* flavoured with cardamom, *dar ni pori* (stuffed with lentils and nuts) and *khajoor ni ghari* (stuffed with dates and almonds). Other sweet teatime snacks include *haiso*, which are made with cracked wheat and nuts, while *khaman na larva* are dumplings stuffed with grated coconut. Also enjoyed at teatime is *kumas* (a semolina cake which contains coconut water).

Savoury snacks include *batata vada*, a fast-food dumpling made by mashing boiled potatoes with green chillies, ginger, garlic, lime juice, turmeric and fresh coriander, then dipping in a besan (gram flour) batter and deep fried, served either with a green chutney or fried green chillies. *Kharo ravo* is a savoury semolina snack and there is also *choora* (savoury pressed rice) and *saria* (rice crackers).

The Parsis have also borrowed dishes from Gujarat and Maharashtra. One such is the *bhajia* or pakora (using vegetables such as potatoes and spinach), fried in batter and served with a mint or sweet and sour chutney. Samosas are also popular at teatime but it is perhaps not surprising that the Parsis of Bombay and Hyderabad have their own version. These are stuffed with vegetables or minced lamb but they might add all sorts of ingredients to make them their own, including a thick rich Mornay sauce. Stuffed *puris* such as *batata puri*, which are not usually eaten by Parsis during their meals, are often served as a teatime snack.

Irani cafés

A SECOND WAVE of Zoroastrian immigrants came from Persia to Bombay at the end of the nineteenth and early twentieth century. Like the Parsis, they too were persecuted for their religion in Persia and came in search of a better livelihood. They came from the smaller villages of Persia, such as Yezd – not from the cities – and were not well off. They became known as Iranis and, like the Parsis, brought with them their own food traditions, including tea traditions, and fused their own tastes with the flavours of India. The Iranis were good businessmen and quick to recognize a good business opportunity in providing the workers of Bombay with refreshing cups of tea, served with a variety of snacks from small street stalls. Later they moved into cafés which became known as Irani cafés. They were usually on a street corner. The Iranis benefited from a

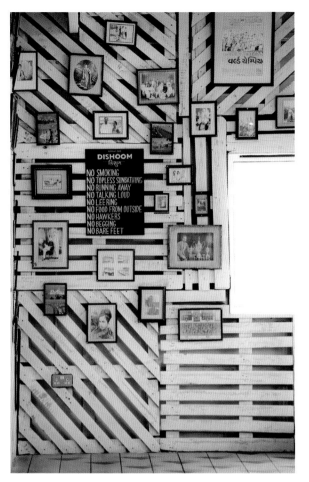

Notice board at Dishoom, at one of their Irani cafés in London.

talking loud, no spitting, no bargaining, no cheating. No gambling, no combing hair.'

Irani cafés serve quite a simple menu but provide a place to read the newspaper or watch the world go by. They became well known for their strong milky sweet tea called *paani kum chai*, and for their *brun maska*, which is often served with the tea. *Brun* or *gutli pao*, a local bread that is unique to Mumbai, is crisp, hard and crumbly on the outside and soft on the inside. The *brun* is sliced and spread lavishly with *maska* (butter). Some people sprinkle it with sugar. The *brun maska* is then dunked into the tea. Biscuits such as the sweet or savoury biscuit Osmania, *nankhatai* and *khari* are served, as are cakes such as *mawa*. *Mawa* are small buttery cardamom-flavoured cakes made using *khoya* (milk reduced to its solids). Irani cafés are also famous for their spicy snacks such as *keema*, a spicy mince, and other Parsi specialities such as *akoori* (spicy scrambled eggs).

Irani cafés were renowned in Bombay and later in Hyderabad but sadly, from an estimated 350 cafés in the 1950s, barely twenty survive today. It seems Kyani and Merwan have reopened.

superstition among their Hindu business competitors – that it was unlucky to place a shop on a street corner – but in fact this was a great advantage as these cafés are visible on two sides and have lots of natural light, thus attracting many customers. The cafés are furnished with marble-topped tables and bentwood chairs; the walls are typically decorated with portraits of Zoroaster and full length mirrors.[19] Also displayed on the walls, or over the sink where you wash your hands in the back, might be an officious notice spelling out a list of 'house rules' such as 'No smoking, no fighting. No

A man enjoying his *paani kum chai* with *brun maska* in the oldest surviving Irani café, Kyani & Co in Fort, South Mumbai.

Afternoon tea out

APART FROM the Irani cafés for tea and snacks, afternoon teas reminiscent of the British Raj can still be enjoyed in a number of hotels and restaurants in many parts of India. Here are just a few notable examples.

Darjeeling, a hill resort in the heart of the eastern Himalayas, with its snow-clad mountains in the distance and tea bushes stretching across its picturesque landscape of steep slopes and green valleys, is famous for its delicately flavoured teas likened to muscatel and often called the 'champagne of teas'. They are generally considered to be the best in the world. Jeff Koehler in his book *Darjeeling* (2015) writes eloquently about afternoon teas served at the Windamere Hotel and The Elgin. The Windamere, which was established in the 1880s as a cosy boarding house for bachelor English and Scottish tea planters, was converted into a hotel in 1939. Afternoon tea is served every day at precisely 4 p.m. in Daisy's Music Room:

The Windamere's tradition began seventy-five years ago by copying the British fashion and has carried on with little change since. A server wearing a frilly lace pinafore and white gloves pours out tea from a silver pot and offers platters of macaroons, Bundt cake with candied cherries, and scones to slice open and generously spread butter and clotted cream across their soft crumb face. Arranged in orderly layers on silver platters are petit triangular sandwiches that have been filled with cucumber, boiled egg, or cheese and had their crusts shaved off with a long, serrated knife.

Sandwiches are also on the afternoon tea menu at The Elgin hotel, which was originally built as the summer palace of the maharaja of Cooch Behar. Koehler describes the surroundings:

a snug interior bedecked with etchings and lithographs, period teak furniture from Burma, oak floor paneling, plus red sofas with ample throw pillows, and fireplaces that crackle in the winter . . . the Elgin's waiters – clad not in frilly lace but turbaned, regimental uniforms – serve afternoon tea on the heavy, polished wood side tables inlaid with mother-of-pearl. Among the monogrammed cups and saucers and silverware covered in a gossamer of spidery patina, waiters set down a stacked tea tray (known in Edwardian days as a curate) with three hoops to hold plates of delicacies and a loop handle on top to carry it.

He goes on to say:

While the Windamere might prepare moister scones and clotted cream that can suspend a spoon upright, the Elgin serves just-fried *pakoras* (fritters) made of onions, vegetables, or boiled eggs to accompany their selection of sweets and savouries, and, along with a long list of fine, single estate Darjeeling teas – including Margaret's Hope, Balasun, and Puttabong (Tukvar) – a sublime masala chai that's aromatic and perfectly spiced.

Kolkata (formerly Calcutta) is regarded as India's cultural and intellectual capital. It is a city of contrasts too. Alongside the poverty, rich Bengali gentry still, for example, frequent the gentlemen's clubs reminiscent of the British Raj and go out for 'tea' at tearooms such as the legendary Flurys. Founded in 1927 by Mr and Mrs

J. Flurys, it soon became a popular meeting place for people of all ages. As the only tearoom of the prosperous British and affluent Indian alike, it was renowned for its authentic Swiss and international delicacies. Flurys was given a makeover recently, recalling the style and decor of the 1930s, and exotic cakes, creamy pastries and Swiss chocolates are still on the menu. At the same time some of the savouries reflect that same mixing of Eastern and Western tastes, with puffs and patties, masala egg scramble and even baked beans on toast, which are spiced up with freshly chopped chillies and onions on the side. The teas also reflect Western and Eastern teas and include Darjeeling, green tea, Earl Grey, masala tea, lemon and iced lemon.[20]

Dolly's, on the other hand, is a small, quaint, iconic tea shop in Kolkata, popular with students and shoppers, with tea chests serving as table tops, teak panels and rattan chairs. The tea shop caters for many tastes and provides a wide range of iced or hot teas including 'Dolly's Specials' such as Shalimar tea and Kashmiri *kahwa*.[21] Savoury snacks include plain sandwiches such as cucumber or cheese or the more substantial club sandwich. Both types can also be toasted. For those who like something sweet with their tea there is chocolate or orange cake with the possible addition of ice cream.

Jammu and Kashmir

IN THE NORTHERN part of India and Pakistan, Jammu and Kashmir, the much-disputed land so famous for its picturesque snow-clad mountains and tranquil lakes, is well known for its tea culture. Kashmiri people start the day with tea and tea is served again as a meal at about four o'clock. The Kashmiris prepare and drink tea in three different ways. *Kahwa* (*qahwah*) is the favourite and it is made with green tea called *bambay*

Kashmiri *noon chai* ('pink tea') sometimes known as *gulabi chai*.

chai (because it used to be imported from Bombay, now Mumbai). It is traditionally brewed in a samovar and served in small metal cups called *khos*. It is sweetened with sugar or honey and is flavoured with cardamom and shredded almonds. *Kahwa* is a speciality for weddings and festivals, when rose petals or saffron from the local crocus flowers might be sprinkled in too. *Dabal* (meaning double) *chai* is also made with green tea, again sweetened with sugar and flavoured with cardamom and almonds, but milk is added. *Sheer chai* (also known as *gulabi* or *noon chai*) is popular too. Green or oolong tea is brewed over a fire and with the addition of salt, bicarbonate of soda and milk makes a distinctly pink beverage which is rich and frothy. It is flavoured with cardamom and sometimes garnished with nuts such as pistachios. It can be bought in many kiosks during the winter months.

A variety of flatbreads are enjoyed with tea, usually bought from the bakery (*kandur*). Pieces of *bakirkhani* (a round nan-like bread but crisp and layered and sprinkled with sesame seeds) or *kulcha* (a light bread, topped with poppy seeds), are broken off and dunked in the tea. Also dunked is *czochworu*, a doughnut-shaped soft round bread with a crispy lower crust. The top is sprinkled with sesame seeds or poppy seeds. Best served hot, *czochworus* are delicious especially if spread with butter or jam.[22] Even everyday breads such as *czot* (sometimes called *girda*, a kind of roti) and the unleavened *lavasa*, when spread with butter or jam, make a tasty teatime snack, as does *sheermal* (also known as *krippe*), a flaky bread leavened with yeast, mixed with milk and sugar and flavoured with saffron. Sometimes the top is brushed with a little bit of warm saffron-infused milk, giving it a golden colour, and sprinkled with sesame seeds. There are also sweet *kulcha*, including *khatai*, which has a sugary taste and melts in the mouth.

Pakistan

DRINKING BOTH GREEN and black tea is popular all over Pakistan. Black tea, which is usually served with milk and often sugar, was originally introduced and popularized during the Raj. Different regions throughout Pakistan have their own flavours and ways of drinking tea. In Karachi, the strong presence of Muhajir cuisine has ensured that masala chai is popular. In the Punjab *doodh pati chai*, which translates as milk and tea leaves, is preferred. The tea and milk, laced with sugar, are boiled together and sold at tea shops. The Pashtun areas of Pakistan and Baluchistan call their green tea *kahwah* or *sabz choi*, while in the northern regions of Chitral and Gilgit, a salty buttered Tibetan-style tea is often consumed. Tea is drunk throughout the day: at breakfast, during lunch breaks and in the evening at home. Teatime snacks are often very similar to those in India and include not only cakes and various kinds of biscuits (*kulcha*), either sweet or salty, but spicy snacks as well such as pakoras, samosas, spicy potato sticks and sometimes *paan* (a stimulant which is a mixture of betel

leaf with areca nut, sometimes with tobacco added; it is chewed before being spat out or swallowed).

High teas are common at hotels and restaurants, usually as a buffet-style meal with light snacks, and club sandwiches are also a common feature in many restaurants throughout the country. The Pak Tea House in Lahore (a city which had one of the most vibrant tea cultures in the mid-twentieth century) is perhaps more well known for being frequented by prominent artistic and literary personalities than for its teatimes.

Bangladesh

BANGLADESH is an important tea producing country. However, although in 2002 Bangladesh was among the world's top tea exporting nations, today with growing domestic demand and production stagnant Bangladesh hardly exports any tea at all. Its tea industry dates back to 1840 when European traders established tea gardens in the port city of Chittagong. Commercial cultivation of tea began in the Malnicherra Tea Estate in Sylhet in the mid-1850s and the Sylhet region emerged as the centre of tea cultivation.

Bangladeshis are a tea drinking people. The tea is often taken at little tea stands throughout the country, usually with snacks. Tea is served mainly with condensed milk and sugar. There is a famous seven-layer tea, only to be found at Nilkantha Tea Cabin outside of Srimongal. The recipe is a secret but combines three varieties of black tea and one of green. Condensed milk and spices such as cinnamon and cloves, a sprinkling of lemon and a hint of asafoetida make up the other layers.

Sweets are especially popular at teatime. Dhaka, the capital of Bangladesh, West Bengal's neighbour, is as famous as Kolkata for its *moira* who make sweets such as *sandesh*, *rosogullah* and *pithas*, which are little cakes made from rice flour, *khoya* and jaggery and then fried or steamed.

Sri Lanka

SRI LANKA (formerly Ceylon), a tropical island just thirty miles from the Indian mainland, produces tea still called Ceylon, the name synonymous with fine teas. Coffee was, however, the main crop on the island until, in 1869, a coffee-rust fungus called *Heliliea vastratix* attacked the coffee plants and devastated the coffee industry. James Taylor, an adventurous Scotsman who had come to the island in 1852 to grow coffee, was selected by the owners of Loolecondera estate to experiment in planting some tea seeds on 19 acres of land in 1867. His pioneering spirit and perseverance led to him being largely responsible for the success of the country's tea business.

The tea industry expanded rapidly in the 1870s and '80s and there was much interest from large British companies in taking over many of the small tea estates. In 1890 one man, Thomas Lipton, bought four estates. The son of poor Irish immigrants, who had grown up in the slums of Glasgow, he became a successful businessman selling groceries, including tea. In Sri Lanka he began packaging and shipping the tea to Europe and the USA at low costs, cutting out the middleman. He was the first to sell tea in brightly coloured packages bearing the clever slogan 'direct from the tea garden to the teapot'.

In Sri Lanka tea is always served to guests at gatherings and festivals such as Christmas and birthdays with local cakes and sweets honouring Portuguese, Dutch and English traditions. (Sri Lanka was colonized successively by the Portuguese, the Dutch and the British, all of whom left their mark on the cuisine.) Recipes

have been handed down through the generations. Baked goods made with wheat flour, sugar and eggs, such as cakes, tarts and biscuits (cookies), reflect the European influence whereas the use of coconut, rice and palm in the local sweet dishes reflects an older, pre-colonial tradition.[23]

Menu card of the Sundae Tearooms, *c.* 1930. These tearooms were enthusiastically described in a letter written by Carol Wilson, a Wren, to her parents, when she arrived in Ceylon in 1944: 'Lovely fruit salads here consisting of pineapple, banana, water melon and so on. Also they have lovely fruit drinks, lime, orange or passion fruit with great lumps of ice in them. Absolutely "lush"!'

Love cake, perhaps the most popular cake in Sri Lanka, is a traditional Sri Lankan birthday cake. No one seems to know where its unusual name came from. What is known is that the cake probably dates back to the fifteenth century and is Portuguese in origin. One of its traditional ingredients is a kind of candied pumpkin called *puhul dosi*, which was almost certainly adapted locally from the Portuguese squash preserve *doce de chila*. The Sri Lankans adopted this foreign cake fusing the European flavours of lemon and honey with Eastern spices, cashews and rosewater. It is a rich and sweet cake so it is recommended that it be cut into small squares. Birthdays are celebrated with much enthusiasm in Sri Lanka and apart from love cake, savoury, meat filled, curry-flavoured pastries called patties are 'a must' for parties. The Sri Lankans give the pastry their own twist by the inclusion of coconut milk. Another savoury, popular as a snack and sold piping hot from the oven at almost every tea boutique, are yeast buns filled with curried meat called *mas paan*. Hoppers, the Sri Lankan version of pancakes or crepes, were a favourite of the British tea planters. Made with rice flour, coconut milk, sugar, salt and yeast and smeared with jam, they are a popular teatime snack.

Other rich cakes are *bolo de coco* (coconut cake flavoured with spices), traditional Christmas cake, the Dutch *breudher*, a rich yeast cake also traditionally served at Christmas and New Year, and *bolo folhado*, a rich layered cake which is much prized by the Burghers who are descendants of the Dutch and Portuguese. *Bibikkan* is a sort of fruitcake made with semolina, rice flour, treacle, coconut, raisins and spices. *Foguettes* are deep fried pastries with a sweet filling of pineapple or melon jam with cashews and raisins mixed together. Sweets served at teatime are often made with rice or rice flour and include *athirasa*, a crisp, deep fried, spicy sweet made with coconut and jaggery; *kalu dodol*, made with coconut and jaggery; *arsmi*, made with honey; and *aggala*, made with treacle and black pepper, which is particularly popular for teatime in the villages.

Despite Sri Lanka's colonial past, having tea out is a relatively new experience and caters mainly for tourists. There are a number of places providing afternoon tea or high tea and, as to be expected, they serve a good selection of teas and a wide range of teatime treats. For example, tea at the Galle Face Hotel in Colombo, one of Asia's oldest hotels and still retaining its colonial Old World charm, consists of Western-style sandwiches, scones and cream served alongside love cakes and hoppers.

Six

Tea Roads and Silk Roads

TEA DRINKING CUSTOMS spread from China during the Tang dynasty (618–906) when a thriving inter-Asian trade developed and trade in tea became big business. There were two main routes from China. One was the ancient *Chamadao* (the Tea Horse Road) which led from southwest China to Tibet, Burma and beyond. In the north, starting from the magnificent city of Chang'an (now Xi'an), the Silk Road was the highway to Central Asia, the Middle East and the Mediterranean. The Tea Road which opened much later in the seventeenth century was another trading route that led to Russia via Siberia.

The tea was usually transported in the form of brick tea (tea leaves pressed into bricks, often with a design imprinted on the surface). Tea bricks were preferred in trade prior to the nineteenth century in Asia since they were more compact than loose leaf tea, kept better and were more easily carried and less susceptible to damage while being transported overland. They could be sewn into yak skins to withstand knocks and bad weather. The universality of tea bricks in these regions led to its use as a form of currency. Tea could be bartered for practically anything.

Many of the places along these trading routes have strong tea drinking traditions and teatime generally means drinking tea at different times of the day, though usually not in the form we have come to know it in the West with snacks or a full meal. Each of the trading routes has its own distinctive teatime traditions, including Tibet where the tea is churned and made into a sort of 'soup'; Burma with its distinctive pickled tea called *lephet*; Afghanistan for its *chai-e-digar* (afternoon tea) and *qymaq chai* (tea with cream); and tea-loving Russia where the samovar reigns supreme.

Tea bricks were made in different shapes and sizes. Some, like this one, had a decorative pattern or motif on one side and marks on the other to guide people where to break off chunks either to make a brew or to use as currency.

Tea Horse Road

THE CHAMADAO, sometimes called the South Silk Road, was never a single path but a patchwork of trails crisscrossing the mountains and jungles. Two main routes went to Nepal and India via Lhasa, the capital of Tibet. One began from Yunnan and the other from Sichuan. Other routes linked China with Burma, leading to India, Laos and Vietnam, and one route went north to Beijing. During the Tang and Song dynasties trade flourished along these routes and trade continued until the twentieth century but declined naturally as horses ceased to have a major military use and as roads were paved for more efficient transport. Today, however, this road with its history has a new life as it has become a vital component in a drive to promote tourism. The road has become *Chamagudao* – the Ancient Tea Horse Road.

Tea and horses were the most important commodities traded. Tea cannot be grown in Tibet because of the rugged climate and cold winters so merchants made the long arduous trek to China to obtain supplies. The Chinese, for their part, needed strong horses which Tibet could supply for fighting hostile tribes to the north and west.

Tea is said to have been first introduced to Tibet in AD 641 when the Chinese princess Wencheng married the Tibetan king Songtsan Gambo. The people of Tibet welcomed this new addition to their diet, which consisted mainly of meat and dairy products and few vegetables, which are hard to grow in the harsh climate. Instead of following the Chinese style of tea drinking, the Tibetans devised their own way of preparing tea to give extra nutrition – in the form of butter tea (*bo-jha* or *po cha*), which perhaps could be better described as a sort of soup. Ladakh, a region of northern India bordering Tibet, makes butter tea called *gur gur cha* in a similar way.

Butter tea, which can be made in a number of ways, is usually made with brick tea. Chunks of tea are broken off the brick and toasted over a fire to destroy any infestation by moulds or insects. The tea is then boiled in water until dark and strong, then strained into a wooden or bamboo tea churn. Yak milk, yak butter and salt are added and the mixture is churned vigorously. When ready the tea is poured into a teapot, then served in wooden tea bowls. Before drinking, the butter, which is floating on top of the tea, is blown to one side and saved so that after finishing the tea, some *tsampa* (roasted flour, usually barley) is mixed with the reserved butter and eaten. Rinjing Dorje explains that 'at least three to five cups of tea are considered necessary for everyone in the morning. And we always say a prayer of offering to the holy ones before drinking.'[1]

Everyone drinks tea in Tibet, including monks. Monasteries have been among the largest consumers of tea. Between periods of chanting or reciting texts, attendants serve tea from large brass or copper jugs into individual tea bowls placed on low tables in front of them. Forty cups a day is quite common, etiquette dictating that guests should never be allowed to have an empty cup, with guests placing their hand over the cup when they have had enough.

Tea rituals in the regions of Tibet, Ladakh and Bhutan continue today. Tea is still boiled and churned although modern ceramic or glass containers might be used instead of wooden cups and the introduction of the thermos as a means of keeping tea hot has seen the disappearance of the brazier and teapot. Tibetans – especially the younger generation – living in exile in India have also taken to drinking Indian chai (with

Ornamental and decorative Tibetan-style teapot used mainly for ceremonial rituals, probably from Kashmir or Ladakh, 19th century, with ornate silver decoration and an elaborately crafted handle in the shape of a dragon.

tea, milk and water, often with sugar added) although butter tea is still popular on festive occasions.[2]

One route on the Tea Horse Road linked China with Myanmar (formerly Burma), which is one of very few countries where tea is eaten as well as drunk. It is known for its unusual fermented tea leaves called *lephet*, which are traditionally served with a cup of hot tea, especially after a rich meal to clear the palate. It plays an important role culturally as Myanmar's national and traditional food and this is reflected in a traditional rhyme:

> Of leaves the tea, or lepet,
> Of meat, chicken or kyet,
> Of fruits the mango or thayet.[3]

According to historians fermenting tea leaves dates back to the ancient Bamar kings (1044–1287). The Bamar people, who are of East Asian descent, settled in the upper Irrawaddy valley in the early ninth century. Since ancient times people have sent invitations to each other for social occasions of sorrow or joy. The journalist Sue Arnold remembers her Burmese mother sending traditional party invitations accompanied by a tiny chunk of ceremonial *lephet*, made by pounding dried tea leaves with garlic and salt, wrapped in a jasmine leaf secured with a clove.[4] In Bamar folklore, a prospective bridegroom would carry a dish of pickled tea-leaf salad to the bride's home for his betrothal. The bride could, however, refuse this offering. For wakes or weddings, or just for tea, *lephet* is not only considered delicious, but acts as a stimulant.

Lephet is made by steaming young tea leaves, then pressing them tightly into clay vessels or large bamboo stems. These containers are stored in the ground,

Modern Burmese lacquered *lephet* tray containing pickled tea leaves (*lephet*) in the centre compartment, surrounded by the other traditional accompaniments.

preferably close to a riverbed to ensure moist conditions and an even temperature. When ready to eat *lephet* is usually kneaded with a little salt and some sesame oil until it is soft and fine. *Lephet* is accompanied by a variety of garnishes and all are traditionally served in a special lacquer box (some of which were exquisitely crafted and made for court use). Inside the box are different compartments filled with *lephet*, dried shrimps, fried slices of garlic, toasted sesame seeds, fried crisp broad beans (*pegyi*), roasted peanuts, dried peas fried crisply (*pelon*) and salt.[5]

Lephet is eaten by taking a pinch, with the tips of three fingers, with two or three items of the garnishes. In between bites the fingers are wiped and sips of tea are taken. Finger bowls are provided at the end. Sometimes the garnishes and *lephet* are mixed together as a salad called *lephet thoke* and served on a serving dish. Lots of variations have developed and ingredients vary from region to region. Sometimes, for example, ripe tomato or minced cabbage is added or some minced papaya leaf, boiled egg or boiled corn. Instead of salt, some people use fish sauce, or sesame or peanut oil, with a squeeze of lime or lemon and a bit of chilli. Some like it served with plain white rice.

Lephet thoke, which is particularly popular with women, is sometimes found on the menu at the numerous tea shops where many Burmese go not only to drink tea and eat snacks but to socialize. Teashops, with their low tables and plastic stools, were originally the domain of men where they talked politics and discussed the news, but are now often frequented by women. Here one can ask for green or black tea, or 'sweet tea', which is also popular; it is strong and thick and made with condensed milk. One can ask for 'mildly sweet', 'mildly sweet and strong', 'sweet and rich', or 'Kyaukpadaung' (very sweet and thick). 'Sweet tea' is also available from

stalls, originally run by Indian immigrants. A variety of snacks can be eaten with the tea at tea shops such as Chinese steamed buns, fried noodles, Indian breads such as puri and parata, samosas and soups, especially mohinga, the country's national dish of delicate rice noodles in a pungent fish broth with toppings, some of them deep fried.

Travelling on to Vietnam, today you are more likely to see people drinking coffee but tea drinking has a long history and is still very much part of the culture. Although tea has been enjoyed for centuries, it has only been produced within the country since the 1880s when French colonists established the first tea plantations. The Vietnamese tend to prefer teas with light, delicate flavours. Green tea is the favourite and is enjoyed plain, without flavourings. However, flower-scented teas are also popular, including lotus tea (traditionally prepared by sealing green tea leaves within a lotus flower), jasmine and chrysanthemum.

While the tea ceremony is not elevated to a religious status as it is in Japan, the preparation, serving and drinking of tea has great social importance. It is an important ritual at celebrations. It is customary practice to serve tea along with several items of food to the bride's family at an engagement party and it is often given as a gift wrapped up in beautiful bags and placed into a *qua son* (a circular lacquered container). It is served at marriage ceremonies and funerals. It is believed that drinking tea together is a medium for uniting friends and relatives and in offering condolences to family members of the deceased. Tea is served at the start of business meetings. It is an essential part of daily life and is drunk throughout the day at home.

Tea houses are popular and diverse in style, ranging from Chinese, and Japanese to traditional Vietnamese. Many are furnished in the typical South Asian style with large tables and numerous chairs to cater for big groups, and the choice of teas varies from the traditional green tea to scented, herbal or exotic imported teas. Tea is often drunk in makeshift tea shops which also sell cakes and sweets.

Many people enjoy hot or iced tea (often served with peanut candy) at *quán cóc*, roadside makeshift shops situated near bus terminals, train stations, schools, offices and so on. Another kind of tea shop called *quán hong trà* (red tea shop) has appeared in major cities offering a sort of tea cocktail consisting of flower petals, sugar, honey or milk and grated ice. Tea is then blended in until a froth appears. Another new trend popular with young people is to meet their friends at tea shops and drink *trà chanh* (tea with fresh lemon), sometimes served with a small dish of roasted sunflower seeds. *Trà chanh* is so popular that it has become slang meaning 'hang out'.

The Silk Road and Central Asia

THE SILK ROAD is the name of a network or web of important trading routes that weaved their way across the mountains and deserts linking China and the Far East, Central Asia, India, the Middle East and the Mediterranean. As the name suggests, silk was the most important commodity traded along these routes, but other precious goods were exchanged such as jade and lapis lazuli. Animals, vegetables, fruits, spices and tea were also traded. Culinary traditions were exchanged too, including the rituals of tea drinking.

At the eastern end, where the great caravans with their precious cargoes started out on their journeys, stood the magnificent capital city of Chang'an (now Xi'an). The goods were usually carried on the backs of Bactrian (two-humped) camels, often called 'ships

Modern but charming ornament showing four Uzbek men enjoying tea, bread and apples at a *chaikhana*. Made for tourists, it was bought in Fergana, Uzbekistan, in the 1990s.

of the desert'. Caravans stopped at strategically placed caravanserais where weary traders and travellers could rest and refresh themselves with tea. Eventually the caravans would reach major cities such as Kashgar, then continue to Kashmir or Afghanistan and on to such fabled cities as Samarkand, Baghdad and Constantinople (now Istanbul).

It seems, however, that tea did not penetrate to western parts of Central Asia in any great quantities and the ancient city of Balkh in northern Afghanistan seems to have been the western terminus of tea trading. Further west in Iran and the Middle East *qahwa* (coffee) was the preferred beverage. Tea drinking was to be adopted much later and arrived by other routes.

Many of the regions along the Silk Road share tea drinking customs. Tea is drunk copiously and plays an important role in hospitality and business dealings. In many places tea is served with sugar lumps which are placed on the tongue and the tea sipped through them.

Tea houses (*chai khana*) are popular places for men to sit and relax or discuss the politics of the day over tea. (They are the preserve of men; women drink their tea at home.) The tea is usually served from a constantly boiling samovar into individual teapots and poured into small Chinese-style porcelain bowls or glasses. In many places of this region porcelain teapots and bowls are from the Russian Gardner Factory, especially those decorated with floral motifs. The factory was founded at Verbilki, near Moscow, by the Englishman Francis Gardner in 1766.

Kashgar was a major junction on the Silk Road and an important trading centre. Merchants and traders would stop there to rest, trade and take fresh supplies

Postcard of a *chai khana* in Afghanistan with large samovar and an impressive array of teapots, *c.* 1970s.

for their onward, arduous journeys. Kashgar also lies at the heart of the Uighur world. The Uighurs are an ancient Turkic people who settled a long time ago along the Silk Road, especially in what is now called Xinjiang province. They drink tea, both green and black, and make it in different ways: with salt and milk or with cream or sour cream and butter added to the tea in big bowls. Black tea is often flavoured with spices such as cardamom, cinnamon and sometimes saffron and rose petals. Green tea is preferred by Uighurs living in the Ferghana Valley. Tea is served to guests before a meal, accompanied by snacks of dried fruits, nuts or perhaps *nan* (bread) sprinkled with black nigella seeds. Tea is also served with sweets after a rich meal.

Lady Macartney, who lived in Kashgar from 1890 to 1918 as the wife of the British consul, wrote a charming and fascinating account of her life there in her book, *An English Lady in Chinese Turkestan* (first published in 1931). She describes a *chai khana*:

> Of course, the inevitable tea shop or Chai-Khana, was everywhere, where people sat and drank tea while they listened to dreamy native music played by a band consisting of perhaps one or two long-necked mandolin-shaped instruments that produced very soft fairy-like music, accompanied by a small drum. Or they listened to a professional story teller . . . I suppose it was just this way that the Arabian Nights romances were first told.

In Afghanistan, which lies at the heart of Central Asia and at a crossroads of the Silk Road, the *chai khana* plays an important role in the lives of Afghans. They are found all over the country, even in out of the way places, so that weary travellers can obtain refreshments after long and dusty journeys. They are also the place for the locals (men) to meet and exchange news and gossip. The standard and fare of Afghan *chai khana* vary considerably. Some are very basic and serve only tea, either green or black, but some are quite large and even provide tables and chairs rather than the customary traditional carpet and cushions for people to sit on. *Chai khana* can be noisy places too, often playing Afghan and Indian taped music. Tea is always served, usually with individual teapots, a small glass or tea bowl and a bowl for dregs. When the tea is served the customer first rinses out his small glass tumbler with the hot tea. Sugar is then usually added to the glass (often quite a lot even though this is charged extra). The tea is then poured. The first glass is very sweet but as the glass is regularly topped up with tea, the sweetness decreases and the last glass drunk will be quite bitter. Sweets, including sugared almonds (*noql*), are often served with the tea and in some of the larger *chai khana* more substantial food is available, such as fried eggs, kebabs, pilau or soup served with *nan*.

Brass samovar from Afghanistan (made in Russia), next to a Gardner teapot, tea in a small porcelain and a bowl of *noql* (sugared almonds).

In the home, as in the *chai khana*, tea is usually drunk without milk but often sweetened and sometimes flavoured with cardamom. Tea is drunk throughout the day – for breakfast, after a midday meal, after the evening meal and at other times such as in the afternoon when a snack or a light meal called *chai-e-digar* (afternoon tea) might be taken. For affluent families teatime in the afternoon can mean something much more substantial, especially for special occasions and guests.

Guests are always offered tea, which is sometimes served in small glasses (*istakhan*) or small porcelain handle-less bowls (*piala*), like the Chinese tea bowl. Western-style cups are sometimes used, especially in the cities. The first cup of tea is usually served with an enormous amount of sugar – the more sugar, the more honour. Another Afghan custom is to drink the first cup of tea sweet, *chai shireen*, followed by another cup without sugar, called *chai talkh*.

The glass or cup is constantly refilled by the host and guests must remember to turn their glass or cup over when they have had enough; otherwise the refilling will continue. Sometimes tea is served in individual teapots allowing the guest to pour out as much or as little tea as he or she needs or requires. A small bowl is provided for the dregs.

Sweets (*shirnee*) and savoury snacks are usually offered with tea. *Noql* – almonds, pistachios or chickpeas coated in sugar – are traditional. *Noql-e-badomi* (sugared almonds) are the most popular. Sometimes a mix of nuts (such as walnuts and almonds) and dried fruits (such as green and red raisins) will be served. Cakes and biscuits (*kulcha*) might also accompany the tea but these are rarely made in the home as few families have ovens. They are usually bought from the bazaar where there are many different types, including the crumbly *ab-e-dandon*, which means 'melt in the mouth'. Some fried biscuits or pastries are, however, made at home and for special occasions light and crispy pastries called *goash-e-feel* (literally 'elephant's ear') are made. Delicate fritter-like pastries called *kulcha-e-panjerei*, lightly dusted with icing sugar, are also popular.

While the guests are sipping their tea and nibbling on snacks the women and girls of the household are busy preparing food. For *chai-e-digar*, fried stuffed pastries called *boulani* might be prepared. Common fillings are *gandana* (a type of Chinese chive), or mashed potatoes with spring onions. Other popular teatime savoury pastries are pakoras (sliced vegetables such as potatoes or aubergines dipped in a spicy batter and fried) and *sambosa* (fried pastries stuffed with a filling of spicy minced meat, or they can be sweet, stuffed with halwa or dried fruits). Kebabs such as *shami kebab* (a kind of rissole made with minced meat, potatoes, onions and split peas, formed into a sausage shape and fried) or *kebab-e-daygi* (lamb cooked slowly in a pan with onion, yoghurt and spices until soft and succulent) are commonly served. All these savoury dishes are served with home-made chutneys and fresh *nan* and often accompanied by spring onions, lemon wedges, lettuce or herbs.

Guests often turn up for tea on special occasions such as religious festivals (*Eid-ul-Fitr* and *Eid-e-Qorban*) or for *Nauroz* (New Year), which falls on 21 March, the spring equinox. Rice biscuits called *kulcha-e-Naurozee* (also known as *kulcha-e-birini*) are traditional. Other sweet pastries and cakes include baklava, *qatlama* (a fried pastry) and *khajoor* (fried cakes, a bit like a doughnut). *Sheer payra* (a rich sweetmeat made with milk and sugar) is often served with tea when celebrating the birth of a baby. *Roht* (a sweet round flattish bread)

is also traditionally made for the festivities celebrating the fortieth day of a newborn child. Engagement parties (*shirnee khoree* – 'sweet eating') are often given at teatime. Sweets, biscuits and sweetmeats are served with tea and sometimes an unusual sweetmeat called *abrayshum kebab* (meaning 'silk kebab') is made. It is made with beaten egg in such a way that 'silken' threads are formed in hot oil and then rolled up and sprinkled with syrup and ground pistachio.

For these occasions *qymaq chai* (*qymaq* is like the Middle Eastern *kaymak*, a sort of clotted cream) is often served. It is made with green tea and by the process of aeration and the addition of bicarbonate of soda the tea turns dark red. Milk and sugar are added and it becomes a purply-pink colour. It has a strong, rich taste. The *qymaq* is floated on the top.

The late former king Zahir Shah (who reigned from 1933–73) often entertained prominent Afghans or visiting VIPs with *chai-e-digar* at the palace. Despite his opulent surroundings he is said to have had quite down-to-earth tastes. Laila Noor remembers having tea at the palace with Princess Bilqis, his eldest daughter. The guests were first of all given a cup of *qymaq chai*. After this rich tea, savoury snacks such as kebabs, *boulani* and *shour panir* (a white salty cheese served with mint) were served with *nan* and chutneys as accompaniments. These were followed by plain sponge cake, *roht* and a range of biscuits including *kulcha namaki* (salty biscuits) and *kulcha-e-jawari* (made with yellow cornmeal and more like a bread than a biscuit). Cream rolls (puff pastries with a whipped cream filling and sprinkled with icing sugar and ground pistachio nuts) – a real treat – were also served, and more tea, of course.[6]

The Tea Road

IN 1689 WHEN the Treaty of Nerchinsk was signed between Russia and China, what is called the Tea Road (sometimes the Great Tea Route or the Siberian Route) was opened. The road, which started in Kalgan in northern China, crossed Mongolia and the Gobi Desert, then continued west across the taiga of Siberia, eventually arriving at the cosmopolitan centres of the Russian Empire. Travelling this road was a long and arduous journey taking more than a year, but it soon became a major trading route with camel caravans carrying fur and other goods to China, traded for Chinese valuables such as silk, medicinal plants (especially rhubarb) and tea.

The first samples of China tea are said to have been brought to Russia in 1616 by a Cossack called Tyumenets returning from a diplomatic mission to Mongolia. He reported that his mission 'drank warmed milk and butter, in it unknown leaves'. Two years later, in 1618, the Chinese Embassy presented several chests of tea to the Russian court in Moscow. In 1638 the Mongol Khan sent via the Russian ambassador, Vassily Starkov, two hundred packets of tea as a precious gift to Tsar Mikhail Fedorovich. It became popular at court but at that time very little was known in Russia about China and tea.

The amount of tea imported into Russia gradually increased. During the eighteenth century, especially during the reign of Catherine the Great (1763–96), tea

Russian tea served in a glass with a metal holder (*podstakannik*) and served with sugar lumps and chocolates.

became fashionable among the Russian nobility, but it was to take until the nineteenth century to become universally popular. Russians evolved their own tea drinking customs, the most important of which is the use of the samovar.

Children were, and still are, allowed and even encouraged to drink tea from their saucers, so as not to burn their lips. Today tea is usually served in glasses at restaurants and cafés, but in cups at home.[7] Tea was also served at public performances. The ballerina Tamara Karsavina, writing in 1896 about a matinee performance, noted the welcome provision of tea on a cold St Petersburg day: 'Huge samovars steamed outside the stage door . . . In the interval tea and refreshments were served in several foyers and the waiting staff wore their gala red livery with the Imperial eagles.'[8]

Russians drink mainly black tea, the best of which is grown on the mountain slopes of Georgia and Azerbaijan. Most of the tea is sold loose, or in packets, but occasionally one encounters *plitochnyi chai* or brick tea. Tea drinking punctuates the day, starting first thing in the morning and served with bread, butter and sometimes cheese. The day closes with tea too, sometime after dinner, with the last meal of the day called 'evening tea'.

Russians often serve a slice of lemon (or sometimes apple) with their tea. It is rarely taken with milk. But most of all they love to sweeten the strong black tea with sugar. They say it brings out the flavour of the leaves. Some like to drink the tea with a cube of sugar clenched between the teeth. The tea is sucked through it and the sugar melts. 'Ecstasy', wrote Pushkin, 'is a glass full of tea and a piece of sugar in the mouth'. The Russian craving for sweets has meant that tea must be served with jam at the very least. The jam is usually very thick with whole pieces of fruit suspended in it and served on tiny, flat, crystal jam dishes called *rozetki*. It can either be eaten right from the dish with a small spoon or stirred into the tea itself, giving the drink a fruity aroma and taste.

The tea table may also be graced with biscuits such as Russian tea biscuits – plain biscuits covered with jam and then topped with meringue and nuts. Souvorov biscuits, named after a famous Russian military commander, are two biscuits sandwiched together with a layer of thick jam, the whole then dusted with icing sugar. There are also crisp biscuits called almond rings and crisp hazelnut rusks. Pastries might include walnut crescents called *rogaliki* ('little horns'), which are stuffed with sugar and nuts. Buns, cakes, tortes and tarts are

Russian samovar, probably 19th century, from Afghanistan.

The samovar

THE SAMOVAR is usually considered to be exclusively Russian but is used in the Central Asian states, Iran, Afghanistan, Kashmir and Turkey as well as other Slavic nations. Its origin is a matter of dispute. Some people believe it is of East Asian origin and suggest that Chinese and Korean vessels used for heating food were the forerunners. Other theories suggest that the ancestor of the samovar was a Chinese teapot that sat atop a brass charcoal burner, or the Mongolian firepot which it resembles.

The samovar, which means 'self-boiler' in Russian, is a portable water heater traditionally made of brass (although some were made of silver and even gold). It is said that Catherine the Great's horse-drawn troika travelling in midwinter from St Petersburg to Moscow included a vast ornate silver samovar, constantly on the boil to warm Her Imperial Majesty, bundled up against the bitter cold in sable and fox furs at the back.[9]

However, the samovar was never restricted to the homes of the wealthy. Even the lowliest peasant hut housed a samovar – perhaps tinplated instead of brass, or perhaps not made in Tula, the city which became the centre of manufacture and renowned throughout Russia for its finely crafted samovars. Today in Russia samovars can still be found, but more often than not electric ones have replaced the original charcoal-heated urns. The Trans-Siberian Railway places a samovar at the disposal of travellers, who are allowed to bring their own tea. Train stations also provide hot water for making tea from a large kettle called a *kipjatok*.

also popular at teatime, such as raisin buns, sweet boiled buns called *bubliki*, lemon cake, apple cake, curd cheese tartlets called *vatrushki*, apricot tart, delicate poppy seed torte or rich Russian caramel torte. Sweets such as *pastila*, which are light airy meringue puffs with a delicate apple flavour, and almond caramels, are also taken with tea by the sweet-loving Russians.[10]

Tea is also enjoyed outside the home. According to the food scholar Darra Goldstein,

Most cities and towns have tea rooms (and most of the tea rooms are less than imaginatively named either 'Samovar' or 'Russian Tea'). Often they are decorated in the old style with brightly

The tea-loving Russians found the samovar far too efficient to be ignored, and by the late eighteenth century it had been adapted to everyday use and become an essential part of Russian life. It was always kept burning, ready to refresh guests with a cup of hot tea. Many great Russian authors, from Dostoevsky to Tolstoy and Gorky, have written about the warm intimacy created by a samovar.

Contrary to popular belief, tea itself is not made in the samovar; the samovar serves only to heat water and keep it hot. The water, which is poured into the samovar's reservoir, is heated by pine cones or charcoal fired through a central funnel. Once the water boils the samovar is brought to the table. The tea is brewed separately in a small teapot and made into a strong concentrate or *zavarka* which is kept warm on top of the samovar. To make tea, a small amount of the concentrate is poured into a cup or glass, and then diluted with hot water from the samovar's ornate spigot. In this way the strength of the tea can be adjusted according to taste.

The samovar was integral to Russian entertaining and always occupied a place of honour at the table next to the hostess who would pour the tea into porcelain cups for the ladies and into glasses for the men. The glasses were inserted into metal or often beautiful filigreed silver holders called *podstakanniki*, so that the hot tea could be held comfortably. Noble families often had their own *podstakanniki* designs and some were even made of gold and decorated with precious stones.

painted ceilings and embroidered tablecloths. Typically the tea rooms contain one or two huge samovars, standing several feet tall. On top of the samovars perch tea cosies made in the round shape of Russian peasant women with disarming faces. Behind the samovars stand the real thing – rotund, matronly women dispensing the tea.

After sitting down with one's tea, one can choose from a variety of sweets displayed on the tables.[11]

The samovar and tea drinking spread to Iran, the Middle East and Turkey, although coffee drinking in many places is still preferred. Coffee, which was known in Iran by the sixteenth century, was the favoured drink

Konstantin Korovin, *At the Tea Table*, 1888, oil on canvas. Family and friends gather round the tea table to enjoy conversation and discuss matters of the day. The table is set with a samovar, tea glasses in their holders, jam, fruit and saucers from which Russians frequently sip their hot tea.

Postcard, *c.* 1906, showing Russian villagers, with two of the women drinking tea from saucers, while listening to a young man playing an accordion.

Boris Koustodiev, *Merchant's Wife at Tea*, 1918, oil on canvas. A well-dressed merchant's wife enjoys a lavish meal of fruits, an assortment of poppyseed rolls and a portion of *kulich*, a type of yeast cake filled with dried fruit and almonds. The shiny samovar and delicate porcelain tea service portray affluence and she has poured her tea into a saucer to cool it before sipping.

for centuries, especially in coffee houses. And although tea drinking was enjoyed by the upper classes in the early nineteenth century it was a luxury commodity and was used for entertaining special guests. Tea only became universally popular in the twentieth century.

Various Iranian governments had frequently suspected coffee houses of fostering degeneration and political dissent. In the 1920s the former Shah's father decided to discourage coffee houses and sought to convert people to drinking tea. He encouraged the Iranian tea industry and even imported new strains of tea from China as well as some fifty Chinese families to oversee tea production. He was successful in his aims. Coffee has largely been relegated to a mourning drink while tea has become the nation's favourite beverage.

Tea is served with breakfast, after meals, between meals and last thing at night. It is served in the bazaars, shops and offices. No serious transaction can take place without tea. It is served in tiny glasses called *estekan*, without milk or sugar, although sometimes it is sipped through a sugar lump placed on the tongue. However, sweetmeats, sweet pastries, sugared almonds, dried fruits or fruit syrups often take the place of sugar. Guests are always offered tea on arrival and for formal entertaining the tea is sometimes flavoured with cinnamon or rose petals.[12]

Turkey is usually associated with coffee drinking but the Turks are also great tea drinkers. It is thought that tea originally came to Anatolia as early as the twelfth century. However, the earliest mention of tea in Turkish literature was in 1631 by the famous Ottoman travel writer Evliya Çelebi, when he mentions that the servants at the customs offices in Istanbul offer visiting officials of the Empire beverages like coffee from Yemen, saleb and tea.[13] Tea only became important in the daily life of the Ottoman Turks in the nineteenth century. Sultan Abdulhamid II (1876–1909), although a coffee addict, showed a keen interest in tea and realized its economic importance. Tea seeds and saplings were brought from Russia and, although originally a China tea, it became known as Moscow Tea. The cultivation of tea had its ups and downs but eventually Turkey became self-sufficient. Virtually all the tea produced comes from Rize on the Black Sea coast.

The samovar came to Turkey from Russia and tea is still served this way at the many tea houses and tea

Ladies Around a Samovar, painted *c.* 1860–75 by the Iranian artist Isma'il Jalayir, oil on canvas. The painting shows a group of harem ladies making music and drinking tea. On the carpet is a selection of fresh fruit, together with the samovar and teapot necessary for making the tea. There is also a bowl of what seems to be sugar lumps or sugared almonds.

Decorative Iranian
tea glass with sugared
almonds.

Turkish tea served in the
traditional tulip glass
with sweet rich baklava.

gardens, and also in the home. For those who do not have a samovar, water is boiled in a kettle (*çaydanlik*) and poured over tea leaves in a tea pot (*demlik*), which is then placed on top of the kettle and allowed to brew. Tea is served light or strong according to taste. For most Turks the ideal tea is made strong with a transparent rich red colour. A little tea is poured from the teapot into tulip-shaped glasses called *ince belli*, or occasionally porcelain cups, and then diluted according to the desired strength with boiling water from the tea kettle. The glass is usually held by the rim in order to prevent the hot tea from burning the drinker's fingers. The tea is often sweetened with sugar and sometimes served with a thin slice of lemon but milk is never added. Serious tea drinkers go to a tea house where a samovar is kept constantly on the boil. Food is not usually served with tea at the numerous tea gardens which are also an integral part of Turkish social life. Istanbul boasts many where people can sip their tea with spectacular views of the Bosphorus or the Sea of Marmara.

In the home, however, savoury or sweet things are often served with tea in the afternoon. Food writer Ayla Algar describes a number of 'teatime specialities or favourites' taken at the 'distinct tea hour in the afternoon'. She says that some people take savoury things with their afternoon tea, while others prefer lightly sweetened cakes or biscuits. Often savoury and sweet are served together, such as savoury pastries filled with cheese or meat called *poğaça*; cheese rolls (*kaşar peynirli çorek*); sesame and caraway sticks (*susamlı çörekotlu çubuk*); yoghurt cake with hazelnut (*fındıklı kek*); apricot cookies (*marmelatlı mecidiye*); almond crescents (*bademli kurabiye*) and sugar cookies (*kurabiye*).[14] Other sweetmeats which may be served with tea include baklava, Turkish delight (*lokum*) and *kadayif*.

Seven

China, Japan, Korea and Taiwan

THE RICH TEA DRINKING CULTURES of China, Japan, Korea and Taiwan have developed their own distinct tea time rituals and traditions. In China, where the story of tea and tea drinking began thousands of years ago, the tradition of public tea houses began as early as the Tang Dynasty (AD 618–906), leading to the custom of *yum cha* and *dim sum*. Japan evolved its own elaborate tea ceremony and the meal taken with it called *cha kaiseki*. Korea and Taiwan have developed their own tea ceremonies and teatime rituals. The Taiwanese love of tea also led to the now worldwide quirky trend of 'bubble tea'.

China

CHINA EVOLVED its own tradition of teatime in the form of *yum cha* and *dim sum*. *Yum cha* (meaning 'drink tea') is the custom of serving tasty bite-sized snacks called *dim sum* (*dian xin* in Mandarin), with tea served in tiny porcelain cups. The meaning of *dim sum* defies translation into English and there are various versions such as 'touch the heart', or 'light of the heart'. Some say 'heart warmers' or 'dot heart', poetically 'heart's delight' – something just to touch upon or satisfy one's appetite whenever the heart (and stomach) desired. *Dim sum* and *yum cha* are inextricably linked, so much so that the two phrases are used interchangeably.

But how did this culinary tradition begin?

Tea drinking, according to legend, began long ago with Emperor Shennong. When some leaves from a tea tree were blown into a pot of water he was boiling, he tasted this infusion and found it to his taste, declaring that 'Tea gives vigour to the body, contentment to the mind and determination of purpose.'

Sichuan was probably where tea was first cultivated and drunk. Successive dynasties produced different styles of tea drinking. At first the fresh unprocessed leaves were simply boiled in water; later they were steamed and compressed into cakes.

In the eighth century tea had become such a passion for the Chinese and so important in trade that tea merchants commissioned Lu Yü, a poet and scholar, to write the first treatise on the subject, *Ch'a Ching* (The Classic of Tea). Lu Yü's book not only contains practical and detailed information such as how tea should be made, what tools should be used, what water to use and how to drink tea, but poetic descriptions such as how tea has myriad shapes: 'tea may shrink and crinkle like a Mongol's boots. Or it may look like the dewlap of a wild ox,' and how the water should look on making tea: 'When the water is boiling, it must look like fishes' eyes and give off but the hint of a sound. When at the edges it chatters like a bubbling spring and looks like pearls innumerable strung together.'[1]

During this time a better quality tea emerged and began to be drunk by members of the upper class, scholars and priests as a refreshing and stimulating beverage. It was also at this time that the tradition of public tea houses emerged and with it the start of the tradition of *yum cha* and *dim sum*.

Yum cha and dim sum

TEA HOUSES started to spring up along the ancient Silk Road during the Tang dynasty (618–907). They provided a place of relaxation and refreshment for weary travellers. Xi'an (formerly Chang'an, the capital of China under the Tang dynasty) was at the eastern end of the Silk Road and it was from here that the great trade caravans set out with their precious cargoes of silk, jade and other commodities, including tea.

It took several centuries for the culinary art of *dim sum* to develop. Tea houses in China do not traditionally serve snacks with tea and in the early days of tea drinking some said that tea should not be combined with food as this would lead to excessive weight gain. However, the benefits of tea drinking as an aid to digestion became known and tea houses began offering snacks to accompany the tea. Some suggest that the idea of serving snacks with tea came about when the owner of a tea house made some snacks for one of her customers which were so delicious and were soon in such demand that a neighbouring tea house started to compete by making their own, even more delicious, to attract customers.

The sort of snacks which may have been on offer appear in accounts of Chang'an. *Wun tun* (wonton), probably in the form of dumplings, were made by the Su family and sold at a particular street corner. Chang'an had two vast market areas where sesame cakes – 'crisp and fragrant from the oven' – were sold. There were bamboo-wrapped packets of glutinous rice made by the Yu family, and a wide variety of pastries, including cherry pastries, were on sale. Elsewhere in Chang'an hawkers sold cakes, both fried and steamed. Unleavened buns called *shaobing* were a common snack – a type of flatbread made in a round or oval shape, sometimes stuffed and sprinkled with toasted sesame seeds. Already the relationship between small snacks and tea drinking had been established.[2]

By the time of the Song dynasty (CE 960–1279), a period of the greatest flowering of art in China's history when Hangzhou in the east was China's capital, tea drinking and tea houses had become well established. A wide range of snacks were served. *Baozi* (leavened steamed buns) with various fillings such as crab or prawns, spring rolls, *shaobing* and mooncakes

Village cooperative having a tea party under Chairman Mao.

all appeared in Song menus.³ The tea house tradition continued to flourish, although not always with snacks. Many tea houses became places of artistic culture, places to socialize and perhaps discuss politics and, of course, to drink tea. Calligraphy and paintings often decorated the walls. Tea houses became open to everyone: labourers and craftsmen, scholars and artists, who came to relax after a hard day's work. In Hangzhou the tea houses were noted for their scholarly atmosphere while those of Chengdu, the capital of Sichuan, were well known for their storytelling, ballad singing and *kuaiban* (rhythmic verses accompanied by bamboo clappers).⁴ Other tea houses specialized in theatrical performances, or chess, while others were renowned as a rendezvous

for prostitutes and their clients. Up until the 1940s tea houses were at the centre of Sichuan's social life. Some were frequented by members of Sichuan's secret societies, who used the arrangement of their teacups as an elaborate secret code. After the Communists came to power in 1949 business in tea houses declined because most people were too busy working or building for the future. During the Cultural Revolution they were seen as 'subversive' and most closed altogether.

Since the late 1970s a revival and a more relaxed attitude and desire for some of the old traditions to return have ensured that tea houses are thriving once again in China, although many are now different from the past – more modern and with a different focus.

Although *yum cha* is enjoyed all over China, it is in Hong Kong and the Cantonese south where it is the most renowned and popular. *Yum cha* is focused as much on the food items (*dim sum*) served with the tea as the tea itself. The tea houses serving *yum cha* were first opened in the 1840s in Hong Kong but only began to flourish after 1897 when the British authorities abolished their night-time curfew for Chinese people. From the 1920s until the 1940s they sprang up all over the territory and provided a vital social function in the post-war economic boom. The tea houses were cheap and convenient and could provide meals for families who at that time were living in cramped accommodation with shared cooking facilities or none at all. Tea houses were also useful for entertaining guests or discussing business.[5]

Snacks of course can be eaten at any time of the day but *dim sum*, unlike appetizers in the West, are not usually eaten before a principal meal. In Hong Kong

Hu Xing Ting tea house, situated in Yuyuan Gardens in the old town of Shanghai, is famous for its zigzag bridge (Jiu Qu Bridge, or Bridge of Nine Turnings). Also known as the first tea house of China, it has attracted lots of celebrities such as Queen Elizabeth II and foreign leaders such as Bill Clinton. Many noted public figures and ordinary tourists go there not just for the sense of history but to taste the fragrant tea.

many tea houses open as early as 5 a.m. to cater for the night-shift crowds in need of a pick-me-up. People on their way to work also might stop off for some breakfast snacks. Men go early in the morning for *yum cha* and, as the saying goes, over 'a pot of tea and two *dim sum*', discuss business, perhaps until lunchtime. However, the most traditional and the busiest time is from about 11 a.m. to 2 p.m. for what is often called a 'tea lunch'. Workers, businessmen, housewives and students go to the tea house either for a quick snack or a leisurely lunch. *Dim sum* are not served after 5 p.m. On Sundays whole families or parties of six, eight or even twelve go to a big restaurant for *yum cha* at lunchtime and sit around a large round, often crowded table.

With the rise of Canton and Hong Kong as bustling trading ports in the nineteenth century, tea houses developed into emporium-type restaurants or 'tea palaces' on several floors. They are noisy places and along the aisles waiters (usually young girls) push trolleys laden with different types of *dim sum* kept warm by heaters. The range of *dim sum* is quite varied. Dishes are usually steamed or fried and may be savoury or sweet. Each trolley carries a different type. Ken Hom, the famous chef and food writer, describes a typical *dim sum* dining ritual:

> Drinking tea is the norm when enjoying *dim sum*. And in the tea houses, where the pace is noisy, leisurely, and informal, it is interesting to watch the social interaction. People sit with their friends at a table and the waiter brings the desired teas. This is no casual choice. The five-thousand-year-old history of tea in China has led to a reverential attitude toward the beverage . . . Whether one prefers Iron Goddess of Mercy, Dragon Well, or White Peony, or any other of a great number of

Dim sum being served from a trolley in a restaurant in Duongguang, Guandong.

teas with special flavors, strengths and fragrance, the choice is thoughtfully made.

Once the tea is selected, it is followed by the dim sum dining ritual. As the carts containing the various delicacies are wheeled around, the diners, alerted by the servers' cries on the foods available, point to the desired dishes, which are then placed on the table. Such eating is a leisurely affair. There is no rush; business and social conversation is one of the main reasons for the tea house. And, given the din of the place, the conversation seems to take place at the top of everyone's lungs. All the foods and beverages served are totalled up at the very end; the servers, with unerring memories, recall everything that has been placed on your table. The trick to their seemingly magical calculation is that they count the empty plates on your table, keeping a sharp eye to see that none has been moved to a neighbouring one![6]

Nowadays in tea houses or restaurants the carts are not used so much: customers choose a selection of *dim sum* from a menu and the dishes are brought to the table as they are cooked. The serving sizes are usually small and normally served as three or four pieces in one dish, which makes *dim sum* easy to share among members of the party, and a wide variety can be tasted.

It takes many years for chefs to learn the art of making *dim sum*. Many of the dumplings are complicated and laborious to make and nimble fingers are essential. The range of *dim sum* is countless and restaurant menus easily offer several dozen. New combinations of ingredients are appearing all the time. Here is a small selection.

Among the steamed variety, which are often made in fanciful shapes and served in small bamboo baskets, are *siu mai* (*shao mai* in Mandarin). These are open-topped dumplings made in thin, round wrappers with a filling usually of pork, shrimp or a combination of the two, mixed with a scant amount of finely sliced or chopped vegetables such as bamboo shoots, mushrooms and green onions. *Har gow* are made with thin, translucent wrappers of wheat starch and cornstarch. They are stuffed with shrimp and made into a crescent shape with multiple delicate pleats on one side (they are often known as shrimp bonnets because of this.) Chicken buns called *gai bao jai* are bread dough filled with chicken and Cantonese sausage and twisted at the top. This snack is a member of the larger-sized *bao* family that originated in northern China, typified by thick, bready wrappers and hefty fillings. Cantonese *bao* were first sold as snacks in Guangzhou teahouses before appearing in Hong Kong. According to legend, *bao* were invented 1,800 years ago by the great strategist Zhuge Liang of the Three Kingdoms. He and his troops came to a raging river that could only be crossed when the evil water spirit had been appeased with 49 human heads. Unwilling to sacrifice his soldiers, Zhuge got his men to make dumplings stuffed with meat in the shape of heads, steamed them and offered them to the river spirit. The spirit was appeased and the water of the river calmed and they were able to cross.[7]

Char sui bao are also steamed buns made with flour and stuffed with 'charsui' or roast pork. Also steamed are *cheong fun*, which literally means 'intestine noodles' because when these large, thin, steamed rice noodles are rolled around meat or shrimp, they glisten and do look somewhat like their namesake. They are sought after for their silken, slippery texture. Sweet soy sauce is poured over the dish just before it is cut and served.

Potstickers (*wo tip*; *guo tie* in Mandarin) are a northern Chinese style of dumpling. Thin rounds of wheat pasta, usually with a ground meat and cabbage filling and crimped along the top, are steam fried. The name comes from the crust that forms on the bottom of the dumplings as they brown and stick to the pan. Potstickers are not considered as traditional Cantonese *dim sum* by some people.

Dumplings are usually accompanied by dipping sauces such as sweet and sour.

Besides dumplings there are other steamed dishes such as pork spareribs, chopped into small cubes and flavoured with black bean or plum sauce. There are also steamed beef balls flavoured with tangerine, and so on. Some *dim sum* are enjoyed more for their texture than their flavour, such as beef tripe or chicken feet.

Deep fried *dim sum* include favourites such as spring rolls, taro croquettes and *hom sui gok*. These are round dumplings made with glutinous rice flour, slightly sweetened and filled with a loose mixture of meats, dried shrimp and vegetables, bound together in a light gravy. Formed into slightly elongated ovals with gentle points at each end, the dumplings are fried until they are golden brown and puffed up.

Selection of *dim sum* in bamboo containers.

Roast meats such as roast duck are also liked. Cantonese-style roast duck is usually served in portions of a half or quarter bird. There are a number of different styles of roasting the duck but whichever style, the skin is usually fairly crisp and the meat pink. The duck is cut roughly into slices before serving, but the bones remain in the duck and the whole thing is reassembled to look complete. It is served with a sauce, most often a sweet plum sauce which contrasts with the savoury and succulent duck.

Chicken feet (*fung zao*), referred to as 'phoenix claws', are popular with the Chinese, although perhaps an acquired taste for Westerners. With claws removed, they are deep-fried then braised in a rich black bean sauce until tender.

'Cakes' made out of radish, taro and water chestnut also appear on the *dim sum* menu. Radish cakes (sometimes referred to as 'turnip') are made from mashed white radish (called mooli or daikon) mixed with dried shrimp and pork sausage, steamed and then cut into slices and pan fried. Cakes made out of crispy water chestnut are see-through and clear.

Some sweet *dim sum* probably derive from either British or Portuguese influences and include mango

Mooncakes and tea.

pudding and custard tarts, but there are also Chinese-style ones such as sesame balls made of sweetened glutinous rice dough covered with sesame seeds before being deep fried. These are a popular Chinese New Year treat. Mooncakes are baked specially to celebrate the mid-autumn festival with its full moon. There are different types: the Cantonese mooncake is made from a rich pastry case filled with a sweet and dense paste made from red bean or lotus seed. Traditional mooncakes have an imprint of a good luck symbol on top.

Chopsticks are the traditional eating utensils for *dim sum*. *Dim sum* dishes are served in small portions which makes them convenient for eating with chopsticks. The drinking of tea is as important to *dim sum*

as the food. The server typically asks first what tea the customer would like to drink. Several types of tea are offered: green teas such as Dragon Well, oolong teas such as Iron Goddess of Mercy, earthy Pu-erh teas and scented teas such as chrysanthemum, rose and jasmine. Jasmine tea is probably the most popular tea served at *yum cha* restaurants.

There are certain customs or etiquette with regard to drinking tea in tea houses and restaurants. It is most gracious to be the first to pour tea and customary to pour tea for others before filling one's own teacup. A common custom among the Cantonese to thank or show appreciation to the person pouring the tea is tapping the bent index finger (if you are single), or tapping both the index and middle finger (if you are married). This symbolizes the gesture of bowing and is known as 'finger kowtow'. This gesture is said to recreate a tale of imperial obeisance, traced to Emperor Qianlong, who used to travel incognito. As the story goes, the Emperor, while visiting South China, went into a tea house with his companions and in order to maintain his anonymity he poured his companions some tea, which was a great honour. His stunned companions did not want to give away the Emperor's identity in public by bowing. Finally, one of them tapped three fingers on the table (one finger representing their bowed head and the other two representing their prostrate arms) and the clever Emperor understood. From then on this has been the practice. It is also a practical way of showing appreciation, given the number of times tea is poured during a meal. It is a timesaver in noisy restaurants, as the person being served might be speaking to someone else or have food in their mouth. If a diner does not wish for a refill at that time, the fingers are used to 'wave off' or politely decline more tea. Teapot lids should be left open or ajar to signal for a refill.

Cha chaan teng – tea food halls

DIM SUM snacks are very much Chinese and the tea served is traditional Chinese tea, but since the 1950s Hong Kong has become famous for another type of tea restaurant. In the early days of Hong Kong Western-style food was regarded as a luxury and served only in high-class restaurants, most of which did not serve local people. After the Second World War, Hong Kong became increasingly cosmopolitan. The Westernized middle classes began to broaden their palates. *Cha chaan teng* were set up and became popular, particularly in Hong Kong, Macau, Taiwan and parts of Guangdong. They provided a variety of tastes – a fusion of the cuisines of the various transient populations. They were also regarded as 'cheap Western food', sometimes nicknamed 'soy sauce Western food'. The service is fast and efficient, resembling Hong Kong's fast-paced lifestyle, and they remain open from 7 a.m. to 11 p.m.

When customers are seated they are first served with tea (usually weak tea called 'clear tea', made from inexpensive black tea). Although the tea is for drinking some customers use it to rinse their utensils before eating. However, the favourite tea drunk at these establishments is Hong Kong-style milk tea which originates from British colonial rule over Hong Kong; the British tradition of afternoon tea, where black tea is served with milk and sugar, grew popular in Hong Kong. The Hong Kong tea is, however, usually made from a mix of several types of black tea (the proportions usually kept as a commercial secret) and, instead of ordinary milk, evaporated milk and sugar, the last of which is usually added by the customer. It is called milk tea to distinguish it from Chinese tea, which is served without milk. It is sometimes called 'silk sock' or 'silk stocking' milk tea because it is brewed and filtered in a large tea sock. The tea sock is reputed to make the tea smoother; it gradually develops an intense brown colour as a result of prolonged tea making and resembles a silk stocking. (Some say that originally a silk stocking was used to filter the tea.) Some versions of the tea use condensed milk instead of evaporated milk and sugar, giving the tea a richer, silkier taste. It is then sometimes called *cha chow*. Milk tea is sometimes served iced but not with ice cubes. A glass of the tea is placed in an icy water bath so that the tea becomes cold without getting diluted by melting ice. This tea is called 'ice bath milk tea'.

Another drink served, which also originated in Hong Kong, is a mix of coffee and tea called *yuangyang* (yin-yang). According to Chinese medicine, coffee is 'hot' and tea is 'cold' in nature and this mix therefore makes the best combination to drink. Other drinks served include lemon tea, coffee and soft drinks.

Customers are spoiled for choice when they eat at a *cha chaan teng*. Menus are scrawled on all four walls, etched into the mirrors or perched in plastic holders on the table. Dishes vary from simple toast (but topped with condensed milk or peanut butter or jam and butter) or French toast to macaroni or spaghetti to egg tart. The French toast comes 'Hong Kong style' with variations. A common version is a sort of syrup-slathered, deep-fried peanut butter sandwich. Another version comes stuffed with satay beef slices and a sweet version called Kaya is made by smearing sweet coconut jam between two slices of bread which are then fried. Other Hong Kong sandwiches, including the club sandwich, almost always consist of lightly toasted, crustless white bread slices with various fillings such as egg, tuna, ham or other meat. Fried rice and noodle dishes (including instant noodles) are served up in endless variations, including in soup dishes. A feature of *cha chaan teng* is the set meals. There are sets for different meals throughout the day: for breakfast, lunch, afternoon tea and dinner. Other 'sets' include a 'nutritious set', 'constant set', 'fast set' (immediately served) and 'special set', which is the chef's (or manager's) recommendation. Each of the sets usually includes a soup, main course and a drink. The Cantonese love of poetry comes out in some of the names of dishes, such as phoenix claws for chicken feet, and the pineapple bun takes its name from its vague resemblance to a pineapple, even though it does not contain any pineapple. It is a regular bun topped with a sweet crusty pastry.

Recently Hong Kong's *cha chaan teng* restaurants have started to disappear, mainly because of the limited land and expensive rents. They are gradually being replaced by chain restaurants.

Japan

TEA DRINKING and the rituals connected with it play an important part in the Japanese way of life. They have evolved their own special teatime in the form of the tea ceremony, *cha-no-yu*, which means 'hot water tea' and is also called *chado*, 'the way of tea'.

The tea ceremony owes its unique role in Japanese culture to the Zen priests who developed the ritual of tea drinking and made it into a vehicle for Buddhist philosophy in the eighth and ninth centuries. Monks drank powdered tea from a communal bowl before an image of Bodhidharma. In the fifteenth century a Zen priest called Shuko created the tea ceremony and became the first great tea master. He combined the rituals of preparing and drinking tea with a spiritual sense of humility and tranquillity. It was a poetic response to nature, a way of celebrating and appreciating the natural environment. In the sixteenth century Zen tea master Sen no Rikyu (1522–1591) amended the principles for the tea ritual into the form practised today. It is less elaborate and focuses on harmony and respect, purity and serenity. At its most profound, the tea ceremony is a quest for spiritual fulfilment through devotion to the making and serving of tea. When asked by one of his disciples what the most important things were in following the 'Way of Tea', he proposed the observance of seven rules:

Make a delicious bowl of tea:
Lay out the wood charcoal to heat the water.
Arrange the flowers as they are in the fields.
In summer evoke coolness; in winter, warmth.

Anticipate the time for everything.

Be prepared for rain.

Show the greatest attention to each of your
   guests.

The tea ceremony influenced all of Japan's fine arts, including garden design, flower arrangement, architecture, calligraphy, painting, lacquer and ceramic arts. Specially built tearooms were constructed, set amid traditional Japanese gardens. The tearooms were intended to have an austere simplicity with no furniture, just mats. The walls were sliding partitions and the doors only 36 inches high, so all must bow to enter,

Ginkaku-ji (Silver Pavilion), Kyoto.

acknowledging they are equal before the tea. The rooms were decorated with flowers of the season and poems were read celebrating the season. The food served was also not only seasonal but represented the season in its form and appearance. Dumplings were made to look like chestnuts in the autumn; rice cakes resembled bamboo shoots in spring.

The first tea house was Ginkaku-ji, or the Silver Pavilion, built in Kyoto by the eighth Shogun, Yoshimasa, in the fifteenth century. It was here that Yoshimasa practised the rites of the *cha-no-yu* during his later years in retirement.

There are two types of tea ceremony: one is called *chakai*, which is an informal tea drinking that usually lasts under an hour. *Usucha*, a thin tea made with matcha (Japanese powdered green tea) is served with sweets called *wagashi* which are eaten to offset the tea's bitterness.

The second type of tea ceremony is *chaji*, the full tea ceremony, which can last for up to four hours. Since it is not desirable to drink the strong powdered green tea made with matcha – which is not steeped but whipped in a bowl with a small bamboo whisk, described as a 'froth of liquid jade' – on an empty stomach, the practice arose of serving a meal beforehand. This meal is called *cha kaiseki*.[8]

The tea ceremony takes place in a special pavilion (*chashitsu*), which is reached via a winding garden path symbolic of a mountain path and begins with *cha kaiseki*. Hot dishes are served in various courses. First there is a tray bearing a bowl of rice, miso soup and a dish of vinegared fish or vegetables, or sashimi. Sake is poured by the host, then *nimono* (simmered food) is served. There are many different kinds of *nimono* according to the seasoning used (sake, soy sauce, egg yolk, ginger and miso) and it is one of the principal

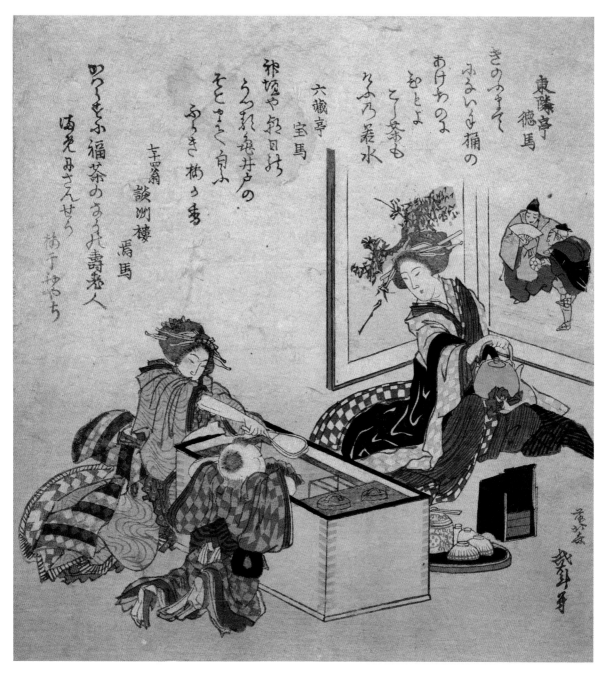

Wakamizu no fukucha (First Tea of the Year), a Japanese print from a woodcut by artist Hokusai Katsushika, 1816, depicting a tea party with two women, one holding a teapot, and a child. The first tea of the year is called *shincha*, the fragrance of spring. According to the time of harvest Japanese tea growers distinguish three types of tea: *shincha*; *niban cha*, the second tea of the year; and *sanban cha*, the third tea of the year.

Wagashi

THESE ARE the Japanese equivalent of confectionary, cakes, cookies and candy. They are not just savoured at the tea ceremony but also typically enjoyed in combination with a cup of green tea at any time.

Wagashi comes from the Japanese word *kashi* (the character pronounced 'wa' denotes things Japanese, while the characters for 'gashi', an alliteration of *kashi*, have come to mean sweets). Originally *kashi* meant literally 'fruit and nuts', which were Japan's earliest snacks. These snacks included dried persimmons, chestnuts and Japanese nutmeg (*kaya*). They were eaten between meals in the ancient period (dating back to the Yayoi Era, 300 BCE–300 CE) but later were served as 'sweets' for the tea ceremony in the 1500s.

Japanese confectionery developed mainly during the time when Japan was exposed to foreign trade. Trade with Portugal and Spain brought new ingredients and recipes, including the development of *wagashi*. The Portuguese popularized the use of sugar and disseminated the knowledge of its use in confectionery, allowing the traditional savoury snacks to be sweetened.

Wagashi have evolved into an exquisite art form, especially in the ancient imperial capital, Kyoto. They represent the beauty of Japan and the essence of Japanese culture. The shapes, colours and designs are inspired by Japanese literature, painting and textiles. They often represent evocative images from nature and are literally a feast for the eyes. They are appreciated for their subtle aromas, texture and appearance, and even the sound made when being eaten. Artistic names are given, derived from classical prose or poetry; some may reflect the various faces of nature, such as flowers or animals.

Wagashi are made with a diversity of ingredients (though largely from various beans and grains that are the staples of the traditional Japanese diet) and methods of preparation (which includes steaming, baking and

Selection of *wagashi*.

frying). They are delicate and fragrant and their textures vary from softness to moistness or crispness. By changing their colours and shapes confectioners developed many varieties and new types continue to be created.

Types of *wagashi* include *namagashi*, *han namagashi* and *higashi*. *Namagashi*, literally raw *kashi*, are classified as 'moist'. Apart from the use of refined sugar, highly milled rice flour is used and a paste (*an*) made from starchy pulses and sugar gives the sweets their soft texture. The delicate and beautiful forms of *namagashi* are hand-made and reflect the nature of Japan's four seasons. February is the time for plum blossom motifs, March for peach and April cherry blossoms. In autumn there is the golden beauty of leaves and also chrysanthemums and persimmons, while winter is the time for winter plum blossoms.

Han namagashi, literally half-raw *kashi*, are less moist and *higashi* are 'dry' sweets made from a paste of rice flour, sugar and starch. The paste is pressed into moulds. It is these sweets which are often used in the tea ceremony but *higashi* can also refer to any kind of dry sweets, such as toffee.

The appreciation of the *wagashi* art forms is an important part of enjoying these confections, especially in the tea ceremony.

ways of serving vegetables and fish. This is followed by *yakimono* (grilled food such as fish). Further rice and a clear soup called *suimono* is then served 'to wash the chopsticks'. Rare delicacies follow representing the bounty of both land and sea. Finally a pickle called *ko no mono* is served with *yuto* (hot washings of the rice pot served in a lacquerware container shaped like a teapot without a handle).[9] At the end of the meal the host offers everyone the sweet confection *namagashi*.

After *cha kaiseki* the guests retire to the garden. This gives the host time to tidy up after the meal and prepare for the main part of the ceremony – *cha-no-yu*. The etiquette is quite complicated and elaborate; tea-making utensils (kept in a box called a *chabako*) and tea bowls,

as well as the decorations in the tearoom, are carefully chosen and coordinated in keeping with *wabi* aesthetics (*wabi* meaning understated beauty).

The host handles all the required instruments carefully. Water is heated in a kettle placed on a charcoal stove sunk into the middle of the floor. When all is ready the guests are invited to re-enter the tearoom for the drinking of matcha – powdered green tea. First a very rich, thick, paste-like mixture called *koicha* is made by kneading matcha. The host does not partake and he prepares for each guest in succession, the same bowl being cleaned and reused. The guest must hold the bowl in both hands, with the porcelain pattern turned towards the host. The tea is bitter and strong and is

Hiroshige Andō, woodcut print of the Teahouse Hiraiwa at Mukojuma, 1835–7.
The print shows the exterior view of the teahouse, with three women returning
from viewing the cherry blossoms and two men trying to attract their attention.

Japanese tea ceremony with four businessmen.

drunk in its entirety. It is considered mandatory to make some appreciative comment on the beauty of the setting, the utensils and so on. The tea ceremony concludes with the host offering a sweetmeat (*namagashi*) to each guest followed by a weaker tea called *usucha*, a foamy infusion which is made using less matcha and more water, served in a different bowl. The matcha, which is

Adachi (Shōsai) Ginkō, woodblock print of the tea ceremony, Meiji period (1890). A group of ladies in exquisite kimonos attending a tea ceremony.

kept in a lacquered tea box or caddy called a *chaire*, is scooped into the tea bowl (*chawan*) by a special teaspoon or scoop called a *chasaku*. Hot water is added and then whisked vigorously with a bamboo whisk (*chasen*) to produce a pale green liquid with a light surface froth.

Learning to perform the tea ceremony requires lengthy training. Instructors must serve long years of apprenticeship before becoming qualified masters.

Although the tea ceremony is still practised today, it obviously encounters some difficulties in modern Japanese life. The tea ceremony can only be performed in a private tea house which conforms to certain proportions and materials and is set in a garden. However, the mistress of an ordinary house can perform the ceremony if a room has been set aside specifically for that purpose. She can invite guests, in writing, three or four

Tea time under the cherry blossoms in Tokyo, Japan.
Woodcut printed on tissue paper by Helen Hyde, *c.* 1914.

weeks in advance to celebrate an occasion such as the blossoming of cherry trees or to honour the arrival of a friend in town, or even just to admire the moon.[10]

Kissaten

MANY JAPANESE PEOPLE still like to go to traditional, old-style tea houses called *kissaten* (literally 'tea drinking shop') although today many people, especially the young, consider them old-fashioned and run-down and they seem to be dying out.

The decor often dates back to the early to mid-twentieth century up to about the mid-1970s. Some are elegant or retro or perhaps a bit shabby but at the same time can appear charming. They are integral to Japanese culture and serve not just tea (green or black) but also coffee. The menu is Western-influenced Japanese food with items such as old-fashioned sandwiches made with *shokupan*, the ubiquitous white and pillowy square-shaped sliced bread with a soft crust. One such sandwich is *katsusando* (pork cutlet sandwich with a sweet and savoury sauce). Light meals are available such as spaghetti Napolitan (spaghetti with ketchup, stir-fried onions, ham and pureed tomato), *omurice* (rice omelette) or curry rice. Western-influenced desserts that have been known and loved in Japan for generations are also available, such as *kasutera* (Castella cake), a sweet sponge cake which was introduced to Japan in the sixteenth century by the Portuguese. Because the Japanese did not have ovens and used an improvised one, the cake has the texture of a steamed cake. *Purin* (caramel custard or flan) is also popular.

As *kissaten* are dying out, cafés are becoming more popular. There is a distinct difference. Cafés are seen as more modern, with chic and contemporary decor and with trendy menus attracting more young people. While the coffee served in a *kissaten* might stick to old-fashioned filtered coffee, in a café the selection is likely to include more recent coffee drinks such as espresso and cappuccino. The tea drunk is now more likely to be an oolong or black or, the latest craze, scented or flavoured teas, often imported from France and known as French tea.

Many kinds of tea are now drunk in Japan. Most are green teas but some black teas are imported from Ceylon and India and are popular on the menus of leading hotels and restaurants. Teas are also imported from Britain, including from the Tregothnan estate in Cornwall which grows tea for blending. Black tea is always drunk from Western-style teacups, whereas green tea is drunk from Japanese-style cups or, if the tea is powdered, from tea bowls.

Korea

KOREA HAS A rich tea drinking culture. During the reign of Queen Sŏndŏk (CE 632–47) green tea (*nok ch'a*) was introduced from Tang China although it was not until the reign of King Heungdeok (826–36) that a royal envoy, Kim Taeryom, returned from a mission to China bearing seeds of the tea plant. The king ordered the seeds to be planted on the warm slopes of Mount Chiri, which is still the centre of tea cultivation in Korea.

At first tea was drunk by the privileged classes such as royalty, warriors and high-ranking Buddhist monks, who used it as a meditational aid. It was prized for its medicinal properties and reserved for special occasions or served to esteemed guests. Tea was considered a gift, a means to discipline the mind and body. The philosophy of tea art, or the 'way of tea', was already developing during this period. Tea drinking was viewed as a spiritual, religious activity leading to higher levels of inner awakening, if not total enlightenment. Buddhist monks

Korean and Western women having tea outside the Nak Tong Mission
House in Seoul, Korea, in 1910. The Western women are missionary
teachers from the Society for the Propagation of the Gospel.

offered tea to the Buddha three times daily and for important rites. Visitors to temples were served tea instead of wine. Villages called *tach'on*, literally 'tea villages', sprang up near temples to supply the great amount of tea the monks consumed.

Tea became an essential part of state rites. A special office, the Tabang (tea chamber), was set up to deal with all matters of tea and also to officiate over tea rites at important national events such as royal weddings, funerals, coronations and diplomatic receptions.

Royalty developed an elaborate ritual for tea drinking. Ceremonies related to drinking tea at the royal court and elsewhere developed into an elaborate and decorous but also solemn tea ceremony, accompanied by music when it was the king or crown prince who were having the tea. Pavilions and arbours were built in the palace for the purpose of holding tea parties and poetry readings for court officials.

Other people such as aristocrats and officials had their own way of enjoying tea in a more relaxed manner, taking the form of parties at scenic locations. There was music, dance, poetry and even wine. The tradition of composing verses in praise of tea started at this time.[11] The ceremonies related to tea drinking developed into the custom known as the tea ceremony (*tado* or *dado*). Specialized implements were developed, such as a brazier for boiling water, bowls, spoons and pots. Types and qualities of tea were developed, as well as a grading system for the taste of water. The etiquette for the tea ceremony is important but central to the ritual is the harmony of water and tea. Ūisun (1786–1866), the famous monk and tea-master, wrote: 'In brewing, delicacy, in storing, aridity, in steeping, purity. Delicacy, aridity, and purity are essential to the tea ceremony.'[12] At tea ceremonies confections called *dasik* (literally meaning 'eatery for food') are normally served to offset the bitterness of the tea. *Dasik* are bite-sized confections made with two main ingredients: a powdered plant base such as rice flour or mung bean starch and honey. *Dasik* are pressed in a wooden or porcelain mould into round shapes and impressed with a pattern such as flowers and Chinese characters for longevity, wealth, health and peace. They are made in different colours representing the five elements of nature: red, green, yellow, white and black, using natural ingredients such as flower extracts. Pine pollen, a costly additive, turns the *dasik* yellow.[13]

Other 'teas' popular with Koreans are not true teas. There are three types of other 'teas': medicinal herb teas made with ginseng or ginger, fruit-based teas made with fruits such as jujube, citron, plum and quince, and grain-based teas such as barley tea (*pori ch'a*). *Omija cha* (*omija* means 'five flavours' – sweetness, sourness, bitterness, saltiness and pungency) is a fruit tea made with magnolia berries and can be served hot or cold. All are drunk for their medicinal properties. Barley 'tea', made with roasted barley and boiling water, is the standard beverage drunk with a meal and is served hot or cold.

Although South Korea has been embracing coffee culture in recent years, all these different teas are available today in the numerous South Korean tea houses in places such as Seoul, Bukchon and Insadong. A variety of snacks to be taken with tea can be ordered, such as steam pumpkin cake and red bean soup. Dawon in Insadong is a well-known traditional tea house that operates in a *hanok* (traditional Korean house). Various 'teas' are on offer with traditional snacks such as assorted *ttoek* (rice cakes) and *yugwa* (a deep-fried sweet rice cake).

Taiwan

TAIWAN (FORMERLY FORMOSA) produces some of the most sought-after teas in the world but is best known for its oolong teas with their exceptional flavours and scent. One of the most famous and rarest is 'Oriental Beauty' (the name, it is said, was bestowed upon it by Queen Elizabeth II when she was presented a sample by a British tea merchant). This tea is also sometimes known as Champagne Formosa and with its deep reddish gold liquor and rich and smooth taste is highly appreciated by connoisseurs. Other renowned oolongs include Oolong Imperial, Grand Oolong Fancy, Tung Ting and a lightly fermented tea – pouchong – which is often scented with rose or jasmine.

The first Europeans to land on the shores of Formosa in the sixteenth century were Portuguese sailors. They were so impressed by the island's beauty that they called it Isla Formosa, meaning 'Beautiful Island'. The island has ideal conditions for growing tea owing to its geographical position, the mountainous terrain and a sub-tropical climate, but it was not until the mid-1850s that Chinese settlers from Fujian Province brought seedlings and began to grow tea on a large scale. They brought not only their tea-growing and processing skills but their tea culture as well.

The tea-loving Taiwanese have a rich culture with tea ceremonies and tea houses; tea is part of the social fabric of Taiwan. It is essential during business negotiations, wedding banquets and funeral services. 'Come in and drink tea' is a standard greeting for guests. The government has opened tea museums, holds tea competitions and throws tea festivals.

The Taiwanese have developed their own tea ritual. Like the Chinese and Japanese tea ceremonies, it should be performed in a tranquil environment to aid the appreciation of the tea. The various stages of the ceremony must be performed with great respect. In the 1970s the fragrance or aroma cup was created. It is distinguished by its cylindrical shape, which enhances the fragrance of the tea. The fragrance cup is paired with a small drinking cup. This way of preparing tea was specifically designed for appreciating the aromas of fragrant Taiwan oolongs.

The fragrance cup, the drinking cup and the tea vessel (which can be a teapot or bowl with a cover called a *gaiwan*) are warmed with hot water. Tea is steeped and allowed to infuse for a few moments. The tea is then poured into the fragrance cup, which is then covered with the drinking cup by inverting the drinking cup so that the pair resemble a mushroom. The two cups are lifted together with the thumb and middle finger of one hand and then quickly flipped over, transferring the tea into the drinking cup. The aroma cup is lifted off the drinking cup and is wafted a little before sniffing and enjoying the fragrance and then drinking the tea from the drinking cup.

Recently this ritual has waned somewhat and many people just smell the lid of the teapot or *gaiwan* when the tea is brewing.[14] Many Taiwanese enjoy their tea at the numerous tea houses which are designed to cut out the hustle and bustle of the hectic pace of city life and provide a peaceful atmosphere for relaxation. They have no outside windows and are constructed around a central courtyard that usually has a large fishpond. Here people linger and chat over pot after pot of good oolong tea, and perhaps watch the fish. Tea houses are

Wu wei tea house in Taichung, Taiwan. *Wu wei* means 'effortless' and the tea house aims to be a 'classic' Chinese tea house. It is a wooden construction of two storeys around a fish pond.

also cultural establishments and are often used to promote traditional arts. Calligraphy and paintings are often on display and some tea houses offer concerts of traditional music.

One famous tea house combining fine tea, history and nostalgia is the Wistaria Tea House in Taipei. This charming former Japanese-era wooden house was built in 1920 as a dormitory for naval personnel. The building was renovated in 1981 as a tea house and became a meeting place for political dissidents. Since then it has been and continues to be popular with artists and writers. The tea house, which has a 1930s decor, serves a fine selection of oolongs plus green teas and some rare Pu-erh teas. To accompany the tea an assortment of snacks are available such as mung bean cakes, coconut balls, Phoenix's Eyes (cakes made with sugar and glutinous rice) and plums preserved in tea.

The Taiwanese love of tea has also resulted in a popular trend called 'bubble tea' which has not only caught on in many places where there is a large Chinese population, such as North America and the Philippines, but in other places including Britain. The drink originally started as a treat in the late 1980s for thirsty children who after lessons would buy refreshing tea at tea stands outside the school. One innovative concession holder, to the joy of her clientele, started to add different fruit flavourings to her iced milky tea which she then shook vigorously to mix everything together. Bubbles formed on top. The children loved the new

dimension to the sweet, cool taste of their tea and other concession holders followed suit. Someone then had the idea of adding tapioca pearls to the tea. These pearls sank to the bottom of the cup, thus creating bubbles on the bottom as well. Bubble tea is usually served in see-through plastic cups or containers with an extra wide straw to suck up the pearls, which have a soft and chewy consistency. And, for even more fun, the children sometimes like to blow the balls out from the straw to shoot at targets or even each other! Bubble tea has acquired many names, some of them wacky, such as *boba*, *QQ* (which means chewy in Chinese) and in the West 'booboo'.

Bubble tea can be made with different types of tea: black, green or white. Different flavourings include fruits such as mango, strawberry, lychee, coconut and so on and other non-fruit flavours such as chocolate, barley, almond, ginger and rose. Some are made with coffee. One version which originated in Hong Kong

A variety of colourful flavoured bubble teas.

consists of half black tea and half coffee. Milk is now optional. Some cafés use a non-dairy milk substitute for those who avoid dairy products.

Although bubble tea originated in Taiwan, bubble tea 'mash-ups' are becoming popular, inspired by flavours from other cuisines, such as saffron and cardamom from India, rosewater from Persia and hibiscus flowers from Mexico. Other ingredients are now also used instead of tapioca balls, such as jelly in small cubes, stars or strips. Another version does not contain any tea or coffee. The base is a flavouring blended with ice making a slushy-like drink to which tapioca balls are added. These drinks are often called 'snow bubble'. The variations are endless and no doubt bubble tea will continue to be enjoyed around the world.

Eight
Other Teatimes from Around the World

THE RITUAL OF TEA DRINKING and teatime is as diverse around the world as the different ways of preparing it. As tea migrated from the East, tea drinking absorbed national influences and took on different styles and uses. So too have customs surrounding the ritual of teatimes: the different foods and how they are served with tea. These are illustrated in this short round up of teatimes in other places from Africa to Indonesia and on to South America.

Morocco and North Africa

NONE OF THE COUNTRIES in North Africa produce their own tea and the history of tea drinking in Morocco is debatable. Some writers, including John Griffiths in his book *Tea: The Drink That Changed the World* (2007), have recounted the story that in 1854 British ships with cargoes of green tea from China were bound for Scandinavia and the Baltic states when they were refused permission to dock and unload. Looking for another market it seems the ships ended up in the ports of Morocco and managed to sell their tea, thus launching tea drinking there. The Moroccans, who had been drinking herbal infusions for centuries, took to drinking green tea with enthusiasm, making their own refreshing drink by flavouring the tea (usually gunpowder green tea) with fresh mint – a native herb already being used as an infusion – and adding plenty of sugar. The mint used is spearmint, *Mentha viridis*, and is considered by many to be the only variety that should be used.

The making of this tea, called *shai bil nana* (tea with mint), which is drunk at various times throughout the day and after meals, is steeped in ritual and considered an art. It is usually made by the master of the house and is traditionally made in a richly engraved silver teapot to which he will add green tea. The tea is sweetened in the pot by adding a chunk of cane sugarloaf and a handful of mint is also added before pouring in boiling water and allowing it to infuse for a few moments. The art is to pour the tea from the pot from a height into small colourful glasses, usually set on an ornate silver tray, in order to form a froth (*keshkusha*) on the surface. Traditionally, three glasses of tea are drunk. The amount of time the tea has been steeping gives each of the glasses of tea a unique flavour, as described in this famous Maghrebi proverb:

The first glass is as gentle as life,
the second is as strong as love,
The third is as bitter as death.

Sweet pastries are often served with tea, such as gazelle horns which are stuffed with almonds and cinnamon, or *ghoriba*, a small round biscuit made with almonds. Stuffed dates are also popular.

The drinking of tea infused with mint spread from Morocco to Algeria, Tunisia, Libya and to the nomadic tribes of Berbers and Tuareg in the Sahara. Black tea, made strong and sweet but without milk, is also drunk and is sometimes infused with mint. In Egypt, where tea is also called *shai*, green tea, which is a fairly recent arrival, is not so popular. Black tea is preferred – drunk strong and sweet, with no milk, but often flavoured with mint. In cafés herbal teas or tisanes are also often served.

Moroccan mint tea served in decorative glasses with pastries and dates.

Teatime in Patagonia

WELSH TEATIME traditions can also be found in Patagonia, a region which is at the southern end of South America, shared by Argentina and Chile. In 1865, 153 Welsh men, women and children boarded a tea-clipper, the *Mimosa*, in Liverpool and set out on an 8,000-mile journey. They were fleeing cultural and religious persecution and were hoping to find a new home where they could worship in their own way, speak the Welsh language and retain their national identity.

After eight weeks they landed in the Golfo Nuevo in northeastern Patagonia. They had been expecting a green and fertile land like Wales but found a barren and inhospitable pampa. They faced bitterly cold winters, floods, crop failures, no water, food shortages and no forests to provide shelter. However, the settlers persevered and founded a colony in the Chubut Valley and with irrigation and water management the tiny band of Welsh settlers survived. Today, almost 150 years later, there are more than 50,000 people claiming Welsh descent in this corner of Patagonia. The town of Gaiman has a key attraction – a collection of traditional Welsh tearooms. These *casas de té* serve up the finest afternoon teas with *torta galesa* (sometimes called *torta negra*), a rich fruitcake made with nuts, candied fruit, molasses, spices and alcohol. Other teatime specialities include Patagonian cream tart and Patagonian carrot pudding. Also on offer are items such *bara brith*, sweet and savoury scones, hot buttered toast, home-made jams and preserves, as well as – of course – a pot of perfectly brewed tea.

Tea flavoured with mint is refreshing in hot climates and is popular in other Arab countries such as Iraq. Tea is often served as the finale to Arabian feasts. In the Gulf states guests are sometimes welcomed with pitcher-shaped flasks filled with a weak, delicate tea infused with saffron. Regional tastes vary and other spices and herbs are often used to flavour tea, such as cinnamon or dried limes.

East Africa

ALTHOUGH ETHIOPIA IS PRIMARILY a coffee-producing and coffee-drinking country, tea is drunk throughout the day. Spicy wholewheat bread or fried pastries are often an accompaniment. In Kenya tea is one of the main exports and much of it comes to Britain. Teatime is a colonial holdover from the British, but the style of tea comes from India and is called *chai*, made with milk and sugar added and sometimes flavoured with spices such as cinnamon, cardamom and ginger. Tea is the national drink of Uganda and is also a major export. Tea drinking reflects British, East Indian and Arab influences. Wealthy Ugandans drink tea the British way with milk and sugar and it is sipped from porcelain cups and saucers. Ugandans of East Indian culture make *chai* – milky and sweet. Some Ugandans drink black tea with lots of added sugar, reflecting the Arab influence. Snacks to be served with tea include samosas, peanuts and bread.

Indonesia

TEA IS GROWN in many parts of Indonesia and is light and fragrant. The best-quality ones are exported to Japan, North America and Europe, where they are usually used in blends or in making tea bags.

Tea is the main beverage and drinking customs vary according to the region. Some Indonesians drink tea without any sugar (*teh pahit* or *teh tawar*, meaning 'bitter tea') but in Java, where there are sugar plantations, *teh manis* (tea with sugar) is drunk. Milk or sweetened condensed milk is sometimes added to tea (*teh susu*). Tea is drunk from cups, sometimes made of clay, and glasses. Teatime here is not really at a specific time; it is enjoyed throughout the day. In many restaurants tea is automatically served to customers without charge. It is really a substitute for water, partly for health reasons, since the quality of drinking water is poor in some parts of the country and the water has been boiled to make the tea. In busy public areas such as railway stations or bus terminals street vendors sell sweet, perfumed tea or glasses of iced tea (*teh es*) sweetened with sugar, a welcome drink when the weather is hot. At home, at about half past four in the afternoon, tea is often served with snacks. Rice cakes are popular and there are numerous varieties including *nagasari*, a rice cake with banana, and *ondé ondé*, small rice cakes rolled in grated coconut. Fried bananas (*pisang goring*) are also popular with tea, as are sweet sago rolls with palm sugar syrup called *ongol-ongol* and a sort of crêpe called *dadar guling* which is made with pandan and has a sweet coconut filling.

South America

ALTHOUGH A NUMBER OF COUNTRIES in South America now produce tea, it is not universally drunk. Brazil, the largest coffee producer in the world, is primarily a coffee-drinking nation. However, tea drinking has been increasing in popularity since the early 1970s among the middle classes. In the big cities tea houses (*casa de cha*) have sprung up and women can enjoy meeting their friends while drinking tea with cakes, biscuits, chocolates or bread. Some tea houses serve salads, sandwiches and light meals. Tea can be ordered with or without milk and sugar. Iced tea is also popular, as well as green tea.

In contrast, on the other side of the Andes, in Chile, teatime is well established. Called *onces*, teatime is a tradition inherited from the British who settled in Chile in the 1800s to mine for saltpetre. Taken in the late afternoon, usually any time between four and eight o'clock, *onces* is as popular today as it was a century ago. *Onces* can range from a simple cup of tea with a biscuit or a slice of cake, to something more substantial, with some toasted *marraqueta* (traditional Chilean bread, sometimes called *pan batido* (whipped bread) or *pan francé* (French bread), composed of a pair of attached soft rolls baked with another pair attached spread with butter, mashed avocado, jam, cheese or *manjar* (milk caramel, like *dulce de leche*). *Sopaipillas*, deep-fried pastries or bread, are topped with various sauces or ingredients such as avocado, cheese, *manjar* or a sweet sauce called *chancaca*. *Chilenitos*, traditional Chilean wafers filled with *manjar* or caramel and sprinkled with icing sugar, are also popular with the sweet-loving Chileans.

Onces is now also taken outside the home. Cafés have sprung up in the towns and cities where friends meet to chat and discuss the news of the day and enjoy *onces* together.

Recipes

Tea Drinks

Tea is a versatile beverage and there are many different ways of preparing it depending on the type of tea (white, yellow, oolong, black, purple and Pu-erh), the region, the occasion and individual tastes. In Britain and Ireland most people prefer black tea with milk. In Russia they drink tea without milk but add a slice of lemon. In America they like it iced. In India and Central Asia spices are often added. In North Africa they add mint. The Chinese and Japanese have a preference for green tea. These different styles have been described in the relevant chapters of this book.

The quality and temperature of the water is also important. Some people use bottled spring water and a thermometer. Some teas are better infused for a short time, others for longer.

Tea is often an ingredient in hot and cold punches or fruit cups.

Tea à la Russe

Tea à la Russe (tea 'Russian style') became popular in the United States in the mid-nineteenth century. Marion Harland (1886) gave this recipe.

Slice fresh, juicy lemons; pare them carefully, lay a piece in the bottom of each cup; sprinkle with white sugar and pour the tea, very hot and strong, over them.

Or,

Send around the sliced lemon with the cups of tea, that each person may squeeze in the juice to please himself. Some leave the peel on, and profess to like the bitter flavour which it imparts to the beverage. The truth is, the taste for this (now) fashionable refreshment is so completely an acquired liking, that you had best leave to your guests the matter of 'peel on' or 'peel off'. There are those whom not even fashion can reconcile to the peculiar 'smack' of lemon-rind after it has been subjected to the action of a boiling liquid.

Tea à la Russe is generally, if not invariably, drunk without cream, and is plentifully sweetened. It is very popular at 'high teas' and 'kettledrums', so much in vogue at this time, – tea being to women, say the cynics, a species of mild intoxicant, of which they are not to be defrauded by evening dinners and their sequitur of black coffee.

Masala Chai

In India masala chai (spiced tea) is popular and there are a number of ways of making it. There are, however, a few key ingredients and there is a basic method. The key ingredients are: strong black Indian tea; a sweetener (sugar, molasses, honey or artificial sweetener); milk or cream or condensed milk; and spices such as cardamom, cinnamon, anise, cloves, pepper, ginger, coriander. These are added according to taste.

The basic method of preparing masala chai is usually to boil the spices with the sweetener in water then add the tea and milk and bring back to the boil. The tea mixture is often left to infuse for several minutes, resulting in a very rich brew.

The following recipe makes about five to six cups.

4 cloves
2 cardamom pods
2 cinnamon sticks
pinch ground black pepper
1 l (4 cups) water
180 ml (¾ cup) milk
3 tbsp honey (preferably clover or orange) or sugar
3 tbsp black tea leaves

Crush the spices and then place in a pan with the black pepper. Add the water and bring to the boil. Remove from the heat and allow to steep for 5 minutes. Add the milk and honey or sugar and bring back to the boil. Remove from the heat and add the tea. Stir, cover and let steep for about 3 minutes. Strain into a warmed teapot or serve directly into teacups.

Qymaq Chai
(Tea with Clotted Cream)

This tea is made in Afghanistan for special occasions such as engagements. It is very similar to the *sheer chai* (*gulabi* or *noon chai*) of Kashmir.

Qymaq (the same as the *kaymak* of the Middle East) is similar to clotted cream and although the taste and texture are not quite the same clotted cream can be substituted.

Qymaq:
450 ml (16 fl. oz) whole milk
½ tbsp cornflour
75 ml (3 fl. oz) double cream

Add the milk to a pan and bring to the boil. Reduce heat and stir in the cream. Sieve in the cornflour, stir to mix, then whisk until frothy. Leave on a low heat. A thick skin will form on the top of the milk. This should be removed from time to time and collected in another pan until there is only a small amount of milk left. Place the pan with all the collected *qymaq* again on a low heat and leave for a couple of hours more. Set aside in a cool place until it is needed.

For the tea:
680 ml (24 fl. oz) water
6 tsp green tea
¼ tsp bicarbonate of soda
280 ml (10 fl. oz) milk
4–8 tsp sugar, according to taste
1–2 tsp ground cardamom
8 tsp *qymaq*
ice cubes

Put the water in a pan and bring to the boil. Add the green tea and boil for about 5 minutes until the leaves have opened up. Add the bicarbonate of soda and continue to boil for a couple of minutes more. The tea will rise to the top of the pan while boiling. Each time it does add an ice cube to reduce the temperature.

Remove the pan from the heat and allow the tea leaves to settle. Strain off and discard the tea leaves.

Put an ice cube into another pan and pour the tea into it from a height in order to aerate the tea. (A ladle could also be used to do the aeration.) Repeat, pouring from a height from pan to pan, several times, adding an ice cube each time until the tea becomes dark red.

Put the pan back on the heat and add the milk. The colour of the tea will now be a purply-pink colour. Slowly heat it to just below boiling point, then stir in the sugar and cardamom according to taste.

Pour the tea into teacups and float two teaspoons of *qymaq* on top.

Tea Cups and Punches

The tradition of drinking punch and cups was brought to England from India by officers of the East India Company where these refreshing drinks were popular, often at tea parties. The name 'punch' is thought to be derived from the Persian *panj* or Hindi *panch*, meaning 'five', from the five ingredients of the drink: sugar, spirits, lemon or lime juice, water and spices. Some later variations included green or black tea, such as the Sarghoda Club tennis cup. Punch also became very popular in North America, especially in the southern states. It was served at grand tea parties and Charleston became particularly famous for its Otranto Club punch (made with strong green tea, lemons and plenty of alcohol – peach brandy, Jamaica rum, brandy or rye whiskey) and St Cecilia punch (made with dark rum, champagne and club soda, stirred together with brandy-marinated lemon and pineapple slices and a green-tea-infused simple syrup).

Not all punches contain alcohol including, again from Charleston, Dixie tea (with tea, lemon, oranges and spiced with cloves) and Fairy Punch (in *Recipes*

from the Old South, 1961) made with tea, fresh pineapple, grape juice, oranges, lemon, banana, sugar, a few cherries, carbonated water and ice. The below Tea Punch recipe, however, is from India, adapted from Gool K. Shavaksha in *The Time and Talents Club Recipe Book* (1962).

4 cups (1 l) water
4 tsp black tea leaves
8 tsp sugar
2 sticks cinnamon
6 cloves
10 mint leaves
ginger ale or lemonade
sprigs of mint to decorate
chopped fruits such as apples, strawberries,
    peaches (optional)

Bring the water to the boil, pour over the tea leaves and allow to infuse for a couple of minutes. Strain into a large jug and while still hot sweeten with the sugar. Tie the cinnamon, cloves, mint leaves in a muslin bag and add this to the jug of sweetened tea. Set aside to cool for about 6 hours. When ready to serve pour in the ginger ale or lemonade according to taste and the chopped fruit if desired. Stir well and pour into tall glasses containing some ice cubes and decorate with a sprig of mint.

Serves 4

Teatime Savouries

Tea Sandwiches

Tea sandwiches are small, dainty sandwiches eaten for afternoon tea. Traditionally, white bread is used, but other breads can be used such as brown, pumpernickel, sourdough or rye. The bread should be tight-grained and thinly sliced. A thin layer of butter is spread on the bread to seal it from the moist filling ingredients. Fillings should be light and delicate in proportion to the amount of bread. Other spreads that are used include cream cheese and mayonnaise mixtures. Fillings vary considerably. Popular fillings include egg and cress, cucumber, tomatoes, asparagus, cheese, smoked salmon, ham and chicken. When assembled the crusts should be removed and the sandwich cut into the required shape: long, narrow 'finger' sandwiches, triangular half sandwiches or other decorative shapes made with a biscuit cutter. The sandwich should be easy to handle and capable of being eaten delicately in two bites.

Cucumber Sandwiches

Cucumber sandwiches are considered to be the quintessential afternoon tea sandwich. The daintiness of tea sandwiches is associated with the British aristocracy or upper class – a symbol of leisure and privilege. Some writers have used cucumber sandwiches in novels and films to identify upper-class people. In Oscar Wilde's *The Importance of Being Earnest* (1895), the character of Algernon Moncrieff had voraciously eaten all the cucumber sandwiches which had been ordered and prepared for his aunt Augusta's (Lady Bracknell) visit. He is forced to tell a little fib, with his butler's connivance, saying that 'there were no cucumbers in the market this morning . . . not even for ready money.'

The popularity of the cucumber sandwich reached its upper-class zenith in the Edwardian era, when cheap labour and plentiful coal enabled cucumbers to be produced in hotbeds under glass through most of the year. They are still popular, especially in the summer months for formal afternoon teas, at cricket teas and picnics.

Traditionally the cucumber sandwich is composed of paper-thin slices of cucumber placed between two thin slices of crustless, lightly buttered white bread. There are some modern versions. Brown bread is now often used and sometimes extra ingredients are added such as cream cheese and chopped herbs (dill or mint) or spices.

1 large thin cucumber
salt
a little vinegar
8 slices brown bread, thinly sliced
8 slices white bread, thinly sliced
110 g (4 oz) fresh unsalted butter, softened
a pinch or two of white pepper
1–2 tsp finely chopped fresh mint or dill
   (optional)

The bread should preferably be a day old or it won't cut well.

Peel the cucumber and slice in paper-thin rounds. Sprinkle the rounds lightly with salt and vinegar and place in a colander for 15 minutes. Drain well and press to remove excess water then pat dry with paper towels.

Spread the butter on the sliced bread. Place two layers of cucumber slices on the bottom slice, sprinkle lightly with salt and white pepper to taste, and the mint or dill (if using). Top with another buttered slice and press lightly with palm of hand.

Cut all the crusts off with a sharp knife and then cut either into four triangles or three rectangles per round. Place neatly on a plate in alternate rows of brown and white bread. Cover with a damp cloth until ready to serve.

Egg and Cress Finger Sandwiches

This recipe comes from Helen Graves's *101 Sandwiches: A Collection of the Finest Sandwich Recipes from Around the World* (2013). You can, of course, cut the sandwiches into triangles and use brown bread if preferred. The amount of cress can also be increased and it is nice to sprinkle some cress over the finished sandwiches for a decorative effect.

2 cold hard-boiled eggs

1 tbsp mayonnaise

1 tsp snipped fresh chives

3 pinches of salad cress

sea salt to taste and a pinch of white pepper

4 slices white bread, thinly cut

Peel the eggs, mash them with a fork, then stir in the mayonnaise, chives and salad cress. Season with salt and white pepper. Spread the filling onto 2 slices of bread, then top with the remaining slices. Remove the crusts and cut into finger sandwiches. Serve immediately.

Makes 6

Smoked Salmon and Cream Cheese Mini Pinwheel Sandwiches

Food writer and journalist Bee Wilson, author of *Sandwich: A Global History*, showed me how to make these elegant little sandwiches which are perfect for a special afternoon tea party.

1 × 400 g (14 oz) medium-sliced loaf of bread (can be white or wholemeal, some use a light rye bread)

170 g (6 oz) light cream cheese with chives

280 g (10 oz) thinly sliced smoked salmon

Trim the edges of the bread slices, removing any crusts, then, using a rolling pin, press down and 'roll out' the slices of bread to make thin and supple. Cover the bread slices with a dampened towel to prevent from becoming dry. Spread the cream cheese onto the bread slices. Place smoked salmon slices on top, using as many slices as necessary to cover in one even layer. Spread a little more cream cheese over the surface of the salmon. At one end of the bread slice, in order to help roll up the sandwich tightly, make a dent across the width of each bread slice close to one end, using the blunt edge of a knife blade. Lift up the end to form the beginning of a roll. Fold the end of each sandwich tightly over the dent. Roll up the sandwiches tightly. Wrap them individually in plastic film and place in the refrigerator to become very cold and firm for cutting. When you are ready to serve, remove the rolled sandwiches from the fridge, remove the plastic film from each roll and, with a sharp knife, cut diagonally into round slices about 5 mm thick. Arrange the slices on a platter, and garnish with springs of parsley.

Makes about 48

Delhi Sandwich

Sandwiches for afternoon tea parties in India during the Raj often combined the spiciness of Indian food with more traditional ingredients. Many people brought this kind of 'fusion' food back with them to Britain. Delhi sandwiches were typical. This recipe is from *The Gentle Art of Cookery* by C. F. Leyel and Olga Hartley (1929).

Six anchovies, three sardines, one teaspoonful of chutney, one egg, one ounce of butter, one small teaspoonful of curry powder.

Free the sardines and anchovies from bones. Pound them with the seasonings, the chutney and butter. Beat up the yolk of the egg and stir this in, with a pinch of cayenne. Heat the mixture, stirring it into a smooth paste.

This is excellent spread between toast. The toast should be made in rather thick slices, split in two, and the soft side buttered.

Welsh Rabbit

Welsh rabbit (or rarebit) was, and still is, a popular savoury dish for high tea. How it got its name is uncertain and there is no evidence that the Welsh actually originated this dish. It is said that it may have started life as a dish resorted to when meat was not available. The word 'rarebit' came later (first recorded in 1785) and was an attempt to give the dish a more fitting name.

There are many variations – the type of cheese used, the liquid (beer, ale or wine). The cheese mixture may be served with toast on the side or poured on top of toast and grilled until golden brown and bubbling. Other variations include Buck rabbit, a Welsh rabbit with a poached egg on top, and Yorkshire rabbit with bacon and a poached egg.

225 g (8 oz) diced or grated Cheddar cheese
2 tsp ready-made English mustard
dash of Worcestershire sauce
25 g (1 oz) butter
3–4 tbsp brown ale
pinch cayenne pepper, optional
toast

Put all the ingredients in a pan (except the toast). Heat very gently until the cheese melts to a smooth consistency. Serve immediately with or on toast.

Irish Potato Cakes

The love of potatoes in Ireland has ensured that there are many varied potato dishes including boxty, champ, colcannon and stampy. Irish potato cakes, also known as 'tatties' or 'parleys', are also enjoyed throughout Ireland for breakfast or at teatime. They are also a popular way to use leftover mashed potatoes. This recipe is from Regina Sexton's *A Little History of Irish Food* (1998).

450 g (1 lb) potatoes (Golden Wonders or Kerr's Pinks are good)
1 tsp salt and a pinch of freshly ground black pepper
25–55 g (1–2 oz) butter
110 g (4 oz) plain flour
a little butter or bacon fat (if frying)

Wash and scrub the potatoes, but don't peel, and boil in slightly salted water (making sure there is enough water to cover the potatoes) until they are tender. Once cool enough to handle, drain and peel potatoes. It is important to use potatoes that are still hot as they make the best potato cakes.

Mash the potatoes to a smooth consistency, ensuring that there are no lumps. Season with salt and freshly ground pepper and pour in the melted butter. Add and knead in enough flour to make a pliable and easily manageable dough. (Don't overdo the kneading or the finished cakes will be tough and heavy.)

Roll out onto a lightly floured board to form a round of about 0.5–1 cm (¼–½ in.) thickness. Cut the round into triangles or farls, or make small individual round cakes. Cook on a hot dry griddle until both sides are mottled and golden brown. The cakes can also be fried on a hot pan in some melted butter or bacon fat.

Serve hot, spread with butter and honey or sugar and a sprinkling of ground ginger or split them with a little butter and eat them with smoked bacon and fried juicy mushrooms.

Pakoras

These tasty snacks are eaten all over north India, Pakistan and Afghanistan. They can be made with many different vegetables, such as sliced potatoes, aubergines, bell peppers, onions and cauliflower, as in Colleen Sen's recipe below which appears in the e-book we wrote together: *Turmeric: The Wonder Spice*.

1 small cauliflower, broken into small florets
For the batter:
120 g (1 cup) chickpea flour
¼ tsp chilli powder
½ tsp turmeric
¼ tsp baking powder
½ tsp salt
225–450 ml (1–2 cups) vegetable oil, as needed

Mix the batter ingredients in a bowl and gradually add water until the batter has a thin smooth consistency. (It should drip easily when dropped from a spoon). Heat the oil in a wok or deep frying pan over a medium to high flame. Coat each floret in the batter, gently drop into the oil and fry until it is golden brown and slightly crunchy. Serve with ketchup, chutney or your favorite sauce.

Warning: be careful not to drip any batter on your clothes, as it will leave permanent stains.

Akoori
Spicy scrambled eggs

Akoori is a Parsi speciality and is often served in Irani cafés in the big cities of India.

6–8 eggs
salt and black pepper
1 tbsp vegetable oil
6 spring onions, finely chopped
1–2 green chillies, seeds removed and finely chopped
1 tsp grated fresh ginger
¼–½ tsp turmeric
¼–½ tsp ground cumin
1 tomato, peeled and chopped (optional)
1 tbsp fresh coriander, finely chopped

Beat the eggs in a bowl and season with salt and black pepper. Set to one side.

Heat the oil in a large frying pan over a medium heat. Add the onion and fry, stirring frequently, until soft. Stir in the chillies, ginger, turmeric, cumin and tomato, if used, and fry for another couple of minutes.

Stir the eggs into the onion mixture in the frying pan. Add half of the chopped fresh coriander and cook over a low heat, stirring and lifting the eggs as they begin to set into thick curds. Do not overcook. Garnish with the remaining coriander and serve immediately with chapati, paratha or toasted bread.

Sweet Things: Cakes and Pastries

Duchess of Bedford's Tea-cakes
This recipe comes from Lady Llanover's *The First Principles of Good Cookery* (1867).

Take two pounds of fine flour, three ounces of pounded sugar, four ounces fresh butter, four eggs well beaten, one large tablespoonful, or half an ounce, of barm (or German yeast), one pint of new milk; melt the butter in the milk, which must be warmed, mix all together and beat it well; let it stand one hour, then put it in well-buttered small round tins; let them be *well proved*. Bake in a quick oven twenty minutes.

Victoria Sandwiches

Victoria sandwiches are light sponge cakes sandwiched together with jam. Named after Queen Victoria in the mid-nineteenth century, it is said the Queen was fond of eating them at teatime. It has, however, also been suggested that these sponge 'sandwiches' originally started out as a nursery teatime treat. Later, the round Victoria sponge cake became popular, to be cut into wedges. Today the fillings can be varied and many also have a layer of buttercream or whipped cream as well as jam. The top is usually dusted with icing sugar.

Mrs Beeton gives a recipe in the first edition *Mrs Beeton's Book of Household Management* (1861).

INGREDIENTS.– 4 eggs; their weight in pounded sugar, butter, and flour; ¼ saltspoonful of salt, a layer of any kind of jam or marmalade.

MODE.– Beat the butter to a cream; dredge in the flour and pounded sugar; stir these ingredients well together; and add the eggs, which should be previously thoroughly whisked. When the mixture has been well beaten for about 10 minutes, butter a Yorkshire pudding tin, pour in the batter, and bake in a moderate oven for 20 minutes. Let it cool, spread one half of the cake with a layer of nice preserves, place over it the other half of the cake, press the pieces slightly together, and then cut it into long finger pieces; pile them in cross-bars on a glass dish and serve.

Balmoral Cakes and Tartlets

How or why these cakes and tartlets got their name is not exactly known but they are associated with Balmoral, which was Queen Victoria's home in Scotland.

Balmoral cakes should not be confused with Balmoral tartlets. The cakes, a Victorian favourite, were made in special moulds, shaped a bit like a Nissen hut. The moulds are much the same as a rehrücken cake pan, which suggests perhaps that these cakes, which were flavoured with caraway, were the influence of Prince Albert. The cakes were cut into slices and toasted before the fire. The following recipe is from Robert Wells, *The Bread and Biscuit Baker's and Sugar-boiler's Assistant* (1890).

Balmoral Cakes

3½ lbs. of flour, 1 lb. of butter, 1 lb. of sugar, 5 eggs, nearly 1 quart of milk, a few caraway seeds, with 1½ oz. of carbonate of soda and tartaric acid, mixed in proportion of 1 oz. of soda to ¾ oz. of acid.

Mix the soda and acid well with the flour, then rub in the butter and sugar; make a bay with the flour, add the seeds, beat up the eggs with the milk, and make all into a dough. Put into buttered pans according to the size; dust with castor sugar, and bake in a moderate oven.

Balmoral tarts or tartlets probably first appeared in the mid-1850s. Elizabeth Craig in her book *Court Favourites* (1953) gives a recipe for Balmoral cheese cakes dated 1850, which are very similar to a recipe for Balmoral tarts that appeared in *Good Housekeeping* magazine in October 1954. Here is the recipe slightly adapted:

175 g (6 oz) sweet shortcrust pastry

25 g (1 oz) butter

25 g (1 oz) caster sugar

1 egg, separated

10 g (½ oz) cake crumbs

25 g (1 oz) shredded glace cherries mixed with candied peel

20 g (¾ oz) cornflour

1 tsp brandy (optional)

Preheat the oven to 190°C (375°F).

Line 10 to 12 patty tins with the pastry, reserving some for decoration. Cream the butter and sugar together. Beat in the egg yolk. Add the remaining ingredients. Whip up the egg white until stiff and fold into the mixture. Fill the pastry cases, and put a thin pastry strip over the top. Bake in the oven for about 20 minutes.

Rich Fruit Scones

The scone originated in Scotland. The word is thought to derive from the Dutch *schoonbrot*, meaning 'fine, white bread'. Scones cover a wide range of small, soft, flat cakes made with flour, usually leavened either with baking powder, bicarbonate of soda and an acid ingredient such as sour milk or buttermilk. They can be baked on a griddle or in the oven. Some are savoury (often with added herbs or cheese), some have potato added and are popular in Scotland and Ireland, and some are sweet often with added dried fruit. Scones are famous for the role they play in a traditional afternoon tea when served with jam and clotted or whipped cream. The recipe below is the one my mother used. The secret of a making a good light and airy scone, she said, was not to handle it too much before baking. She liked to serve them while still fresh from the oven with butter or cream and strawberry jam.

200 g (8 oz) self-raising flour

½ tsp salt

50 g (2 oz) butter

25 g (1 oz) sugar

2 tbsp raisins or sultanas

1 egg beaten with enough milk to make ¼ pint liquid

Preheat the oven to 220°C (425°F).

Mix the flour and salt. Rub in the butter. Stir in the sugar and fruit. Add the egg and milk, reserving a little for brushing the tops.

Knead lightly on a floured surface and roll out just over 1 cm (½ in.) thickness. Cut into rounds, re-roll the trimmings and cut more rounds.

Place on a greased baking tray and brush the tops with the beaten egg and milk. Bake in the hot oven for about 10 minutes.

Serve fresh with clotted or whipped cream and jam.

Makes approximately 10 scones

Maids of Honour

Maids of honour are small almond-flavoured tarts. There are not only many different recipes but various stories associated with them. It is said that they were the favourite tarts of Elizabeth I, who sent her ladies-in-waiting out of the palace to collect them from a baker in Richmond. Another story is that Anne Boleyn invented them while she was lady-in-waiting to Catherine of Aragon, and Henry VIII is said to have liked them so much that he called them maids of honour (a maid of honour was a queen's unmarried female attendant). However, the first record of them in print was not until 1769, appearing in the *Public Advertiser* on 11 March as 'Almond and Lemon Cheesecakes, Maid of Honour, Sweetmeat Tarts'. It is possible that these tartlets do derive from close connections to the royal court with the former palace of Richmond (in which town they appear first to have been made) or with the palace at Kew.

The recipe (which remains a trade secret) in use today at The Original Maids of Honour tea shop opposite Kew Gardens came into the hands of the Newens family, the present owners, in the mid-nineteenth century when an ancestor served an apprenticeship at the Richmond Maids of Honour shop. Here is my version:

> 200 g (7 oz) puff pastry
> 50 g (2 oz) curd cheese
> 25 g (1 oz) softened butter
> 2 eggs, beaten
> 1 tbsp orange flower water or brandy
> ½ lemon, juice and finely grated zest
> a pinch of cinnamon and/or nutmeg
> 50 g (2 oz) ground almonds
> 10 g (½ oz) fine flour
> 25 g (1 oz) caster sugar
> a few currants (optional)

Preheat the oven to 200°C (400°F).

On a floured surface roll out the pastry until very thin. Cut out circles using a 7.5 cm (3 in.) pastry cutter. Line patty or tartlet tins with the circles and place in the fridge or cool place while you prepare the filling.

Cream together the curd cheese and butter. Beat the eggs and add the orange flower water or brandy. Add this to the curd mixture. Stir in the lemon juice and zest, almonds, flour, caster sugar and spices and beat well.

Half fill the pastry cases with about 1 teaspoon of the mixture. Sprinkle a few currants on top, if desired, then bake for about 20 to 25 minutes until well risen and golden brown. Remove from the oven and allow to cool for a couple of minutes in the tins then transfer carefully to a wire rack to cool.

Makes about 18

Queen Cakes

Queen cakes are small rich cakes which have been popular since at least the eighteenth century. They were made with flour, butter, sugar and eggs with the addition of currants, and flavoured with orange flower water and mace. They were made in little tins or patty pans. Some later recipes include ground or chopped almonds, lemon zest and rosewater. Queen cakes became popular in the United States and *Miss Leslie's New Cookery Book* of 1857 suggests the cakes be iced with lemon or rose flavoured icing. Here is my recipe:

> 100 g (4 oz) butter
> 100 g (4 oz) sugar
> 2 eggs
> 100 g (4 oz) self-raising flour
> pinch of ground mace (optional)
> 1 tsp orange flower water
> 50 g (2 oz) currants

Preheat the oven to 190°C (375°F).

Cream the butter and sugar together in a bowl until light and fluffy. Beat in the eggs one at a time, adding a little flour with each. Sift together the flour and mace (if used) and gently fold into the mixture. Gently stir in the orange flower water and currants. Half fill paper cases or greased patty tins with the mixture and bake in the oven for 15 to 20 minutes until golden and firm.

Remove from the oven and allow to cool in the tin for a couple of minutes, then transfer to a wire rack. Ice them if you wish or serve lightly dusted with icing sugar.

Makes about 12–16

Gingerbread Men

The history of gingerbread goes back a long way and there are many variations and recipes. This simple recipe is ideal for a children's tea party.

    350 g (12 oz) self-raising flour
    ½ tsp bicarbonate of soda
    3 tsp ground ginger
    100 g (3½ oz) butter
    100 g (3½ oz) soft brown sugar
    3 tbsp golden syrup
    3 tbsp milk
    currants, cherries
    icing to decorate

Heat the oven to 190°C (375°F).

Mix together the flour, soda and ginger, rub in the butter and stir in the sugar. Mix the syrup and milk together and then add to the dry ingredients. Mix and stir and form into a dough, working the mixture together with your hands.

Roll out on to a floured board and with a gingerbread man cutter cut out the shapes. The dough should not be rolled too thickly, nor too thinly. Place on greased baking trays, decorate with the currants or cherries, if desired, and bake in the oven for approximately 15 minutes.

Children enjoy decorating them with coloured icing after they have been baked, giving them different hair styles, outfits and so on.

Shrewsbury Cakes

Shrewsbury cakes were first mentioned in a document in 1561. The story of these cakes was given in a pamphlet published in 1938 entitled 'Shrewsbury Cakes: The Story of a Famous Delicacy'. The cakes, or rather the baker, a Mr Palin who ran a confectionary shop in Shrewsbury during the late eighteenth and early nineteenth century and was renowned for his particular mix, which included spices and rosewater, were made famous in *The Ingoldsby Legends* (first published in book form in 1840):

Palin, prince of cake pounders!
The mouth liquefies at thy very name

Recipes in cookbooks were varied in proportions, ingredients and spicing. Martha Bradley used cinnamon and cloves, Elizabeth Raffald caraway seed, Hannah Glasse favoured rosewater and Mrs Rundell cinnamon, nutmeg and rosewater, as in the recipe below.

Sift one pound of sugar, some pounded cinnamon, and a nutmeg grated, into three pounds of flour, the finest sort; add a little rose-water to three eggs, well beaten, and mix these with the flour, etc.; then pour into it as much butter melted as will make it a good thickness to roll out.

Mould it well, and roll thin, and cut it into such shapes as you like.*

* Mrs Rundell did not give instructions for the actual baking. The biscuits should be baked in a moderate oven 170°C (325°F) for about 12 to 15 minutes until golden and firm to the touch and many would dredge with caster sugar while still warm, then transfer to a wire rack to cool.

Fat Rascals

Fat rascals are a sort of cross between a scone and a rock cake. They were also known as turf cakes. Turf cakes were made on the North Yorkshire moors very simply from flour, lard, salt, baking powder and cream or milk to mix. For harvest time (or pig killing time) currants and sugar were added. They were baked as one cake in a large frying pan with a lid to about 1 cm (½ in.) thick and were turned once. The beauty of these cakes was that they could be made quickly if unexpected visitors arrived. Other names for this type of cake include 'warm cakes', 'turn cakes', 'sod cakes' and 'backstone cakes'. A similar cake popular at teatime and made in the north-east of England is the singin' hinny. Hinny is a term of endearment and the singin' refers to the sound of the sizzling lard or butter when the rich dough is being cooked.

Nowadays fat rascals tend to be made for individuals and are baked in the oven. Bettys of Yorkshire have made them famous. Their recipe is a secret but here is one which is a close relation.

225 g (8 oz) plain flour
½ tsp salt
1 rounded tsp baking powder
½ tsp ground cinnamon, optional
100 g (3½ oz) butter
50 g (2 oz) sugar, preferably golden caster sugar
50 g currants
zest of 1 small orange or lemon
1 beaten egg
4–5 tbsp full fat milk
1 egg yolk beaten with 1 tbsp water for the glaze

For decoration:
glacé cherries or raisins
orange peel and/or whole almonds

Preheat the oven to 220°C (425°F). Sift together the flour, salt, baking powder and cinnamon. Rub in the butter until the mixture is fine breadcrumbs. Stir in the sugar, currants and orange or lemon zest. Add the beaten egg and just enough milk to make a soft dough. Roll out on a floured board to about 2.5 cm (1 in.) thickness. Cut into 7–8 cm (3–4 in.) rounds and place on a greased baking tray. Brush with the beaten egg yolk and water. Make a face on each fat rascal according to your fancy with currants or glacé cherries for eyes and orange peel for the mouth and/or almonds for the teeth. Bake for about 15 minutes until nicely golden brown and then cool on a wire rack.

Makes 5–8 depending on size of cutter used

Petticoat Tails

Petticoat tails are a Scottish shortbread biscuit baked in a round which resembles a bell-hoop crinoline petticoat. Before baking, the biscuit is marked in equal segments, usually with a small circle cut out of the centre which avoids any untidy breakage to the pointed end of each wedge of biscuit.

There are a number of suggestions as to the origin of these biscuits. Dorothy Hartley in *Food in England* (1954) suggests that they originally date from the twelfth century and were called 'petty cotes tallis' – *petty* meaning little, *cotes* meaning a small enclosure, *tallis*, a cut-out pattern formed by cuts on sticks made for measuring or tallying. From this, when the central round was removed and the biscuits were made in the shape of women's petticoats, *petticote tallis* evolved. However, others have speculated that the name is a corruption of 'petits gateaux tailes', small French cakes which it is said were brought to Scotland by Mary Queen of Scots from France in 1560. The name soon became corrupted to petticoat tails.

Christian Isobel Johnstone who wrote *The Cook and Housewife's Manual* in 1826, using as her pseudonym

Mistress Margaret (Meg) Dods, says of petticoat tails: 'In Scottish culinary terms there are many corruptions, though we rather think the name Petticoat-tails has its origin in the shape of the cakes, which is exactly that of the bell-hoop petticoats of our ancient Court ladies.'

250 g (9 oz) plain flour
75 g (3 oz) caster sugar, plus extra for dredging
    on top if wished
175 g (6 oz) butter
caraway seeds (optional)

Mix the flour and sugar in a bowl, then rub in the butter. Knead well to form a smooth, firm dough adding in a few caraway seeds if desired. Roll out into a circle 1 cm (½ in.) thick and pinch the edges.

Cut a small piece out from the centre with a small round cutter. Mark the shaped dough into eight equal portions. Crimp or pinch round the edge of the circle and decoratively prick all over with a fork.

Bake on a greased baking tray at 160°C (350°F) for about 25 to 30 minutes until golden. Dredge with a little more caster sugar if wished and cool on a wire tray.

Seed Cake

Seed cake was particularly popular during Victorian times and was a favourite item on the tea table with its pungent flavour of caraway seeds. However, seed cakes date back centuries, notably in Scotland. Seed cakes were traditionally made for social gatherings, agricultural harvests and feast days, and when the seeds were sown for crops. When caraway seeds were first added to the cakes it was in the form of comfits (seeds encrusted in layers of sugar) and it wasn't until the late seventeenth century or early eighteenth century that plain caraway seeds were used. Seed cakes since the Second

World War have been considered old-fashioned and fallen out of favour. Today they are rarely made, despite being a moist and tasty cake, keeping for days. For those who would like to enjoy a slice of old-fashioned seed cake with their cup of tea, or perhaps serve it for a special tea party, here is Mrs Beeton's recipe from 1861:

A VERY GOOD SEED-CAKE

INGREDIENTS.– 1 lb butter, 6 eggs, ¾ lb. of sifted sugar, pounded mace and grated nutmeg to taste, 1 lb. of flour, ¾ oz. of caraway seeds, 1 wineglassful of brandy.

MODE.– Beat the butter to a cream; dredge in the flour; add the sugar, mace, nutmeg, and caraway seeds, and mix these ingredients well together. Whisk the eggs, stir to them the brandy, and beat the cake again for 10 minutes. Put it into a tin lined with buttered paper, and bake it from 1 ½ to 2 hours. This cake would be equally nice made with currants, and omitting the caraway seeds.

Dundee Cake

Dundee cake is a traditional Scottish fruitcake with a rich flavour and deep golden brown colour ideal for high tea or for special occasions such as Christmas. The top of the cake is typically decorated with concentric circles of almonds giving an attractive finish. The cake was first made in Keillers' marmalade and confectionery factory in Dundee in the late 1800s, when production lines turned from marmalades and jams to festive midwinter baking. Using the Seville orange peel from the marmalade process they made this rich fruitcake which eventually took on the name of the town. As this is a Scottish cake I suggest whisky to flavour the cake but sweet sherry or brandy can be used if preferred.

250 g (9 oz) butter, softened

250 g (9 oz) caster sugar

grated zest of 1 orange and 1 lemon

5 medium eggs, beaten

280 g (10 oz) plain flour

450 g (1 lb) sultanas (or mixed dried fruit)

2 tbsp whisky

1 heaped tbsp thick peel marmalade, pureed

50 g (2 oz) whole blanched almonds for the top

Preheat the oven to 160°C (325°F).

Grease and line a 20.5 cm (8 in.) deep round cake tin with non-stick baking paper.

Cream the butter with the sugar and grated orange and lemon rind until light and creamy. Add the eggs gradually, beating well between each addition. Sift in the flour and lightly stir in, then stir in the sultanas or mixed fruit. Add the whisky and pureed marmalade and mix in gently but well. The mixture should be a soft dropping consistency.

Pour the mixture into the cake tin, spreading it to the sides making a slight hollow in the centre. Arrange the blanched almonds in concentric circles on top. To protect the cake make a strip of thick brown paper which will come just above the height of the cake and wrap around the sides of the tin. Secure with string or tape.

Bake for about an hour. Check the cake and if the top is browning too quickly cover with some grease-proof paper and reduce the heat to 150°C (300°F) and bake for about another one and a half hours or until the cake is a deep golden brown and a metal skewer inserted into the centre of the cake comes out cleanly.

Remove the cake from the oven and place on a cooling rack, leaving the cake to cool in the tin. The cake keeps well when stored in an airtight tin.

Bara Brith

Tea loaves are very good to have with a cup of tea and there are many variations from different regions. *Bara brith* is the traditional rich spiced fruit loaf of Wales. *Bara brith* translates to 'speckled bread', the speckling meaning the fruit.

Originally it was a yeast cake, like many other ancient traditional cakes and breads, before the arrival of chemical raising agents. Some contain butter or lard and many recipes, as in this one, soak the dried fruit in tea. You can use Welsh Brew tea or try using another tea such as jasmine for a different flavour. The loaf is delicious when the slices are spread with salted Welsh butter.

This recipe is slightly adapted from the recipe on visitwales.com.

450 g (1 lb) mixed dried fruit

300 ml (½ pint) cold tea

175 g (6 oz) muscovado sugar

1 medium size free-range egg

2 tbsp orange juice

1 tbsp orange zest

1 tbsp honey

450 g (1 lb) self-raising flour

1 tsp mixed spice

extra honey for glazing

Put the mixed dried fruit into a mixing bowl, pour over the tea, cover and leave to soak overnight. The next day mix together the sugar, egg, orange juice, zest and honey. Add to the fruit. Sift in the flour and spice, and mix well. Pour the mixture into a buttered loaf tin (1.2 l/ 2 pt). Bake in a preheated oven at 160°C (325°F) for about 1¾ hours. The loaf should be golden in colour and firm to the touch in the middle. Baste with the extra honey while still warm. Allow to cool thoroughly before storing in a cake tin.

Lemon Drizzle Cake

Lemon drizzle cake has become a favourite teatime snack in cafés, tearooms and in the home. It can also be made with an orange drizzle; just substitute two small oranges for the lemons.

175 g (6 oz) butter, softened
175 g (6 oz) caster sugar
zest and juice of 2 unwaxed lemons
3 eggs
175 g (6 oz) self-raising flour
a little milk
100 g (3½ oz) granulated sugar

Preheat the oven to 180°C (350°F). Grease and line a 1 kg (2 lb) loaf tin with greaseproof paper.

Cream together the butter, caster sugar and the finely grated zest of one lemon and beat until light and fluffy. Add the eggs, one at a time, beating until well combined before adding the next.

Sift over the flour and fold in. Add just enough milk to bring the mixture to a dropping consistency (so that it falls off the spoon), then spoon into the prepared tin and even out the top. Bake for about 40 to 50 minutes, turning down the heat to 170°C if browning too quickly, until a skewer comes out clean.

Mix together the remaining lemon zest and the juice of both the lemons with the granulated sugar. While the cake is still warm pierce all over the top with a skewer and pour over the drizzle, waiting for the cake to absorb one lot before adding the next. Cool in the tin before turning out.

Madeleines

This recipe comes from *Geraldene Holt's Cakes* (2011). She says in her introduction that 'It is possible that the legendary little cakes baked by Françoise and offered the young Marcel Proust by his aunt Léonie at Combray were made to this recipe from the popular nineteenth-century cookery book, *La Cuisinière de la champagne et de la ville* by Louis-Eustache Audot. It's an appealing notion because this version is both simple and delightful. Serve the madeleines freshly baked – with lime tea, of course.' I like to dust mine very lightly with icing sugar just before serving.

180°C/350°F/gas mark 4/baking time: 15 minutes
Equipment: Madeleine tin with shell-shaped moulds, preferably non-stick – brushed with clarified butter

60 g (2 oz) butter
150 g (5 oz) caster sugar
½ lemon, finely grated zest
3 eggs, separated
1 tsp orange flower water
120 g (4 oz) plain fine white cake flour, preferably French
1 tbsp clarified butter, melted for brushing cake tins

Cream the butter in a warmed bowl and gradually beat in the sugar with the lemon zest. Beat in the egg yolks with the orange flower water. Whisk the egg whites until stiff and fold into the mixture alternately with the sieved flour.

Brush the shaped moulds of the cake tin with clarified butter. Place a rounded teaspoon of the mixture in each and smooth fairly level.

Bake in the preheated oven until golden and the little cakes are just starting to shrink from the tin. Cool in the tin for 1 minute, then transfer to a wire rack. Wash the tin with hot water only, dry and brush with more clarified butter and make the second batch of cakes with the remaining mixture.

Makes 24 cakes

Tea Kisses

These delicate little meringues look pretty on the tea table and have been popular on both sides of the Atlantic. An early recipe in the United States was given by Eliza Leslie in *Miss Leslie's New Cookery Book* (1857). She hollows out the base of the meringue and fills with jelly; 'then clap the two halves together, and unite them at the base, by moistening the edges with a little of the meringue that was left.'

The meringue for tea kisses can be flavoured with scented teas (as in the recipe below) or with lemon, rosewater, orange flower water or vanilla. A few drops of colouring can be added to, say, half of the mixture if desired. (If using rose-scented tea then colour pink, for Lady Grey a pale blue and so on.) Matcha tea can be used to give a green colour and also adds a bit of a kick to the taste. The kisses can also be sandwiched together in twos with some whipped cream. The variations are endless.

1 tbsp tea such as rose pouchong or jasmine
110 g (4 oz) caster sugar
2 large egg whites
food colouring (optional)
whipped cream (optional)

Wrap the tea in muslin and bury it in the sugar. Leave for at least a couple of hours, preferably longer. It can be left for up to two weeks in a sealed container, shaken from time to time. Remove the muslin bag before using the sugar.

Preheat the oven to 130°C (250°F, gas mark ½). Line a baking sheet with non-stick baking paper. Whip the egg whites until stiff. Add the scented sugar, continuing to whip until the mixture is a very stiff, thick and glossy meringue. At this point the mixture can be divided and one half can be delicately coloured as you wish. Drop spoonfuls, or pipe swirls or stars, of the mixture on to the baking paper. Bake for 50 minutes. Leave to cool on the baking sheet, then carefully remove. Sandwich together in twos with whipped cream if desired. Serve in small, pretty paper cases.

Russian Snowballs

These deliciously light 'snowballs' are so-called for their powdery white spherical appearance and melt-in-the-mouth texture. They are a form of jumble, a type of pastry/biscuit which was common in England during the Middle Ages. They are quite simple to make and generally consist of flour, butter, ground nuts and powdered (icing) sugar, flavoured with vanilla.

In the United States they are often made around Christmas. The nuts used can be walnuts, almonds, hazelnuts or pecans. They have several other names: Russian tea cakes, which is a little misleading for they are more like cookies or biscuits and no one seems to know what the connection is to Russia; butterballs; meltaways; and when made with pecans, pecan puffs or pecan balls.

They exist in similar forms in many countries around the world, as Mexican wedding cakes (or cookies), Italian wedding cookies, Polish Christmas crescents and polvorones in Spain.

110 g (4 oz) pecans (or walnuts, almonds or
    hazelnuts)
110 g (4 oz) butter, softened
2 heaped tbsp caster sugar
1 tsp vanilla extract (or you can use 1 tbsp rum,
    whisky or brandy)
125 g (4½ oz) plain (all purpose) flour
icing (powdered) sugar, for coating

Preheat the oven to 170°C (325°F).

Chop the nuts very finely or grind in a food processor. Cream the butter well, then cream in the sugar until light and fluffy. Add the vanilla, then the flour, followed by the nuts. Mix together until all the flour is absorbed. Break off walnut-size pieces of the mixture and roll them in the palm of your hands into a ball. Place the balls on an ungreased baking tray, allowing space between the balls. Bake in the oven for about 20–25 minutes until a light golden colour.

Meanwhile sift plenty of icing sugar into a deep plate. Remove the cookies from the oven and roll them in the icing sugar. Transfer to a wire rack to cool then dust again with icing sugar, coating on all sides. Store in an airtight container.

Newfoundland Tea Buns

These little buns, sometimes called raisin buns, are a sort of cross between a tea cake and a scone. There are many variations, every family having their own 'secret' recipe, many containing rum. In the nineteenth century when merchants shipped their salt cod from Canada and traded it down to the Caribbean, they got rum back in exchange. The buns were often given to children to eat when they came home hungry from school (presumably without the rum) or served for high tea. It is said that the best raisin buns are made with evaporated milk but fresh milk can be used and many Newfoundlanders like to serve with Fussell's canned thick cream.

This recipe has been slightly adapted from a recipe card produced by the Canadian Tourist Board.

150 g (5 oz) raisins
1–2 tbsp rum
300 g (10 oz) plain flour
2½ tsp baking powder
¼ tsp salt
110 g (4 oz) sugar
100 g (3½ oz) unsalted butter
1 egg, beaten with about 110 ml (4 fl. oz)
    evaporated milk

Soak the raisins in the rum for a couple of hours or overnight.

Preheat the oven to 200°C (400°F).

Combine the flour, baking powder, salt and sugar in a large bowl. Rub in the butter until the mixture resembles breadcrumbs.

Add the raisins with their rum followed by the egg and enough milk to the dry ingredients, mixing well together, to make a soft dough. Put the dough on a floured surface and knead four or five times. Roll to 1 cm (½ in.) thickness and cut out buns with a round cutter.

Place on a non-stick cake pan. Bake for 10 to 15 minutes, until golden. Cool on a rack before serving with butter (or thick cream) and perhaps some jam.

Makes 12

Nanaimo Bars

Nanaimo Bars (NBs for short) are one of Canada's favourite confections. They are named after the city of

Nanaimo in British Columbia. The exact origin of the bar is unknown. They probably go back to the 1930s but were then called chocolate fridge cake or chocolate squares or slice. The earliest confirmed printed copy of the recipe using the name 'Nanaimo Bars' appears in Edith Adams's prize cookbook (14th edn) from 1953.

These no-bake, three-layered bars are delicious with their crumb base, followed by a layer of light custard buttercream, topped with a smooth and glossy layer of semi-sweet chocolate. There are many different recipes. In fact, when Nanaimo mayor Graeme Roberts held a contest in 1985 to find the 'ultimate' Nanaimo Bar recipe there were about a hundred entries. Local resident Joyce Hardcastle won and her recipe is now the 'official' Nanaimo Bar recipe.

The recipe below, slightly adapted, was given to me by Noreen Howard. She remembers visiting her husband's parents in Montreal in 1965 and every afternoon her mother-in-law Mary Howard, who was a home economics graduate, would serve tea with some bars, cookies or squares at about four o'clock to keep everyone going until dinner time.

1st layer

110 g (4 oz) butter or margarine, melted

50 g (2 oz) brown sugar

4 tbsp cocoa powder

1 beaten egg

225 g (8 oz) Graham wafer crumbs (or use digestive biscuits, crushed)

75 g (3 oz) desiccated coconut

50 g (2 oz) chopped walnuts

1 tsp vanilla essence

Combine, put in 23 cm (9 in.) square pan and chill for half an hour.

2nd layer

250 g (9 oz) icing sugar, sifted

50 g (2 oz) butter, softened

60 ml (2 fl. oz) cream or milk

2 tbsp Bird's custard powder

Combine all ingredients, beating until smooth and flabby, then spread carefully on top of the first layer.

3rd layer

3 chocolate semi-sweet squares (75 g, 3 oz)

50 g (2 oz) butter

Melt chocolate and butter together, then spread over second layer and chill.

These bars are rich and should be cut into small 2.5 cm (1 in.) squares.

Afghans

Afghans are a traditional biscuit (sometimes called cookie) popular in both New Zealand and Australia. The origin of this biscuit is a mystery and many say that the name has nothing whatsoever to do with Afghanistan or Afghans. However, some say the biscuits were first sent to a British soldier serving in Afghanistan during the Second Anglo-Afghan War fought by soldiers of the British Empire in the late nineteenth century (1878–80). Others have suggested that the biscuit was named for its resemblance to an Afghan male, the colour resembling dark skin, the chocolate frosting the hair and the walnut top his hat (or perhaps his turban). Another theory is that the biscuit was made to honour an Afghan gentleman who visited New Zealand – but who was he? No one knows. Wherever it originally came from, this biscuit is tasty and easy to make.

The recipe has appeared in many editions of the influential New Zealand *Edmonds Cookery Book* and the one given below has been slightly adapted from the de luxe edition of 1955.

200 g (7 oz) softened butter

75 g (3 oz) sugar

175 g (6 oz) plain flour

1 tbsp cocoa powder

50 g (2 oz) cornflakes

chocolate icing (see recipe below)

walnut halves

Preheat oven to 180°C (350°F).

Cream together the butter and sugar. Add flour and cocoa and mix well. Mix in the cornflakes last so as not to break them up too much.

Drop approximately one tablespoonful of mixture in small heaps on a greased oven tray and bake for about 15 minutes. Remove from the oven and leave them to cool.

When cold, ice with chocolate icing and top each one with a walnut half.

Chocolate icing:

1 dessert spoon butter

1 dessert spoon boiling water

50 g (2 oz) finely grated chocolate

225 g (8 oz) icing sugar

essence of vanilla

Warm the butter in a pan. Dissolve the chocolate in water; add to the butter, then sift in the icing sugar and stir until smooth and glossy. Flavour with a couple of drops of vanilla essence.

Anzac Biscuits

This recipe has been given to me by Roger Attwell who, as a little boy growing up in New Zealand, remembers his mother and grandmother baking cakes from the *Edmonds Cookery Book* where this recipe (slightly adapted) comes from.

50 g (2 oz) flour

75 g (3 oz) sugar

50 g (2 oz) coconut

50 g (2 oz) rolled oats

50 g (2 oz) butter

1 tbsp golden syrup

½ tsp bicarbonate of soda

2 tbsp boiling water

Preheat the oven to 180°C (350°F).

Mix together the flour, sugar, coconut and rolled oats. Melt the butter and golden syrup together. Dissolve the bicarbonate of soda in the boiling water and add to butter and golden syrup. Make a well in centre of flour and stir in the liquid. Mix well. Place about a teaspoon of the mixture on cold greased trays leaving space for them to spread. (Or roll rounded teaspoons of mixture into balls and flatten slightly.) Bake for 15 to 20 minutes until golden brown. Remove from the oven, cool for 5 minutes on the baking tray before transferring to a wire rack.

Louise Cake

Louise cake is a traditional New Zealand favourite consisting of a thin layer of cake or biscuit which is spread with raspberry jam (although other jams could be used), topped with a coconut meringue and then baked in the oven. Kiwi cooking bible *Edmonds Classics* rated the Louise cake sixth in the top ten favourite

Kiwi recipes. This recipe has been slightly adapted from the *Edmonds Cookery Book* edition of 1955.

50 g (2 oz) butter
150 g (1½ cup) plain flour
25 g (2 tbsp) sugar, plus 125 g (½ cup) caster sugar
2 eggs, separated
1 level tsp baking powder
raspberry jam
50 g (½ cup) desiccated coconut

Preheat the oven to 170°C (325°F). Cream the butter and sugar until light and fluffy, add the egg yolks then sift in the flour and baking powder. Roll out or press evenly into a greased baking tray or tin. (I used a 20 cm/8 in. square tin.) Spread with raspberry jam. Whisk the egg whites until quite stiff and add the caster sugar and the coconut. Fold in well and spread on top of the jam. Bake for about 30 minutes until the meringue is golden brown and firm.

Allow to cool in the tin. Cut into squares or fingers to serve.

Hertzoggies

Hertzoggies are a traditional teatime treat in South Africa.

250 g (9 oz) plain flour
25 g (1 oz) caster sugar
2 tsp baking powder
¼ tsp salt
125 g (4½ oz) butter
3 large egg yolks
1 tbsp cold water

Filling:
apricot jam
3 egg whites
250 g (9 oz) sugar
160 g (6 oz) desiccated coconut

Sift the flour, sugar, baking powder and salt together into a bowl. Rub the butter lightly with the fingertips into the dry ingredients. Beat the egg yolks together with the water. Add to the mixture, mix well and knead until a soft dough is formed, adding a little extra cold water if necessary. Cover and set aside in a cool place.

Preheat the oven to 180°C (360°F) and lightly grease patty pan tins.

Roll out the dough fairly thinly (about 5 mm (¼ in.) thick) on a floured surface and cut into rounds with a pastry cutter. Line the greased tins with the rounds of pastry. Spoon a small blob of apricot jam (about ½ tsp) into each tartlet.

Whisk the egg whites until stiff. Whisk in the sugar gradually until fluffy. Add the coconut and mix in well. Spoon the mixture on top of the jam to cover.

Place in the oven and bake for about 20 to 25 minutes. Cool slightly in the pans, then carefully lift them out and cool on a wire rack.

Cinnamon Toast

A warming snack in winter, the earliest recipe for cinnamon toast I have been able to find is in Robert May's *The Accomplisht Cook* (1660). Whether or not his cinnamon toast was served with tea is not known as tea had only just arrived in Britain. His instructions are brief. 'Cut fine thin toasts, then toast them on a gridiron, and lay them in ranks in a dish, put to them fine beaten cinnamon mixed with sugar and some claret, warm them over the fire, and serve them hot.'

Cinnamon toast was a common afternoon tea offering during the British Raj in India, but without the claret.

1 tsp powdered cinnamon
1 tbsp sugar
2 tbsp butter (unsalted)
4 slices of bread

Mix the cinnamon and sugar and set aside. Toast the bread lightly and while still hot butter generously. Sprinkle with the cinnamon and sugar and put under a grill for a couple of minutes until the sugar melts. Serve straightaway.

Serves 4

Love Cake

This recipe comes from Pauline Holsinger via Napoleona Teas in Libertyville, Illinois. It has been in Pauline's Sri Lankan family for over a hundred years and is a regular favourite for teatime and to serve guests on the family's tea plantation in Nuwara Eliya. According to Pauline 'the secret is in the slow baking and proper pan'. It is a rich and sweet cake and best served in small squares.

110 g (¼ lb) semolina
225 g (½ lb) unsalted butter
zest of 1 lemon
450 g (1 lb) raw cashew nuts
10 g (½ oz) vanilla
½ tsp almond essence
30 ml (⅛ cup) rose water
450 g (1 lb) pumpkin preserve
10 egg yolks
150 g (¾ cup) soft brown sugar

¼ tsp each nutmeg and cinnamon
40 g (⅛ cup) honey
4 egg whites, stiffly beaten

Toast the semolina lightly; when warm and slightly brown, mix with the butter and lemon zest. Set aside.

Pound cashew nuts (do not mince) with mallet, and add vanilla, almond essence, rosewater and cover with lid. Allow to season for one hour.

Chop preserved pumpkin and beat until bubbles appear; beat in the egg yolks and sugar until light and frothy, then blend in nutmeg and cinnamon. Stir in the honey and the semolina and cashew mixtures.

Whip 4 egg whites until stiff, then fold in gently.

Pour into a greased, parchment-lined 25 × 30 cm (10 × 12 in.) pan and bake at 150°C (300°F) until top is lightly browned. (Note that the traditional way to line this pan is with two layers of newspaper, then one layer of greased parchment paper before pouring in the batter.)

Cool and cut into 2.5 cm (1 in.) squares. This cake can be cut and frozen for up to 3 months.

Serve with Ceylon tea.

Pumpkin preserve is not easy to find in grocery stores and supermarkets. Going under the name *puhul dosi* it may be possible to track down in some Asian supermarkets. However, it is worth noting that some recipes for Love cake contain no pumpkin preserve.

Kulcha-e-panjerei
(also known as rose, rosa or rosette cookies)

These crisp, delicate, deep-fried fritters, often served with tea in Iran and Afghanistan, are made using intricately designed fritter irons, often in the shape of a flower. The iron is heated to a high temperature in oil, dipped into a batter made from flour, eggs, milk, lightly sweetened and flavoured (perhaps with vanilla or rose-water) and then re-immersed in the hot oil, creating a crisp shell around the metal. The iron is removed and the fritter is separated from the iron and placed on a dish. The fritters are usually lightly dusted with icing sugar.

These fritters are found in many other countries around the world. In India they are believed to have been introduced by the Portuguese and in Anglo-Indian circles they are known as rose or rosa cookies. In Christian communities they are traditionally made for Christmas and special occasions. In Kerala they are also known as *achappam*. The milk used is usually coconut milk. In Sri Lanka, known as *kokis*, they are made with rice flour and coconut milk and believed to have originated with the Dutch.

In Sweden, Norway and Finland they are known as rosettes. (Rosettes are popular in the United States among families with Scandinavian ancestry.) In Mexico they are called *buñuelos* and in Colombia *solteritas*. In Turkey they are called *demir tatlısı* and in Iran and Afghanistan, where this recipe comes from, they are *kulcha-e-panjerei* (meaning 'window' biscuits).

2 medium eggs
1 tsp sugar
¼ tsp salt
110 g (4 oz) plain flour
225 ml (8 fl. oz) milk
2 tsp melted butter
oil for frying
icing sugar for dusting

Beat the eggs in a bowl until well blended. Add and mix in well the sugar and salt, then gradually stir in the flour alternately with the milk and the melted butter. Beat well until smooth.

Deep fry in plenty of oil heated to 200°C (400°F). First of all immerse the fritter iron in the hot oil to season. Then dip it in the batter, making sure the batter does not cover the top of the iron. Immerse quickly in the hot oil for about 20 to 30 seconds, until the bubbles disappear and the fritter is golden brown. Remove from the oil and carefully remove the fritter from the iron, if necessary with a fork. Place on kitchen paper to drain. Repeat until all the batter is used up. When cool, dust with icing sugar. They are best served immediately.

Christmas Trifle

Trifles are a popular teatime treat all year round, especially for summer tea parties or in the depths of winter. No Christmas tea table would be complete without a trifle.

250 g (9 oz) fresh cranberries
100 g (3½ oz) caster sugar
8–12 small sponge cakes or madeleines
5 tbsp orange liqueur such as Drambuie
5 tbsp fresh mandarin or tangerine juice
12–16 ratafia biscuits

For the custard:
565 ml (20 fl. oz) double cream
2 tbsp caster sugar
6 egg yolks
2 tsp cornflour
1 tsp vanilla essence (optional)

For the syllabub:
zest and juice of 1 lemon
3 tbsp white wine (dry or sweet, according to taste)

2 tsp orange flower water

75 g (3 oz) caster sugar

280 ml (10 fl. oz) double cream

To finish:

cranberries, angelica, silver dragees

Add the cranberries to a pan containing 150 ml (5 fl. oz) water, reserving a few for decoration. Bring to the boil, then turn down the heat and simmer uncovered for about 5 minutes. Add the sugar. Simmer for another 10 minutes or until the fruit is tender. Remove from the heat and cool a little.

Arrange the sponge cakes in a decorative glass trifle bowl. Mix the orange juice and liqueur together and spoon over the cakes evenly and allow to soak. Spread the cranberries over the top and sprinkle with the crushed ratafias. Leave in a cool place.

Meanwhile make the custard. Heat the double cream in a saucepan. Blend the egg yolks, sugar and cornflour together in a basin and, when the cream is hot, pour it over the mixture, stirring constantly. Return the mixture to the saucepan and stir continuously over a low heat until the custard thickens. Then remove it from the heat and allow it to cool a little. (If it starts to curdle, whisk vigorously until it is restored.)

Pour the custard over the cake and fruit and leave to cool and set.

Next, make the syllabub. Soak the zest in the juice of the lemon for a couple of hours. Whip the cream until stiff. Add the sugar, wine and orange flower water to the lemon juice and then gently mix everything together to make a light frothy cream. Spread this syllabub over the custard.

Decorate with the reserved cranberries, angelica and silver dragees or according to your fancy.

References

1 Britain

1 Sam Twining, *My Cup of Tea: The Story of the World's Most Popular Beverage* (London, 2002), p. 18.

2 Originally a teapoy was a small three-legged occasional table. The word originates from the Persian and Hindi for 'three'. Over time, the name made people associate them with tea, and therefore the phrase was also applied to tea chests on legs.

3 William H. Ukers, *The Romance of Tea: An Outline History of Tea and Tea-drinking Through Sixteen Hundred Years* (London, 1936), p. 80.

4 Kim Wilson, *Tea with Jane Austen* (London, 2004), p. 44.

5 What was often sold as tea was not tea at all, but leaves from trees, most often sloe leaves, boiled, baked, curled, dried and coloured to resemble Chinese green tea. It was called smouch.

6 Edward Bramah, *Tea and Coffee* (London, 1972), p. 132.

7 John Griffiths, *Tea: The Drink That Changed the World* (London, 2007), p. 359.

8 Jane Pettigrew, *A Social History of Tea* (London, 2001), p. 102.

9 English muffins are different from American muffins, which are baked in tins, 'puff up' (baking powder is used as a raising agent, rather than yeast) and are very light. Often fruits such as blueberries are added.

10 For a full history see Bee Wilson, *Sandwich: A Global History* (London, 2010).

11 Pettigrew, *A Social History of Tea*, p. 120.

12 Laura Mason, 'Everything Stops for Tea', in *Luncheon, Nuncheon and Other Meals: Eating with the Victorians*, ed. C. Anne Wilson (Stroud, 1994), p. 72.

13 Dorothy Hartley, *Food in England* (London, 1954), p. 281.

14 Alan Davidson, *North Atlantic Seafood* (Totnes, 2003), p. 466.

15 Mason, 'Everything Stops for Tea', pp. 77–9.

16 Catherine Brown, *Broths to Bannocks: Cooking in Scotland 1690 to the Present Day* (London, 1990), p. 69.

17 S. Minwel Tibbott, *Domestic Life in Wales* (Cardiff, 2002), p. 10.

18 Cambric tea was given to children, supposedly to give them energy, or to help them feel grown up during teatime. It was also often served to the elderly. It got its name from cambric fabric, which was white and thin, just like the tea, and named after the French town of Cambrai, a textile centre. Cambric tea was popular during the late nineteenth to early twentieth centuries. It was also known as white tea. In France *thé de Cambrai* is made with hot tea, cream and boiling water, and sugar added to taste.

19 Quoted in Pettigrew, *A Social History of Tea*, p. 105.

20 Peter Brears, *A Taste of Leeds* (Derby, 1998), p. 53.

21 Peter Brears, 'Of Funeral Biscuits', in *Petits Propos Culinaires*, 18 (1984), p. 10, quoted in J. Nicholson, *Folk Lore of East Yorkshire* (London, 1988), p. 8.

22 Personal communication with food historian Gillian Riley.

23 'Were Cream Teas "Invented" in Tavistock?', *BBC News*, 17 January 2004.

24 See 'The Tea Rooms of London', www. edwardianpromenade.com, 28 December 2009.

25 From William Cowper's *The Task* (1784), this was later used as a slogan promoting tea as an alternative to alcohol in the mid-nineteenth century associated with the Temperance Movement.

26 Perilla Kinchin, *Taking Tea with Mackintosh: The Story of Miss Cranston's Tea Rooms* (Fullbridge Maldon, 1998), p. 68.

27 Catherine Brown, *Feeding Scotland* (Edinburgh, 1996), p. 55.

28 Ibid., p. 56.

29 Susan Cohen, *Where to Take Tea* (London, 2003), p. 41.

30 Elizabeth Crawford, 'WALKS/Suffrage Stories: Suffragettes and Tea Rooms: The Criterion Restaurant, Kate Frye, and the Actresses' Franchise League', http://womanandhersphere.com, 5 September 2012.

31 Beatrice Crozier, *The Tango and How to Dance It* (London, 1914), quoted in Cohen, *Where to Take Tea*, p. 28.

32 Elizabeth Casciani, *Oh, How We Danced!: History of Ballroom Dancing in Scotland* (Edinburgh, 1994), quoted in Hamish Whyte and Catherine Brown, *A Scottish Feast: Anthology of Food in Scottish Writing* (Argyll, 1996), p. 33.

33 Cohen, *Where to Take Tea*, p. 36.

34 Fiona Robinson, 'Teatime in the Trenches', www.ghostsof1914.com, 27 October 2011.

35 'Wartime Children's Meals', www.theoldfoodie.com, 18 June 2015.

36 Quoted from Pettigrew, *A Social History of Tea*, p. 148.

37 Ibid., p. 149.

2 Europe

1 Dawn L. Campbell, *The Tea Book* (Gretna, LA, 1995), p. 155.

2 Gaitri Pagrach-Chandra, *Windmills in My Oven: A Book of Dutch Baking* (Totnes, 2002), p. 113.

3 N. Hudson Moore, *Delftware: Dutch and English* (New York, 1908), p. 16.

4 Campbell, *The Tea Book*, p. 155.

5 Pagrach-Chandra, *Windmills in My Oven*, p. 113.

6 Campbell, *The Tea Book*, p. 157.

7 *The Book of Tea* (Paris, nd), p. 146.

8 English translation of Heine's poem from www.lieder.net, accessed 26 June 2016.

9 Nick Hall, *The Tea Industry* (Cambridge, 2000), p. 63.

10 William H. Ukers, *The Romance of Tea* (London, 1936), p. 65.

11 Ibid., p. 66.

12 Ibid., p. 67.

13 The Wallace Collection in London holds the finest museum collection of Sèvres porcelain in the world.

14 Carole Manchester, *French Tea: The Pleasures of the Table* (New York, 1993), pp. 12–13.

15 *The Book of Tea*, p. 190.

16 Claire Joyes, *Monet's Cookery Notebooks* (London, 1989), translation of *Les Carnets de cuisine de Monet* (Paris, 1989), p. 102.

17 From the definitive French Pleiade edition translated by CK, Scott Moncrieff and Terence Kilmartin (New York, n.d.), pp. 48–51.

18 *The Times*, 13 February 1935, p. 14.

19 Michael Krondl, *Sweet Invention: A History of Dessert* (Chicago, IL, 2011), pp. 234–5.

20 Quoted in Annie Perrier-Robert, *Book of Tea*, English edn (London, 2004), p. 69.

21 Manchester, *French Tea*, pp. 53–4.

22 From the recipe box of Hartson Dowd's Sligo-born grandmother, quoted in Bridget Haggerty, 'Memories of Tea Time', www.irishcultureandcustoms.com, accessed 28 June 2017.

23 See 'List of Countries by Tea Consumption by Capita', https://en.wikipedia.org, accessed 28 June 2017.

24 Tony Farmar, *The Legendary Lofty Clattery Café: Bewleys of Ireland* (Dublin, 1988), p. 13.

25 Ibid., p. 15.

26 Ibid., p. 22.

27 Ibid., p. 28.

28 Haggerty, 'Memories of Tea Time'.

29 Myrtle Allen, *The Ballymaloe Cookbook* (Dublin, 1987), p. 168.

30 Ibid., p. 146.

31 Monica Sheridan, *The Art of Irish Cooking* (New York, 1965), p. 120.

32 Florence Irwin, *The Cookin' Woman: Irish Country Recipes* (Belfast, 1949), p. 5.

33 Regina Sexton, *A Little History of Irish Food* (Dublin, 1998), p. 84.

34 Susette Goldsmith, *Tea: A Potted History of Tea in New Zealand* (Auckland, 2006), pp. 45–7.

35 Campbell, *The Tea Book*, pp. 158–60.

3 United States of America

1 Jane Pettigrew and Bruce Richardson, *A Social History of Tea* (Danville, KY, 2014), pp. 51, 76.

2 Ibid., p. 47.

3 *The Cliffside Inn: Tea and Breakfast Cookbook* (Newport, 2000), p. 15.

4 Quoted in Susan Williams, *Savory Suppers and Fashionable Feasts: Dining in Victorian America* (Knoxville, TN, 1996), pp. 187–8.

5 Marion Harland, *Breakfast, Luncheon and Tea* (New York, 1886), pp. 360–61.

6 Williams, *Savory Suppers and Fashionable Feasts*, p. 127.

7 Ibid., pp. 127–8, from Eliza Leslie, *The Ladies Guide to True Politeness and Perfect Manners; or, Miss Leslie's Behaviour Book* (Philadelphia, PA, 1864), pp. 41–2.

8 Harland, *Breakfast, Luncheon and Tea*, p. 362.

9 Mrs T. J. Crowen, *Mrs Crowen's American Lady's Cookery Book* (New York, 1847), pp. 401–2.

10 Quoted in Williams, *Savory Suppers and Fashionable Feasts*, pp. 186–7.

11 Harland, *Breakfast, Luncheon and Tea*, pp. 356–8.

12 *The Cliffside Inn*, pp. 22–3.

13 Ibid., p. 21.

14 Lucy G. Allen, *Table Service* (Boston, MA, 1920), pp. 74, 75.

15 John Drury, *Dining in Chicago* (New York, 1931), pp. 147, 186.

16 Jan Whitaker, *Tea at the Blue Lantern Inn: A Social History of the Tea Room Craze in America* (New York, 2002), p. 146.

17 Mildred Huff Coleman, *The Frances Virginia Tea Room Cookbook* (Atlanta, GA, 1981), pp. 5–7, 94.

18 Smilax are thorny creeping shrubs. Young shoots can be eaten in salads or boiled. The dried roots are a principal source of sarsaparilla, used extensively for flavouring root beers, soft drinks, ice cream, candies and baked goods.

19 Whitaker, *Tea at the Blue Lantern Inn*, pp. 172–3.

20 Ibid., p. 173.

21 Ibid.

22 Drury, *Dining in Chicago* (New York, 1931), pp. 228–9.

23 Whitaker, *Tea at the Blue Lantern Inn*, pp. 169–71.

24 Ibid., p. 182.

4 Canada, Australia, New Zealand and South Africa

1 *Hudson's Bay* archives, A.24/2, p. 76, quoted in Frances Hoffman, *Steeped in Tradition: A Celebration of Tea* (Ontario, 1997), p. 11.

2 Ibid., pp. 11–12.

3 Ibid., p. 12.

4 Ibid., p. 13, quoted from Charles Francis Hall, *Arctic Researches and Life Among the Esquimaux* (New York, 1866), pp. 161–2.

5 Personal communication with Noreen Howard.

6 Personal communication with Gail Bowen.

7 Personal communication with Noreen Howard.

8 Thomas Lymer Papers, Archives of Ontario, MU 4573-F1035, in Hoffman, *Steeped in Tradition*, pp. 62–3.

9 Ibid., p. 63.

10 Ibid., p. 64.

11 See 'Queen Elizabeth Cake: A Uniquely Canadian Cake', www.cooksinfo.com, accessed 28 June 2017.

12 The tea was Empress Blend and could be bought in tins from Murchie's shop. It is now called Murchie's Afternoon Tea Blend and sold in a box.

13 Lee Jolliffe, ed., *Tea and Tourism* (Clevedon, 2007), p. 239.

14 Ibid.

15 The First Fleet is the name given to the eleven ships that left Great Britain on 13 May 1787 to found the penal colony that became the first European settlement in Australia. It arrived at Botany Bay in mid-January 1788. The fleet consisted of two Royal Navy vessels, three store ships and six convict transports, carrying more than one thousand convicts, marines and seamen, and a vast quantity of stores.

16 Jacqueline Newling, 'A Universal Comfort: Tea in the Sydney Penal Settlement', *Locale*, 1 (2011), p. 19. localejournal.org/issues.

17 Nicholas Martland, 'Milk and Two Sugars: Why Australians Switched from Chinese to Indian Tea', http://britishlibrary.typepad.co.uk/untoldlives, 23 January 2012.

18 G. Earnest, *Two Years Adrift: The Story of a Rolling Stone* (Brighton, 1870), p. 50, quoted in *Eat History: Food and Drink in Australia and Beyond*, ed. Sofia Erikkson, Madeleine Hastie and Tom Roberts (Cambridge, 2014), p. 113.

19 Francis Lancelott quoted in Barbara Santich, *Bold Palates* (Kent Town, 2012), p. 156.

20 See http://trove.nla.gov.au, accessed 29 September 2017.

21 Barbara Santich, 'Sponges, Lamingtons, and Anzacs', *Journal of Gastronomy*, IV/2 (Summer 1988), pp. 97–9.

22 Ironically, Lord Lamington was believed to have hated the dessert cakes that had been named in his honour, referring to them as 'those bloody poofy woolly biscuits'.

23 Santich, 'Sponges, Lamingtons, and Anzacs', p. 99.

24 Santich, *Bold Palates*, pp. 206–8.

25 Janet Clarkson, 'Anzac Biscuits: A Brief History', www.theoldfoodie.com, 25 April 2014.

26 Victoria Heywood, *Possum Pie, Beetroot Beer and Lamingtons: Australian Family Recipes 1868 to 1950* (Victoria, 2011), p. 233.

27 Published for free distribution by the Joint Publicity Committee, representative of the Dried Fruits Industry throughout Australia.

28 Hal Porter, *The Watcher on the Cast-iron Balcony: An Australian Autobiography* (London, 1963), quoted in Santich 'Sponges, Lamingtons, and Anzacs', p. 99.

29 Michael Symons, *One Continuous Picnic: A Gastronomic History of Australia* (Victoria, 1984), p. 64.

30 Santich, *Bold Palates*, pp. 100, 107.

31 Ibid., p. 104; quoted from Agnes Littlejohn, *The Silver Road, and Other Stories* (Sydney, 1915).

32 *Bold Palates*, p. 101.

33 Symons, *One Continuous Picnic*, p. 83.

34 Ibid., p. 84.

35 Susette Goldsmith, *Tea: A Potted History of Tea in New Zealand* (Auckland, 2006), pp. 15–17.

36 Ibid., p. 53.

37 Ibid., pp. 57–9.

38 G.R.M. Devereux, *Etiquette for Women: A Book of Modern Modes and Manners*, revd edn (London, 1920), p. 32, quoted in Helen Leach, *The Pavlova Story: A Slice of New Zealand's Culinary History* (Dunedin, 2008), p. 66.

39 Leach, *The Pavlova Story*, p. 87.

40 Goldsmith, *Tea: A Potted History of Tea in New Zealand*, p. 75.

41 Ibid., p. 71.

42 Leach, *The Pavlova Story* (Dunedin, 2008), p. 67.

43 Tony Simpson, *A Distant Feast: The Origins of New Zealand's Cuisine* (Auckland, 1999), p. 137, quoting Julie Park, ed., *Ladies a Plate: Change and Continuity in the Lives of New Zealand Women* (Auckland, 1991), from the chapter 'Women and Food', p. 145.

44 Jock Philips, Nicholas Boyack and E. P. Malone, eds, *The Great Adventure: New Zealand Soldiers Describe the First World War* (Wellington, 1988), p. 97.

45 Leach, *The Pavlova Story*, p. 88.

46 Bell Tea is New Zealand's oldest tea company, having been founded by Norman Harper Bell in 1898 when he registered the trademark Bell Tea. In an advertisement of 1936 they advertise themselves as the 'Aristocrats of the Tea Table'. In the 1970s Bell Tea purchased other tea companies, including Edglets, Tiger and Amber Tips.

47 Personal communication with Sybille Ecroyd.

48 Goldsmith, *Tea: A Potted History of Tea in New Zealand*, p. 134.

49 Ibid., pp. 131–2.

50 Ibid., pp. 88–91.

51 Ibid., pp. 92–3.

52 Ibid., pp. 94–5.

53 Ibid., p. 95.

54 Ibid., pp. 96–7.

55 Ibid., p. 98.

56 Ibid., p. 134.

57 Ibid., p. 149.

58 Ibid., pp. 150–51.

59 *Hildegonda Duckitt's Book of Recipes*, selected by Mary Kuttel (Cape Town, 1966), pp. 6–7.

5 India and the Subcontinent

1 *The Voyages and Travels of J. Albert de Mandelslo (A gentleman belonging to the Embassy, sent by the Duke of Holstein to the great Duke of Muscovy, and the King of Persia) into the East Indies. Begun in the Year M.D.C.XXXVIII, and finished in M.DC.XL in Three Books, Rendered into English by John Davies of Kidwelly*, 2nd edn (London, 1669).

2 'Gymkhana' is an Anglo-Indian term which originally referred to a place of assembly. During the time of the British Raj gymkhanas were established in large cities such as Bombay, Delhi, Lahore and Karachi, providing facilities for social and intellectual evenings as well as tournaments and sporting activities. In Britain it is the name given to an equestrian event with races and competitions.

3 In colonial India tiffin was a light afternoon meal. The word tiffin derives from both the slang English noun 'tiffing', for eating or drinking out of meal times, and the word 'tiff', which was to eat the midday meal. The word tiffin has been adopted particularly in the Madras area for an afternoon snack. K. T. Achaya, *A Historical Dictionary of Indian Food* (Delhi, 1998), p. 252.

4 Beatrice A. Vieyra, *Culinary Art Sparklets: A Treatise on General Household Information and Practical Recipes for Cooking in All Its Branches* (Madras, 1915), p. 224.

5 Colonel Kenney-Herbert, *Culinary Jottings for Madras* [1878], facsimile edn (Totnes, 1994), pp. 192–3.

6 David Burton, *The Raj at Table: A Culinary History of the British in India* (London, 1993), p. 197.

7 Isobel Abbott, *Indian Interval* (London, 1960), p. 95.

8 Burton, *The Raj at Table*, p. 198.

9 Colonel Kenney-Herbert, *Sweet Dishes* (Madras, 1884), p. 199.

10 As quoted in Dennis Kincaid, *British Social Life in India, 1608–1937* (Newton Abbot, 1974), p. 283.

11 Jennifer Brennan, *Curries and Bugles: A Memoir and a Cookbook of the British Raj* (London, 1992), pp. 179–80.

12 Pat Chapman, *Taste of the Raj: A Celebration of Anglo-Indian Cookery* (London, 1997), pp. 93–5.

13 Carole Manchester, *Tea in the East: Tea Habits Along the Tea Route* (New York, 1996), p. 104.

14 Brennan, *Curries and Bugles*, p. 197.

15 Chitrita Banerji, *Bengali Cooking: Seasons and Festivals* (London, 1997), p. 31.

16 Rani Kingman, *Flavours of Madras: South Indian Cookbook* (Reading, 1995) p. 124.

17 In Persian, *nankhatai* means 'bread of Cathay' or Chinese bread although some historians assert that the name *nankhatai* reflects the recipe, where *nan* stands for bread, and *khat* refers to the six ingredients that were used in the original recipe: flour, ghee, sugar, palm toddy, eggs and almonds. Later palm toddy was dropped, as people thought it may be intoxicating and so were eggs, as many Gujaratis do not eat them. The recipe for *nankhatai* is said to have been developed by a Parsee gentleman in Surat. He started making the biscuits in his bakery. This biscuit became popular among the Gujaratis as a teatime snack and so they started to export it from Surat to Bombay where many Gujaratis lived. During the Raj, the biscuits were liked by the British as they reminded them of shortbread.

18 Toddy (palm wine) is the extract from the sap of various species of palm tree such as date and coconut palms.

19 Suketu Mehta, *Maximum City: Bombay Lost and Found* (New York, 2005), p. 261.

20 For the history of Flurys see Bachi Karkaria, *Flurys of Calcutta* (Kolkata, 2007).

21 Described in the Shalimar tea brochure as 'a subtle blend of green and black teas from China and Sri Lanka, flavored

with vanilla, bergamot, cinnamon, lavender, and natural
aromas of cardamom.'

22 See '9 Kinds of Breads You Have to Try in Kashmir',
http://dialkashmir.com, 7 July 2015.

23 Colleen Taylor Sen, 'South Asia', in *The Oxford Companion
to Sugar and Sweets* (New York, 2015), p. 635.

6 Tea Roads and Silk Roads

1 Rinjing Dorje, *Food in Tibetan Life* (London, 1985), p. 53.

2 John Clarke, 'Tibet and the Himalayas', in *Tea: East and
West*, ed. Rupert Faulkner (London, 2003), pp. 69–70.

3 Mi Mi Khiang, *Cook and Entertain the Burmese Way*
(Ann Arbor, MI, 1978), p. 156.

4 Sue Arnold, review of *Tea: A Global History*, in *Asian
Affairs*, XLIII/1 (March 2012), pp. 113–15.

5 Khiang, *Cook and Entertain the Burmese Way*, pp. 156–7.

6 Personal communication with Laila Noor.

7 Darra Goldstein, *A Taste of Russia: A Cookbook of Russian
Hospitality* (London, 1985), p. 210.

8 Tamara Karsavina, *Theatre Street: The Reminiscences of
Tamara Karsavina* (London, 1930), p. 76, quoted in
Faulkner, ed., *Tea: East and West*, p. 79.

9 Arnold, review of *Tea: A Global History*, pp. 113–15.

10 Goldstein, *A Taste of Russia*, pp. 213–27.

11 Ibid., pp. 210, 211–12.

12 Margaret Shaida, *The Legendary Cuisine of Persia* (Henley-
on-Thames, 1992), pp. 270–71.

13 Saleb or salep is a milky drink thickened with salep, a
starchy powder made by drying and pulverizing the root
tubers of certain plants of the orchid family; O. S. Gökyay,
ed., *Evliya Çelebi Seyyahatnamesi*, vol. 1 (Istanbul. 1996),
p. 261.

14 Ayla Algar, *The Complete Book of Turkish Cooking*
(London, 1985), p. 307ff.

7 China, Japan, Korea and Taiwan

1 Lu Yü, *The Classic of Tea*, trans., with introduction by
Francis Ross Carpenter (Boston, MA, 1974), pp. 70–72,
107.

2 Margaret Leeming and May Huang Man-hui, *Dimsum:
Chinese Light Meals, Pastries and Delicacies* (London,
1985), p. 8.

3 Ibid., pp. 8–9.

4 Carole Manchester, *Tea in the East: Tea Habits Along
the Tea Route* (New York, 1996), p. 12.

5 Fuchsia Dunlop, *Shark's Fin and Sichuan Pepper:
A Sweet-sour Memoir of Eating in China* (London, 2008),
p. 190.

6 Ken Hom, *The Taste of China* (New York, 1990), pp. 155–6.

7 See Carolyn Phillips, 'The Beginner's Field Guide to Dim
Sum', http://luckypeach.com, accessed 26 June 2017.

8 There are two kinds of *kaiseki*. *Kaiseki* can mean 'party
food', often in connection with wedding parties. It
starts off as a drinking party with beer and sake served
with appetizers and a variety of traditional Japanese
dishes such as *sashimi* and *yakimono*. The second kind
of *kaiseki*, composed with different Chinese characters
but pronounced the same, is usually called *cha kaiseki*, to
distinguish it from the former.

9 Richard Hosking, *At The Japanese Table* (Oxford, 2000),
p. 58.

10 Gilles Brochand in 'Time for Tea', *The Book of Tea* (Paris,
nd), pp. 116, 119–20.

11 Suk Yong-un, 'History and Philosophy of Korean Tea Art',
Koreana, XI/4 (Winter 1997), pp. 4–11.

12 Michael J. Pettid, *Korean Cuisine: An Illustrated History*
(London, 2008), pp. 124–7.

13 Chun Su jin, 'Sweet Treats for Teatime Snacks', http://
koreajoongangdaily.joins.com, 26 November 2007.

14 See Bon Teavant, 'How to Use a Tea Aroma Cup', http://
bonteavant.com, 17 November 2010.

Bibliography

Aitken, Rhona, *The Memsahib's Cookbook: Recipes from the Days of the Raj* (London, 1989)

Allen, Ida Bailey, *When You Entertain: What to Do, and How* (Atlanta, GA, 1932)

[Allen, M.] *Five O'Clock Tea* (London, 1890).

Blofeld, John, *The Chinese Art of Tea* (Boston, MA, 1985)

The Book of Tea (Paris, n.d.)

Bramah, Edward, *Tea and Coffee: Three Hundred Years of Tradition* (London, 1972)

Brown, Catherine, *Broths to Bannocks: Cooking in Scotland 1690 to the Present Day* (London, 1990)

—, *Feeding Scotland* (Edinburgh, 1996)

—, *A Year in a Scots Kitchen* (Glasgow, 1996)

Brown, Patricia, *Anglo-Indian Food and Customs* (New Delhi, 1998)

Burnett, John, *Liquid Pleasures: A Social History of Drinks in Modern Britain* (London, 1999)

Burton, David, *The Raj at Table: A Culinary History of the British in India* (London, 1993)

Campbell, Dawn L., *The Tea Book* (Gretna, LA, 1995)

Chapman, Pat, *Taste of the Raj: A Celebration of Anglo-Indian Cookery* (London, 1997)

Chrystal, Paul, *Tea: A Very British Beverage* (Stroud, 2014)

Cohen, Susan, *London's Afternoon Teas* (London, 2012)

—, *Where to Take Tea* (London, 2003)

Collingham, Lizzie, *Curry: A Biography* (London, 2005)

Craig, Elizabeth, *1500 Everyday Menus* (London, n.d. [c. 1941])

Culinary Landmarks, or, Half-hours with Sault Ste Marie Housewives, 3rd edn (Sault Ste Marie, 1909)

Davidson, Alan, *The Oxford Companion to Food*, 2nd edn, ed. Tom Jaine (Oxford, 2006)

Day, Ivan, ed., *Eat, Drink and Be Merry: The British at Table, 1600–2000* (London, 2000)

Drury, John, *Dining in Chicago* (New York, 1931)

Duncan, Dorothy, *Canadians at Table: Food, Fellowship, and Folklore: A Culinary History of Canada* (Toronto, 2006)

—, *Feasting and Fasting: Canada's Heritage Celebrations* (Toronto, 2010)

Ellis, Markman, Richard Coulton and Matthew Mauger, *Empire of Tea: The Asian Leaf That Conquered the World* (London, 2015)

Farmar, Tony, *The Legendary Lofty Clattery Café: Bewleys of Ireland* (Dublin, 1988)

Faulkner, Rupert, ed., *Tea: East and West* (London, 2003)

Forrest, Denys, *Tea for the British: The Social and Economic History of a Famous Trade* (London, 1973)

Freeman, Michael, and Selena Ahmed, *Tea Horse Road: China's Ancient Trade Road to Tibet* (Bangkok, 2011)

Gay, Lettie, ed., *Two Hundred Years of Charleston Cooking* (Columbia, SC, 1976)

Gin, Margaret, and Alfred E. Castle, *Regional Cooking of China* (San Francisco, CA, 1975)

Goldsmith, Susette, *Tea: A Potted History of Tea in New Zealand* (Auckland, 2006)

Goldstein, Darra, *A Taste of Russia: A Cookbook of Russian Hospitality* (London, 1985)

—, *The Oxford Companion to Sugar and Sweets* (New York, 2015)

Griffiths, John, *Tea: The Drink That Changed the World* (London, 2007)

Grigson, Jane, *English Food* (London, 1979)

Hardy, Serena, *The Tea Book* (Weybridge, 1979)

Harland, Marion, *Breakfast, Luncheon and Tea* (New York, 1886)

Hartley, Dorothy, *Food in England* [1954] (London, 1975)

Heiss, Mary Lou, and Robert J. Heiss, *The Story of Tea: A Cultural History and Drinking Guide* (Berkeley, CA, 2007)

Hoffman, Frances, *Steeped in Tradition: A Celebration of Tea* (Toronto, 1997)

Hopley, Claire, *The History of Tea* (Barnsley, 2009)

Huxley, Gervas, *Talking of Tea* (London, 1956)

Isles, Joanna, *A Proper Tea: An English Collection of Recipes and Anecdotes* (London, 1987)

Jameson, Mrs K., *The Nursery Cookery Book* (London, *c*. 1929)

Jolliffe, Lee, ed., *Tea and Tourism* (Clevedon, 2007)

Joyes, Claire, *Monet's Cookery Notebooks* (London, 1989), translation of *Les Carnets de Cuisine de Monet* (Paris, 1989)

Kenney-Herbert, Colonel A. R., *Culinary Jottings for Madras* [1878], facsimile edn (Totnes, 1994)

Kinchin, Perilla, *Taking Tea with Mackintosh: The Story of Miss Cranston's Tea Rooms* (Fullbridge Maldon, 1998)

Koehler, Jeff, *Darjeeling: A History of the World's Greatest Tea* (London, 2015)

Leach, Helen, *The Pavlova Story: A Slice of New Zealand's Culinary History* (Dunedin, 2008)

Lee, Rhoda, *Dim Sum* (San Francisco, CA, 1977)

Leeming, Margaret, and May Huang Man-hui, *Dimsum: Chinese Light Meals, Pastries and Delicacies* (London, 1985)

Leslie, Eliza, *Miss Leslie's New Cookery Book*, facsimile edn (Philadelphia, PA, 1857)

Lovell, Sarah, *Meals of the Day: A Guide to the Young Housekeeper* (Montreal, 1904)

Mair, Victor H., and Erling Hoh, *The True History of Tea* (London, 2009)

Manchester, Carole, *French Tea: The Pleasures of the Table* (New York, 1993)

—, *Tea in the East* (New York, 1996)

Manekshaw, Bhicoo, J., *Parsi Food and Customs* (New Delhi, 1996)

Mariage Frères: The French Art of Tea (Paris, 1997)

Mason, Laura, 'Everything Stops for Tea', in *Luncheon, Nuncheon and Other Meals: Eating with the Victorians*, ed. C. Anne Wilson (Stroud, 1994)

—, with Catherine Brown, *Traditional Foods of Britain: An Inventory* (Totnes, 1999)

Masset, Claire, *Tea and Tea Drinking* (Oxford, 2012)

McKee, Mrs, *The Royal Cookery Book* (London, 1983)

Moon, Rosemary, and Janie Suthering, *Fortnum & Mason: A Fine Tradition of Tea* (London, 1998)

Nicey and Wifey, *Nicey and Wifey's Nice Cup of Tea and a Sit Down* (London, 2004)

O'Connor, Sharon, *Afternoon Tea Serenade* (Emeryville, CA, 1997)

Okakura, Kakuzo, *The Book of Tea* [1906] (New York, 1964)

Palmer, Andrew, *Movable Feasts* (London, 1952)

Patten, Marguerite, *The Complete Book of Teas* (London, 1989)

Perrier-Robert, Annie, *Book of Tea* (London, 2004), translation of *Le Thé* (Paris, 1999)

Pettigrew, Jane, *Afternoon Tea* (Andover, 2004)

—, *Jane Pettigrew's Tea Time: A Complete Collection of Traditional Recipes* (London, 1986)

—, *A Social History of Tea* (London, 2001)

—, and Bruce Richardson, *A Social History of Tea* (Danville, KY, 2014)

R. Twining & Co., *The Book of the Tea Pot* (London, 1899)

The Raj Cookbook (Delhi, 1981)

Repplier, Agnes, *To Think of Tea!* (London, 1933)

Richardson, Bruce, *The Great Tea Rooms of America*, 3rd edn (Perryville, 2006)

—, *The Great Tea Rooms of Britain*, 5th edn (London, 2008)

Saberi, Helen, *Tea: A Global History* (London, 2010)

Santich, Barbara, *Bold Palates* (Kent Town, 2012)

—, 'Sponges, Lamingtons, and Anzacs', *Journal of Gastronomy*, IV/2 (Summer 1988)

Scott, I. M., *The Tea Story* (London, 1964)

Simpson, Helen, *The Ritz London Book of Afternoon Tea* (London, 1986)

Smith, Andrew F., ed., *The Oxford Companion to American Food and Drink* (New York, 2007)

Smith, Michael, *The Afternoon Tea Book* (New York, 1986)

Spry, Constance, *Come Into The Garden, Cook* (London, reprint 1952)

Steel, F. A., and G. Gardiner, *The Complete Indian Housekeeper and Cook* (London, 1921)

Stella, Alain, *Mariage Freres French Tea: Three Centuries of Savoir-faire* (Paris, 2003)

Symons, Michael, *One Continuous Picnic: A Gastronomic History of Australia* (Victoria, 1984)

Tenison, Marika Hanbury, *Book of Afternoon Tea* (Newton Abbot, 1986)

Twining, Sam, *My Cup of Tea: The Story of the World's Most Popular Beverage* (London, 2002)

Ukers, William H., *The Romance of Tea: An Outline History of Tea and Tea-drinking Through Sixteen Hundred Years* (London, 1936)

Whitaker, Jan, *Tea at the Blue Lantern Inn: A Social History of the Tea Room Craze in America* (New York, 2002)

White, Florence, *Good Things in England* [1932] (London, 1968)

Whyte, Hamish, and Catherine Brown, *A Scottish Feast: Anthology of Food in Scottish Writing* (Argyll, 1996)

Wild, Jonathan, *Hearts, Tarts and Rascals: The Story of Bettys* (Harrogate, 2005)

Williams, Susan, *Savory Suppers and Fashionable Feasts: Dining in Victorian America* (Knoxville, TN, 1996)

Acknowledgements

Thanks are due to Michael Leaman, Martha Jay and Susannah Jayes at Reaktion Books. I would also like to thank the following people who have helped me in various ways with advice, information, recipes, illustrations and encouragement: Gail Bowen, the late Henry Brownrigg, Sarah Byrne and Tom Crowley of the Horniman Museum, Charlotte Clark, Graham Day, Karen Dias, Tim Doffay of Postcard Teas, Sybille Ecroyd, Hattie Ellis, Anya Goddard, Helen Graves, Geraldene Holt, Noreen Howard and Karen Howard, Phil and Patsy Iddison, Bobso Kanwar, Maria Emilia Lopes, Siobhan McGuire, John Mulcahy of Fáilte, Ireland, Sharon Meyers of Napoleona Teas, Laila Noor, Gaitri Pagrach-Chandra, Alex Saberi, Nasir Saberi, Oliver Saberi, Regina Sexton, Jenny Staley, the late Rosie Stark, Marietjie and Jaco Swart, and Bee Wilson.

I am particularly grateful to Colleen Taylor Sen who read through my drafts and gave me so many helpful suggestions, comments, encouragement and advice. I am also grateful to David Burnett, Laura Mason, Barbara Santich (Australia) and Mary Williamson (Canada) for generously sharing their expertise and giving many perceptive comments and helpful suggestions.

I owe an enormous debt of gratitude to Hilary Hyman, Kaori O'Connor and Gillian Riley not only for their wit and wisdom but for keeping me going when I was flagging and providing me with books, pictures, postcards and other tea paraphernalia. I also thank the members of the Walks and Talks – History of London group for their enthusiastic support especially Maggie Allen, Roger Atwell, Jenny Cook, Carole Cox, Sheila Gent, Betty Mattes, Myra Morgan, Guy Rowston, Sue Simms, Simon Swindell, Derek Ward and Christine Wolski. We have shared many happy teatimes together after our long walks.

Photo Acknowledgements

The author and the publishers wish to express their thanks to the below sources of illustrative material and/or permission to reproduce it.

Alamy: pp. 17 (The National Trust Photolibrary), 24, 68, 77 (Chronicle), 129 (Picture Partners), 138 (Dave G. Houser), 146 (IMAGEPAST), 151 (Lebrecht Music and Arts Photo Library), 163 (Chronicle), 178 bottom right (Chronicle), 186 (Giles Robberts), 187 (Lou-Foto), 200 (Chronicle), 202 (Philip Game); Courtesy Angelina, Paris: pp. 69, 72; Archives of Ontario: p. 114; Art Gallery of New South Wales: p. 197 bottom left; Asamudra: p. 103; Babingtons Tea Rooms: p. 78; Karen Dias: p. 159 bottom left; Courtesy Dishoom: p. 159 top left; Fáilte Ireland: p. 76; Getty Images: pp. 10 (Culture Club), 49 (H. F. Davis), 197 top left (Buddhika Weerashinghe); Gryffindor: p. 63; Courtesy Horniman Museum, London: pp. 144, 168 top left, 170; iStockphoto: p. 45 (threeseven); Library of Congress, Washington, DC: pp. 82 below right, 83 bottom right, 84, 97, 193, 196, 198; David Loong: p. 28; New York Public Library: p. 100; Mary Evans Picture Library: pp. 19 (A.Koch/Interfoto), 22 bottom right (Illustrated London News Ltd), 29, 39 top right (Retrograph Collection), 53, 55 top right, 58 (Illustrated London News Ltd), 70 (Estate of Edmund Blampied/ILN); Miansari66: p. 161; Museum of New Zealand Te Papa Tongarewa: pp. 131, 134 bottom left; National Portrait Gallery, London: p. 37; The Metropolitan Museum of Art, New York: pp.15, 66, 82 top left, 83 top left, 87; courtesy Postcard Teas, London: p. 155; courtesy Kaori O'Connor: pp. 30, 39 top left, 123, 124; courtesy Gillian Riley: p. 65; Alex Saberi: pp. 16 top left and bottom right, 25, 26, 27, 34, 41, 95, 166, 168 bottom right, 172, 175, 181 top left; courtesy of the Savoy: p. 54; Monica Shaw: p. 134 top left; Shutterstock: pp. 43 (Magdanatka), 62 bottom right (Bjoern Wylezich), 110 (NoirChocolate), 116 (Kelly vanDellen), 122 bottom left (Kylie Ellway), 122 top right (Milleflore Images), 156 (EIRoi), 157 (espies), 174 (mar_chm1982), 181 centre right (Resul Muslu), 188 (KPG_Payless), 189 (Makistock), 192 (Sean Pavone), 195 (Sann von Mai), 203 (stockcreations), 206 (Anneka); State Library of New South Wales, Sydney: p. 128; Courtesy State Library of Victoria: p. 120; Jaco Swart: p. 141; Topfoto: pp. 22 top left, 57 bottom right; Derek Ward: p. 88; Ke.We: p. 64; Wellcome Collection, London: p. 55 bottom left; courtesy Mary Williamson: p. 115; Victoria and Albert Museum, London: p. 180.

Index

Page numbers in *italics* refer to illustrations; page numbers in **bold** refer to recipes

ACM Company 137
Adam, Robert 16
Adkin, Leslie
    Afternoon Tea 134
    Tea on the Lawn 131
Aerated Bread Company (ABC)
    Aerated Bread Shop 46, *47*
Afghanistan 170, 165, *171–3*, 176, 212, 217, 228, 231, 232
Afghans (biscuits) 133, *134*, 139, **228–9**
afternoon tea 12, 20–27, 29, 30, 31, 33, 35, 36, 38, 41, 42,
    45, 51, 52, 58, 60, 62, 64, 66, 70, 71, 73, 77, 79, 83, *83*,
    92, 93, 96, *97*, 102, 104, 107–8, 110, 114, 115, *115*, 116, 117,
    121, 123, 125, 126, 128, 130, 131–2, 133, 135, 136, 138, 139,
    142, 145–9, *146*, 150, 151, 153, 154, 155–6, 160, 164, 165,
    182, 190, 191, 207
    see also chai-e-digar
akoori (spicy scrambled eggs) 159, **217**
American Centennial tea party 84, *84*
Andō, Hiroshige, *Teahouse at Hiraiwa at Mukojuma 196*
Angelina tearoom 69, *69*, 70, 72, *72*
Anglo-Indians 145, 151, 153, 154, 157
Anne of Green Gables 117
Anne, Queen of England 13
Anzac biscuits 121–2, *122*, 133, 139, **229**
'arvo tea' 125
Assam 143, 154
    Assam tea 24, 42, 64, 74
At Homes 27, 30, 39, 107, 108, 131
Atkinson, Captain G. F., *The Cook's Room 147*
Austen, Jane 17–18, 19, 20
Australia 105, 118–30, 133, 228

Babington's tearooms 78–9, *78*
Balmoral cakes 24, **218**
    Balmoral tarts 121, **218–19**
Balzac, Honoré de 66

Bambay chai 161
Bangladesh 162–3
bara brith 33, 207, **224–5**
barley tea 201
Barry's Tea (Ireland) 74
bed tea 155
Beeton, Mrs (Isabella) 26–7, 30, *30*, 31, **218**, **223**
Bell teas (New Zealand) 135
Belmont, Alva Vanderbilt 97
Best, Mary Ellen, *Cottagers at Tea 35*
Bettys
    Bettys café menu card 50–51, *51*, 222
Bewley, Charles 75
Bewley's Cafés 75, 76, *76*
billy tea 118–19, 126
black tea 15, 16, 25, 31, 64, 79, 87, 91, 94, 106, 118, 125, 130, 162,
    169, 171, 175, 190, 199, 204, 206, 208, 211, 212, 213
Blampied, Edmond, *Le Five O'Clock at Deauville 70*
Blechynden, Richard 95
Blue Baths 137–9, *138*
Bohea tea 106, 118
Boston Tea Party 82, *82*, 97
Brazil 208–9
brick tea 165, 167, 175
    see also tea bricks
Brown Betty 34
bubble tea 183, 203, *203*, 204
'builder's tea' 8
Burma 160, 165, 167, 168–9
Bushells tea (Australia) 118
butter tarts 111
butter tea 167, 168

caddy 15, *15*, 41, *82*, 92, 132, 197
    caddy spoon 15, *16*
Canada 23, 64, 105–18, 227

Canadian tea ice 40
caravanserai 170
casa de cha 208
casas du thé 207
Cassatt, Mary, *Lady at the Tea Table 80*
Catherine of Braganza *10*, 12, 13
Catherine the Great 174, 176
çaydanlik 181
Centennial Tea Party *84*
Ceylon 143, 153
Ceylon teas 14, 24, 25, 44, 64, 74, 100, 107, 115, 118, 153, 163, 199,
    231
    see also Sri Lanka
Ch'a ching 184
cha chaan teng 190–91
cha kaiseki 183, 192, 196
chabako 196
chado 191
chai 130, 159, 161, 162, 165, 167, 172, 175, 208
    see also masala chai, *sheer chai, qymaq chai*
Chanel, Coco 70, 74
cha-no-yu 191, 192, 196
chai khana 170, 171–2, *171*
chai wallah 154, *155*
chai-e-digar 165, 172–3
chaire 197
chaji 192
chakai 192
Chamadao see Tea Horse Road
Chamagudao (Ancient Tea Horse Road) 167
chasen 197
chashitsu 192
chawan 197
chevda 141, 156, 157, *157*
Chile 209
China 13, 23, 61, 66, 81, 127, 143, 165, 167, 168, 170, 174, 179,
    183–91, 199, 205
China tea 12, 25, 44, 46, 115, 118, 126, 127, 180
chinaware (porcelain) 7, 13, 26, 30, 36, 40, 41, 47, 61, 62, 63, 64,
    65, 83, 85, 107, 117, 121, 125, 127, 134, 135, 138, 139
Chinese chews 108–9, **109**
Chinese House, Sanssouci 63, *63*
chota hazri 155
Christmas afternoon tea *43*
Christmas trifle **232**
Cinnamon Toast 230–31
club teas 153–4
cockle teas 32
Collins, Richard, *An English Family at Tea* 14
Coronation street party (1953) *58*
Cranston, Kate 47, 48

Cranston, Stuart 46
cream teas 45, *45*, 139
cricket teas 40, 214
Crumperie, The 98
curate 27, 92, 132, 160
Cutchee tea 145

dabal chai 161
Dadd, Philip, *Soldiers and Sailors Buffet at Victoria Station 55*
damper 118, 119, 120
Darjeeling 42, 64, 115, 143, 153, 160, 161
dasik 201
De Quincey, Thomas 11
delftware 62, 63
demlik 181
department stores 47, 49, 93, 99–100, 102, 113, 128, 136–7
Devonshire cream tea *47*
dim sum 60, 105, 183, 184–90, *187*, *188*
'dish of tea' 16
Dragon blend tea 116, 134
Dragon Well tea 186, 189
Drury, John 96, 100
Duchess of Bedford (Anna Maria) 20, 21, 116
    Duchess of Bedford Tea-cakes **217–18**
Duckitt, Hildagonda 140
Dundee cake 42, **223–4**
Dutch East India Company 63, 65, 140

Earnest, G. 119
East Frisia 63, 64
East India Company 13, 74, 144, 213
Eaton's 113–14, *114*
Ebsworth, A. M., *Tea and Damper 120*
Edglets tea (New Zealand) 135
Edmonds Baking Powder 133, *133*
Edmonds Cookery Book 133, 229, 230
Edward VII, King of the UK 113
Elizabeth II, Queen of the UK 41, 58, 114, 132, 186, 201
Elizabeth, the Queen Mother 114
England 7, 12–32, 34–46, 48–58, 60, 61, 74, 78, 79, 81, 82, 83, 98,
    106, 118, 127, 132, 143, 145, 150, 153, 213, 222, 226
English Monkey 112
Estabrooks, Theodore Harding 107
estekan (also *istakhan*) 172, 179
Ethiopia 208

Fat Rascals **221–2**
Fauchon's *Grand Salon de thé* 67
fermented tea 143, 168, 201
    see also lephet
fish teas 31

five o'clock tea(s) 20, 21, 27, 50, 52, 67, 70, 73, *83*, 84, 92, 113, 140
    Five O'Clock Tea, Paris *68*
    Five O'Clock Tea menu (Macy's) *100*
Flurys 160–61
football tea 93
Formosa *see* Taiwan
fortune cookies 103
fortune telling *see* reading the leaves
fragrance (or aroma) cup 202
France 61, 64–74, 75, 199, 222
French tea 64, 71, 73, 199
Fullers 48, 49
funeral teas 44, 46

garden parties 42, 112–13, 132
Gerber, Hilda 140–41
Germany 9, 13, 34, 61, 63–4
gingerbread men **221**
Ginkaku-ji (Silver Pavilion) 192, *192*
Ginkō, Adachi/Shōsai, tea ceremony, Meiji period *197*
Golden Lyon, The 17
green tea 12, 61, 94, 103, 118, 143, 161, 162, 169, 170, 171, 192, 194, 196, 199, 203, 205, 206, 209, 211, 212, 213
Greenaway, Kate, *Polly Put the Kettle on 91*
Greenwich Village tearooms 96, 98, 102
gulabi chai see sheer chai
'gumboot tea' 130
Gunn, Sir James, *Conversation Piece at the Royal Lodge, Windsor 37*
Gypsy tearoom(s) 98, *99*

Hagiwara, Makoto 103
halvais see moira
Hanway, Jonas 17
Harland, Marion 85, 87, 90, 94, 211
herbata 79
Herbert, A. P. 11
Hertzoggies 141–2, *141*, **230**
high tea 12, 30–33, 35, 36, 47, 48, 52, 55, 56, 58, 60, 62, 63, 74, 83, 89, 90, 107, 110, 111, 125, 128, 139, 142, 162, 164
Hopetoun Tearooms 128, *129*
Horemans, Joseph, *Tea Time 62*
hotels 12, 45, 46, 47, 49, 52, 58, 59, 60, 71, 79, 93, 94, 96, 100, 101, 104, 113, 114, 115, 116, 117, 142, 160, 162, 164, 199
Hu Xing Ting tea house *186*
Hudson's Bay Co. 106
Huntley & Palmer biscuits 25, 54, 148, *149*
Hyde, Helen, *Tea Time under the Cherry Blossoms 198*
Hyson 81, 100, 118
    Hyson tea canister *82*

iced tea 39, 40, 92, 94–5, *95*, 96, 104, 105, 113, 116, 170, 208, 209
    Iced Tea à la Russe **94**
Imperial tea 81
ince belli 181
India 140, 143–63, 167, 170, 199, 204, 208, 211, 213, 215, 217, 231, 232
Indian snacks 141, 156, 157, *157*
Indian sweet stall *156*
Indian teas 25, 31, 44, 49, 107, 118, 154, 212
Indonesia 62, 205, 208
Inuit 106
Iran 170, 176, 177, 179, *181*, 231, 232
Irani cafés 158–9, *159*, 217
Ireland 23, 60, 74–8, *77*, 211, 216, 219
Irish potato cakes **216**
Iron Goddess of Mercy 186, 189
Irwin, Florence 77
Italy 78–9

Jalayir, Isma'il, *Ladies Around a Samovar 180*
Jammu and Kashmir 161–2
Japan 61, 183, 191–9
Japanese tea ceremony *197*
    see also tea ceremony
Japanese Tea Garden 100, 103, *103*
Japanese tearoom 100
    see also kissaten
jasmine tea 189
Jefferson, Thomas 81

kahwa 161
Kashgar 170, 171
Kashmir 161–2, 168, 170, 176, 212
Kashmiri tea 161–2, *161*
Katsushika, Hokusai, *Wakamizu no fukucha 193*
kawiarnia 79
Kenney-Herbert, Colonel 145–6, 148
Kenya 208
Kettledrum Tearooms 49
kettledrum(s) 21, *22*, 85, 108, 211
khitmutgar (khidmatgor) 151, *151*
King Cole blend 107
Kissaten 199
koicha 196
Korea 8, 9, 183, 199–201
Korovin, Konstantin, *At the Tea Table 178*
Koustodiev, Boris, *Merchant's Wife at Tea 179*
kulcha-e-panjerei 173, **231–2**

Ladakh 167
Ladurée 68
Lady Baltimore cake 86, *86*

Lake Agnes Tea House 116, *116*
Lamingtons 121, *122*
Le Five O'Clock see Five O'Clock
Lemon Drizzle Cake **225**
lephet 143, 165, 168–9
lephet thoke 168, 169
lephet tray *168*
Leslie, Eliza 87, **226**
Levering, Albert, *Afternoon Tea 97*
Liotard, Jean-Étienne, *Still-life: Tea Set 65*
Lipton, Thomas 162
Louise Cake **229–30**
Love Cake 164, **231**
low tea 83
Lu Yü 184
Lyons tearooms/shop 49, *49*, 71, 56
Lyons, Joseph 48

McIlhenny, C. M., *Five O'Clock Tea 83*
MacIntosh, Charles Rennie 48
Macy's 100, *100*
Mad Hatters Tea (Party) 59, *59*, 60, 115
madeleines 66, 69, 72, 73, **225–6**, 232
Maids of Honour **219–20**
Mandelslo, Albert 143
manuka tea 130
Mariage Frères 28, 72–3
Mary of Modena 13
masala chai 60, 142, 154, 157, 160, 162, **211–12**
    see also chai
'Matchmakin' in Ireland' *77*
meat tea 31
miang 143
milk in tea 25, 65–6
milk tea 190
moira 155, 162
Monet, Claude, *The Tea Set* 66, 67, *67*
mooncakes 184, 189, *189*
Moreland, George, *The Tea Garden 19*
Moroccan mint tea 205, *206*
Morocco 205–6
mote spoon 15, *16*
moustache cup 28, *28*
muffin man 24, *24*
muffin (or cake) stand *see* curate
Murchies (Canada) 115
Myanmar *see* Burma

Nak Tong Mission House *200*
namagashi 195, 196, 197
Nanaimo Bars 110, *110*, **227–8**

Neenish tarts 133
Netherlands 61–3
New Sunshine Cookery Book, The 122–3, *123*, *124*
New Zealand 105, 121, 122, 130–40, 228, 229
Newfoundland Tea Buns **227**
nippies 49, *49*
noon chai 161
Nurmahal Cake **148**
nursery teas 35–8, 218

omija cha 201
onces 209
oolong 100, 130, 161, 189, 199, 201, 202, 203, 231
Orwell, George 25
Ovington, Revd John 143

paani kum chai 159
Pakistan 162, 217
pakoras 43, 154, 155, 156, 158, 160, 162, 173, **217**
Palm Court(s) 52, 53, 104
Parsis 157–9, 217
Patagonia 207
Pepys, Samuel 12
Petticoat Tails **222**
picnic parties/teas 39, 40–41, *42*, 76, 94, 116, 125–6, 130, 145,
    152, *153*
Pitt, William the Younger 18
podstakannik(i) 174, 177
Poland 61, 79
pori ch'a 201
Presidency Cakes **152**
Prohibition 96
Proust, Marcel 64, 69, 225
Pu-erh 8, 189, 203, 211
puftaloons 119, **120**
Pumpkin Scones 123, **123–4**

Qianlong, Emperor of China 190
queen cakes 124, **220**
Queen Elizabeth cake 114
Queen's Sandwiches **112**
qymaq chai 165, 173, **212**

railway tea(s) 57, 139, 154, 176
Raj, the 9, 144–54, 155, 160, 162, 215, 231
reading the tea leaves 21, *22*, 23, 98
Red Rose blend/tea bags 107, *107*
red velvet cake 112
Regency era 18–20, 82
rose (rosa) cookies 154
    see also kulcha-e-panjerei

roti wallah 152–3
rout cakes 18, **19**
routs 18
Rowlandson, Thomas, *Ladies at Tea 21*
Rumpelmayer, Antoine 68, 69, 70, 71
Russell, Lilian 102
Russia 61, 165, 172, 174–7, *178*
Russian punch 94
Russian Snowballs **226–7**
Russian tea 89, 94, 108, 113, *174, 175, 176*
    see also tea à la Russe

salon de thé 67–9, 71, 73, 105, 118
samovar 71, 93, 161, 165, 171, *172,* 175, *175,* 176–7, 179, 180, 181,
    182
sarsaparilla ('sweet tea') 118
Saucer Cake (Saucy Kate) **146**
schotel drinken 62
scones, rich fruit **219**
    see also pumpkin scones
Scotland 12, 13, 17, 21, 23, 33, 52, 115, 218, 219, 222, 223
seed cake 32, 34, 77, 121, 130, 135, 154, **223**
Sen-no-Rikyu 191
Sevigné, Madame de 65
Sèvres 66
shai 205
shai bil nana 206
Shannon, Kitty, *Catherine of Braganza giving a tea party*
    10
sheer chai 161, 212
Shennong, Emperor of China 8, 183
Sheridan, Monica 77
Shrewsbury cakes **221**
shrimp teas 31
Shuko (Zen priest) 191
Sichuan 167, 184, 185
Silk Roads 9, 165, 167, 170–73, 184
    see also Tea Horse Road
silk sock milk tea 190
smoko(s) 125, 130
smuggling 18
Smutsies 141
souchong 81
South Africa 105, 140–42, 230
Sri Lanka 62, 130, 143, 163–4, 231, 232
Steel, Flora Annie 148–51
Stroopwafels 62, 62
suffrage/suffragettes 50–52, 96, 97, 127
sugar cone 88, *88*
Sultaness Head Cophee House 12
Sundae Tea Rooms menu card *163*

Tabang 200
tabloid tea 55, *55*
tach'on 200
tado 200
Taiwan 9, 118, 183, 190, 201–4
tango teas 52–3, *53*
Tart, Quong 126–8, *128*
Taylor, James 162
tea à la Russe 44, 94, **211**
tea bag(s) 58, 95, 106, 107, 114, 208
tea bowls 13, 14, 16, 167, 196, 199
tea bricks 165, *166*
tea caddy *see* caddy
tea cart 26, 92, 108, 132
tea ceremony
    Japan 183, 191–9, *197*
    Korea 200–201
    Taiwan 201–2
    Vietnam 169
tea chest *15*
tea cosies 34, 35, 87, *87,* 177
tea dance(s) 52–3, 70–71, 93, 98, 101–2, 113, 139, 145
tea food halls 190–91
tea gardens 18, *19,* 49, 81, 100, 101, 103, *103,* 130–31, 162, 163, 182
tea glass 9, 64, 79, *178, 181*
tea gowns 29, *29,* 53, 145
Tea Horse Road 165, 167–70
tea house(s) (see also *chai khana*) 63, *63,* 72, 97, 103, 116, *116,* 118,
    126, 127, 162, 169, 171, 180, 182, 183, 184–90, *186,* 192, *192,*
    197, 199, 201, 202, *202,* 203, 208, 209
'Tea in the Nursery' *36*
tea kettle 16, 20, 92, 181
Tea Kisses **226**
tea ladies 57, *57*
tea palaces 186
tea parties 27, 41, 58, 61, 81, 82, 83, 84–93, *84,* 97, 108, 109, 113,
    131, 132, 141, 145, 200, 213, 215, 232
Tea Party under Chairman Mao 185
tea punch 113, **213**
tea rationing 37, 54, 56, 125, 135
tea receptions 27, 93, 132
Tea Road 165, 174
tea salon *see salon de thé*
tea sandwiches
    Cucumber **214**
    Delhi sandwich 42, 100, 103, 155, 213–14
    Egg and Cress **215**
    Smoked Salmon Pinwheel **215–16**
tea sets 36, 61, 64, *65,* 66, *74*
tea shops 17, 46, 49, 56, 58, 60, 73, 96, 98, 117, 154, 161, 162, 169,
    170, 171, 220

tea table 13, 14, 16, 30, *30*, 33, 34, 35, 36, 37, 41, *80*, *83*, 85, 88, 89, 101, 108, 175, *178*, 223, 226, 232

tea trolley 26, 57, *57*, 108, 152
    see also tea cart

tea urn 16, 41, 42, 43, 87, 132

tea wagon *see* tea cart

teacups 16, 62, 81, 85, 87, 92, 97, 126, 139, 185, 199

teagles 29

teapots 13–14, *13*, *14*, 16, 35, *65*, *74*, 79, *80*, *134*, *144*, *167*, *168*, *171*, *171*, *172*, *180*, *193*
    see also Brown Betty

teapoy 16, *17*

tearoom(s) 9, 45, 46–51, *50*, *51*, 59, 60, 64, 69, 72, 78, 93, 96–100, 102–3, 105, 106, 114–15, 118, 126–30, *129*, 136–9, 142, 160, *163*, 192, 207

teaware 25–7, *25*, 26, *26*, *27*, 28, 61, 64, 66, 83
    see also tea sets

tee mit Sahne 64, *64*

temperance 46, 47, 75, 108, 117, 136

Tenniel, John, Mad Hatter's Tea Party *59*

tennis biscuits 142, 133

tennis cake 40, 133–4, **134**

tennis parties 39, *39*, 40, 149–50

tennis tea sets 40, *41*

tennis teas 39, 89

thé dansant
    52–3, *52*, 70–71, 101–2

theetijd 62

thimble teas 108

Tibet 8, 9, 165, 167–8

tiffin 145, 148, 155–6

Tim Tam 125

Tissot, James, *Holyday*, also known as *The Picnic 42*

trà chanh 170

travelling tea service *66*

Turkey 176, 177, 180–82, 232

Twining, Thomas 17

Twining's shop 18, 42, 56

Uganda 208

Üisun 201

United States of America 9, 58, 81–104, 211, 220, 226, 232

usucha 192, 197

Victoria sandwich/sponge cake 7, 24, 43, 108

Victoria Sandwiches **218**

Victoria, Queen of the UK 18, 20, 24, 27, 41, 113, 114, 115, 132, 218

Vietnam 167, 169

wagashi 192, 194–5, *195*

Wales 32, 33–4, 38, 44, 46, 60, 207, 224

Waller, Edmund 12

Washington, George 81, 82

Washington, Martha 81, 82, 84, 85

Welsh rabbit (rarebit) 31, 76, 112, **216**

Welsh tea party *39*
    Welsh tea party fairing *34*

Welsh tea rooms (Patagonia) 207

Wesley, John 17

Willow Tea Rooms 47, 48, *48*

women's suffrage movement *see* suffragette/suffrage 96

Wu-Wei teahouse *202*

Yoshimasa 192

yuang-yang 190

yum cha 183, 184–90